MW01154702

BAPTIST WHY AND WHY NOT REVISITED

Herschel H. Hobbs

VOLUME EDITED BY
TIMOTHY GEORGE AND RICHARD D. LAND
TIMOTHY AND DENISE GEORGE, EDITORS

Nashville, Tennessee

Printed in the United States of America

4212-62
0-8054-1262-x

Dewey Decimal Classification: 286.132
Subject Heading: BAPTIST—DOCTRINES
Library of Congress Card Catalog Number: 97-4403

Unless otherwise stated all Scripture is from the King James Version.

Interior design by Leslie Joslin
Cover Design by Steve Diggs & Friends

Library of Congress Cataloging-in-Publication Data

Baptist Why and Why Not Revisited /Timothy George and Richard D. Land, editors.
p. cm. — (The Library of Baptist classics ; vol. 12)
Includes bibliographical references and index.
ISBN 0-8054-1262-x
1. Baptists—Doctrines. I. George, Timothy. II. Richard D. Land. III. Title.
BX6462.7.B36 1997
286'.132—dc-21 97-4403
CIP

1 2 3 4 5 01 00 99 98 97

Contents

General Editors' Introduction

The Baptist movement as we know it today began as a small persecuted sect in pre-Revolutionary England. One critic labeled them as "miscreants begat in rebellion, born in sedition, and nursed in faction." Excluded by law from the English universities, Baptists developed their own structures for pastoral training. They also wrote hymns, preached sermons, published confessions, and defended their beliefs against skeptics, detractors, and rival religious groups of all kinds. From the popular works of John Bunyan and Benjamin Keach to the learned theology of John Gill and Andrew Fuller, Baptists wrote with a passion and with a purpose. In time, a large body of Baptist literature was developed, writings that both reflected and contributed to the emerging sense of Baptist identity.

The Southern Baptist Convention (SBC) was organized in 1845 for the purpose of "eliciting, combining, and directing the energies of the whole denomination in one sacred effort, for the propagation of the gospel." This was an ambitious undertaking for the 293 "delegates," as they were then called, who gathered in Augusta, Georgia, and embraced this far-reaching vision at the founding meeting of the Convention. Through the years the SBC has suffered numerous setbacks and distractions—the Civil War, Reconstruction, the Great Depression, social unrest, denominational strife, and much more. But through it all, God has graciously blessed Southern Baptists in ways that future historians will surely record as remarkable. By the end of the twentieth century, Southern Baptists had grown into America's largest Protestant denomination, a fellowship of some fifteen million members in nearly forty thousand congregations, supporting more than nine thousand missionaries.

Drawing on this rich heritage, the Library of Baptist Classics presents a series of books reflecting the faith and vision of Southern Baptists over the past 150 years. We are republishing in fresh editions and with new introductions a collection of seminal writings. These works have proven their worth as classics among Southern Baptists in the past and still speak powerfully to Baptists and other evangelical Christians today.

The Library of Baptist Classics includes writings of pastors, theologians, missionary statesmen, and denominational leaders from the past. Some of them are popular, others scholarly in form. They include sermons, doctrinal treatises, missionary biographies, and an anthology of Baptist confessions, covenants, and catechisms. Most of these writings have long been out of print. We present them now in the fervent hope that the Lord will see fit to use them again, as He has in the past, not only to remind us of the great legacy we have received, but also to inspire us to be faithful shapers of the future under the lordship of Jesus Christ.

Timothy George and Denise George,
General Editors

Introduction

TIMOTHY GEORGE AND RICHARD D. LAND

Nearly one hundred years ago, at the dawn of the twentieth century, the Baptist Sunday School Board published a collection of twenty-five essays under the title, *Baptist Why and Why Not.* This remarkable little book was dedicated to "the Baptists of the world in their contending for the faith once for all delivered to the saints." This volume was introduced by J. M. Frost, the executive leader (then called "Corresponding Secretary") of the Baptist Sunday School Board, but it included chapters by both Southern and Northern Baptists. The tone of the volume was at once irenic—recognizing that Baptists shared much in common with other Bible-believing Christians—and at the same time distinctively denominational in its ringing affirmation of Baptist identity.

Now that we are perched on the other side of this same century, a moment that also brings to a close the second millennium of Christian history, we think it is time for thoughtful and committed Baptists to revisit the issues raised by J. M. Frost and his colleagues one hundred years ago. The differences between Baptists then and Baptists now are staggering in many respects. Southern Baptists and Northern Baptists were roughly equivalent in size in 1900, both claiming slightly more than 1 million adherents each. Today Northern Baptists, renamed American Baptists in 1950, are about the same size as they were in 1900. Southern Baptists, on the other hand, have grown dramatically in the last century and now number more than 15 million members in more than forty thousand congregations.

But statistics alone do not tell the whole story. Powerful currents of theology and culture have shaped the development of Baptists in this country, both North and South, white and black. In the early part of this century, white Baptist churches in the North were split apart by the convulsions of the Fundamentalist-Modernist controversies while white Baptists in the South consolidated their strength and streamlined their efforts on behalf of missions and evangelism.

Since World War II, Southern Baptists have moved beyond their traditional regional base to become a truly national denomination. In recent decades, they have resisted assimilation into the mainline Protestant paradigm by reclaiming a high view of biblical authority as the basis for a new denominational consensus.

This realignment, which is often touted as a "conservative resurgence," has given Southern Baptists a much stronger voice in the wider evangelical movement. At the same time, new questions have been posed about issues of denominational strategy, methodology, and even theology. The question of 1900 remains: "Baptist—why and why not?" American Baptist churches, on the other hand, have become more openly identified with mainline Protestant concerns even as their numerical strength continues to wane. At the same time, crosscurrents of change and realignment continue to affect Baptists of all kinds. There is a fledgling renewal movement among American Baptist evangelicals while a minority of Southern Baptist moderates, some more theologically liberal than others, have organized their own infra-denominational efforts in protest to the conservative direction of the Southern Baptist Convention (SBC). Since 1900, African-American Baptists have also divided into several major denominational groupings, though less out of theological than personal and organizational concerns. Most of the essays in this book are focused on issues of renewal within the SBC, but the issues raised are pertinent for all Baptists who live with the tension of identity and adaptability in a changing world.

The opening chapter in this volume, "People of the Book: The Baptist Doctrine of Holy Scripture," is one of the last writings to be completed by the late Herschel H. Hobbs, Baptist patriarch and leading pastor-theologian of the denomination. Hobbs chaired the committee that drafted the 1963 revision of *The Baptist Faith and Message*, the guiding confessional standard of the SBC. For many years Hobbs served as pastor of the First Baptist Church of Oklahoma City. He was dearly beloved and well known as an expository preacher, astute Bible scholar, and faithful teacher of God's Word.

In this posthumously published essay, Hobbs affirms the doctrine of biblical inerrancy, claiming that the historical accuracy of the Scriptures has been confirmed by the evidence of archaeology. Hobbs was revered by all sectors of the SBC, and his unswerving commitment to the total truthfulness of the Bible was a significant factor in the recovery of a high doctrine of scriptural inspiration and authority within the SBC. In this article, Hobbs quotes one of his former teachers, John R. Sampey, who stated that the biblical writers were "preserved from all error by the inbreathed Spirit guiding them." Hobbs was an important personal link between the generation of Sampey and A. T. Robertson, another one of his teachers at Southern Seminary, and the contemporary renaissance of conservative biblical scholarship in the SBC represented by the multivolume New American Commentary project.

Hobbs's view of the Bible echoes the language of J. M. Frost, first published in the original introduction to the 1900 edition of *Baptist Why and Why Not*: "We accept the Scriptures as an all-sufficient and infallible rule of faith and practice, and insist upon the absolute inerrancy and sole authority of the Word of God. We recognize at this point no room for division, either of practice or belief, or even sentiment. More and more we must come to feel as the deepest and mightiest power of our conviction that a 'thus saith the Lord' is the end of all controversy." This statement by Frost has been etched in stone and placed on a plaque just outside the office of the president of the Baptist Sunday School Board—a reminder of the historic Baptist commitment to the Bible.

Timothy George applauds the renewed emphasis on a high doctrine of Holy Scripture, but he also argues that the pronouncement of inerrancy alone will not stop the theological erosion that has been going on for several generations in SBC life. He calls for a renewed commitment to the communitarian character of Baptist life as exemplified by the use of church covenants, confessions, and catechisms. These historic documents can be used by local congregations as a means of reconnecting to the rich theological legacy of the past. Peering into the future, he claims that the recent conservative victory in the SBC will prove hollow unless it is accompanied by genuine spiritual and theological renewal. Such renewal, he asserts, will be marked by five classic principles drawn from the Baptist heritage. These "benchmarks for shaping Baptist theological identity" are orthodox convictions, an evangelical heritage, the perspective of Reformed theology, Baptist ecclesiological distinctives, and a renewed focus on the confessional context of both congregational and denominational life.

Historic Baptist theology supported a strong evangelistic and missionary witness, primary goals of the SBC since its founding in 1845. Chuck Kelley examines four major methods of doing evangelism that have shaped contemporary Southern Baptist practice: decisional preaching, personal evangelism, outreach through the Sunday school, and revivalism. Kelley claims that the genius of Southern Baptist evangelism is not to be found in the methods themselves but rather in their integration, which has proven to be an effective means for reaching lost men and women with the gospel of Jesus Christ. Kelley sets forth several key evangelistic strategies for sharing the gospel with the unreached millions who are yet perishing without hope in Christ. These strategies include renewed focus on church planting, assigning specific responsibility for evangelistic witness, and adopting non-Southern Baptist tools for sharing the gospel with others. At the conclusion of his essay, Kelley declares, "If Southern Baptists are to find the strategies to reach our nation . . . it will come when we are on our knees before a holy, sovereign God and follow his agenda for how to grow churches."

Along with evangelism, missions has been a major priority of the SBC, which resolved at its founding meeting "to organize a Society for the propagation of the Gospel." In the twentieth century, Southern Baptists have emerged as one of the leading missionary-sending bodies in the evangelical world. More than five thousand missionaries are currently serving the cause of Christ throughout the world under the sponsorship of the Southern Baptist International Mission Board. One of those missionaries, Rebekah Ann Naylor, is the coauthor of "Into All the World: Fulfilling the Great Commission."

A physician and longtime medical missionary to India, Dr. Rebekah Naylor wrote this missionary challenge with her father, Dr. Robert E. Naylor, denominational statesman and former president of Southwestern Baptist Theological Seminary. This father-daughter essay presents both a biblical and theological rationale for responding obediently to Jesus' missionary mandate. A succinct historical overview of the Baptist missionary movement is also included. The latter part of this chapter presents the witness of Rebekah Naylor herself. Her ministry through the Bangalore Baptist Hospital is a brilliant example of how God can use one dedicated servant to share His love anywhere in the world.

The first Baptist educational institution in America was Brown University, founded in 1765 as Rhode Island College.

Since that time, Baptists have invested enormous resources to endow and support academies, colleges, and theological seminaries to advance the life of the mind in the context of nurturing communities of faith and love. Henry Dunster, the first president of Harvard College, once said that the primary purpose of that school was "to lay Christ in the bottom as the only foundation of all sound knowledge and learning." That same purpose statement could be made with reference to nearly every Baptist institution founded in this country since 1765. Carl F. H. Henry issues a stirring challenge for Baptist institutions of higher education to remain faithful to the great legacy they have received from the past even as they forge new strategies in shaping the Christian worldview of the coming generation.

Henry himself has been a major voice for theological renewal both within the SBC and in the wider evangelical community. Henry's concern for biblical fidelity in higher education echoes the sentiment of E. B. Pollard who wrote in the 1900 edition of *Baptist Why and Why Not*: "We shall find ourselves forever losing at the top if we do not impart to the youth before he leaves our halls of learning a systematic and stable knowledge of the Bible and an intelligent respect for its teachings. We have no right . . . to doom ourselves to denominational mediocrity by neglecting the Word of God as a potent factor in education."

In his essay on Baptist ecclesiology, Paige Patterson presents a comprehensive overview of the doctrine of the church, with special emphasis on the confessional character of corporate Christian life. While Baptists have historically agreed with the mainline reformers of the sixteenth century on issues of salvation and scriptural authority, on the application of these principles to church life they have sided more with the Anabaptists who sought to restore the New Testament pattern of regenerate church membership. Patterson also reviews biblical images of the church such as the people of God, the body of Christ, the fellowship of the Spirit, and the temple of the Lord. He rightly points out the dynamic understanding of the church based on faithful obedience to the Great Commission, which has motivated Baptist commitment to missions and evangelism. Patterson concludes this essay by applying the biblical principles of ecclesiology to the ordinances of baptism and the Lord's Supper, church governance, worship, and connectional cooperation. While he strongly affirms the congregational model of church polity, he stoutly rejects a false understanding of "church autonomy" that minimizes the lordship of Christ and the authority of Holy Scripture.

In his article on worship, David S. Dockery examines an important dimension of church life that has become increasingly controversial among many congregations in recent years. Diversity in Baptist worship styles is nothing new, as the contrasting traditions of Charleston and Sandy Creek demonstrate. Dockery believes that issues of worship style should not obscure more basic commitments to faithful biblical and God-centered worship. As more and more Southern Baptist congregations are influenced by seeker-friendly models of outreach and church life, the importance of a sound theology of worship is magnified. Dockery's essay offers a good foundation for reflection and further exploration of this timely theme.

T. W. Hunt's article on the ministry of prayer in a local congregation reflects a growing hunger for spiritual life and communion with God in Baptist life today. The phenomenal success of Henry Blackaby's *Experiencing God*, together with numerous conferences and concerts of prayer that regularly convene in many cities, is a further indication of a remarkable spiritual vitality among evangelical Christians. Hunt's article focuses both on the theology of prayer and the methodology of local church prayer ministry. He encourages meditation on the attributes of God and cultivation of the fear of the Lord, humility, purity, and sincerity as part of a proper preparation for prayer. Students of revival indicate that unusual outpourings of God's Spirit have historically occurred following an intense time of prayer and seeking God's face. As Baptists face important issues of outreach, missions, and organization at the dawn of the twenty-first century, no issue is more important than the recovery of an authentic and deep-rooted spirituality. As the traditional hymn puts it, "All is vain unless the Spirit of the Living God comes down."

O. S. Hawkins begins his chapter, "The Preaching Event: A True Baptist Distinctive," by noting the centrality of proclamation in the Baptist tradition. This fact is symbolized in most Baptist churches by the placement of the pulpit on center stage in the sanctuary. Hawkins explores the role of preaching in "an ecotonic period of history" when the traditional approaches of confession and confrontation are being eclipsed by soft-sell and frequently watered-down forms of communication. Hawkins argues for the restoration of a balanced model of apostolic proclamation, citing the biblical example of the apostle Paul. At the heart of this approach is a strong commitment to faithful expository preaching, a method that both honors the historic Baptist commitment to biblical authority and exalts the person and work of Jesus Christ.

Baptist Christians cannot ignore the awesome responsibility they bear as citizens of God's kingdom in a this-worldly society. Richard D. Land calls on Christians to apply the principles of righteousness to every area of human endeavor, citing the classic statement of *The Baptist Faith and Message*, which declares that "every Christian is under obligation to seek to make the will of Christ supreme in his own life and in human society." In recent years, the separation of church and state has been misconstrued to mean the divorce of moral values from the public square. Land shows that this was not the purpose of the First Amendment nor the implication of Christian citizenship based on the teachings of Jesus. When Christians are truly motivated by the compassion of Christ, "that love will savor the salt and energize the light that our Savior has called us to be."

In recent years much attention has been given to "family values" as politicians of varying views have sought to exploit this theme for their own purposes. In her essay on "Family Values in Baptist Life," however, Dorothy Patterson shows that concern for the family is neither new nor essentially political in nature. On the contrary, throughout Christian history God has used the home as the "primary classroom for teaching His people about Himself and the holy lifestyle." The rudiments of Christian nurture and discipleship should be developed within the family circle by godly parents committed to passing on the faith intact to the rising generation. As Baptists face the future, they will need to develop models of countercultural parenting and nurturing if they are to preserve the integrity of the family in an increasingly secularized and feminized culture. Patterson's article provides both biblical and historical resources for developing faithful family commitments in a fragmenting world.

In his informative essay, "Holding the Ropes: A Strategy for Christian Stewardship," Morris H. Chapman challenges Southern Baptists to work together more closely for the sake of the gospel. The expression "holding the ropes" recalls the origin of the modern missionary movement connected with William Carey who agreed to "go down into the mine" while his fellow Baptists back home "held the rope." Thus began a cooperative pattern of missions and ministry that has continued to undergird the work of the SBC to this day. In recent years, Southern Baptists have set new records for missions giving through the Cooperative Program and the two convention-wide annual missions collections, the Lottie Moon Christmas Offering and the Annie Armstrong Easter Offering. For all this, it is imperative that Baptists not forget the biblical basis for Christian stewardship nor the need to give sacrificially so that the work of Christ may continue to go forward both at home and abroad.

The concluding chapter in this volume originated as a message delivered by Robert Reccord at the June 1996 annual meeting of the SBC in New Orleans. "Implementation of the Covenant for a New Century" sets forth the vision and challenge for a major restructuring of the SBC as it prepares to enter the third millennium of Christian history. Reccord based his stirring message on Hebrews 12:1–3, "Let us run with perseverance the race marked out for us" (v. 1, NIV). He called on Southern Baptists to "seize the baton . . . and sprint into the twenty-first century" in order to accomplish the purpose of the denomination set forth by its founders more than 150 years ago, namely, the task of "eliciting, combining, and directing the energies of the whole denomination in one sacred effort, for the propagation of the Gospel." In this connection, Reccord exhorted the messengers to the 1996 SBC to pray for a renewed and passionate thirst for God, to remain faithful to the Cooperative Program as the most effective means for doing missions and ministry together, and to support the Covenant for a New Century as the best means for reallocating resources for evangelism, missions, and church planting. Later in this session of the convention, the messengers voted overwhelmingly to embrace the Covenant for a New Century, thus committing the SBC to a new paradigm for advancing the cause of Christ in North America and throughout the world.

CHAPTER ONE

People of the Book: The Baptist Doctrine of the Holy Scripture

HERSCHEL H. HOBBS

Sir Walter Scott was terminally ill. He asked someone to read to him from "The Book." Since he had a large library the person asked, "Which book?" The reply: "The Bible! There is but one Book, the Bible."

Most Southern Baptists could say the same thing, for we have always been a "people of the Book." This is our heritage.

God's Inerrant Word

The 1963 *Baptist Faith and Message* states that the Bible has "truth, without any mixture of error, for its matter."

Listen to the past. James P. Boyce, first president of Southern Baptist Theological Seminary, said that we should view the Bible as if God had written every word Himself or as if He had spoken it to us directly. John Dagg, nineteenth-century theologian and president of Mercer University, held that inspiration extended to the very words, and not just to the thoughts, of Scripture.

J. M. Frost, first head of the Sunday School Board, in 1906 wrote that Southern Baptists "insist upon absolute inerrancy . . . of the word of God."

J. B. Tidwell, former head of the Bible Department at Baylor University, in 1935 wrote in a Sunday School Board book that biblical writers considered "every verse and line and even every tense of the verb, every number of the noun, and every little particle" as coming from God.

Basil Manly, one of the first four professors of Southern Seminary, espoused "plenary" inspiration.

John A. Broadus, another of the four founders of Southern Seminary, held that biblical writers "were preserved by the Holy Spirit from error."

John R. Sampey, president of Southern Seminary when I was a student there, identified with those who believed that "the writers were preserved from all error by the inbreathed Spirit guiding them."

And A. T. Robertson, the greatest New Testament scholar Southern Baptists ever produced, spoke favorably of the "inerrancy of God's original Scriptures."

Incidentally, I sat within ten feet of Dr. Robertson in senior Greek class at Southern Seminary in September 1934, when he suffered a stroke that took his life ninety minutes later. On the previous Friday, he had given to the class what could have been his last and, perhaps, greatest testimony concerning the Scriptures. He said, "I have been studying, preaching, teaching, and writing about the New Testament for over fifty years. But I never open my Greek New Testament without seeing something I never saw before."

E. Y. Mullins, probably Southern Baptists' greatest theologian and president of Southern Seminary, chaired the committee that drew up the 1925 statement of *The Baptist Faith and Message*. Surely with his approval, the committee borrowed from the 1833 New Hampshire Confession of Faith the statement that the Scripture has "God for its author, salvation for its end, and truth, without any mixture of error for its matter." It was my privilege to chair the committee that presented to the Southern Baptist Convention the 1963 statement of *The Baptist Faith and Message*. We retained that statement in the 1963 Statement.

Of interest is the fact that this inerrancy statement did not come from a pastor or theologian. It came from the English philosopher John Locke. It is found in a bound book of his letters. He had received a letter from a young minister asking what he should do in order to have a successful ministry. Locke's reply is dated in September 1702, one year before his death. He wrote, "Preach the Bible. For it has God for its author, salvation for its end, and truth, without any mixture of error, for its matter." The above statement, "its . . . matter," is found in both the 1925 and 1963 *The Baptist Faith and Message*—borrowed from the New Hampshire Confession of 1833.

When the 1963 Statement was presented to the Convention, not one question was asked about the article on the Scriptures. The only question raised by a small group was about one sentence added to the 1925 Statement on the "Church." It stated that the word "church" is used a few times to refer to all the redeemed of all the ages. This small group voted against the adoption of the 1963 Statement. But it was adopted by an overwhelming majority anyway. The "Preamble" of the Statement is designed to protect Southern Baptists from creedalism. It is simply a statement of basics generally believed by Southern Baptists.

Subsequently, every agency of the Southern Baptist Convention has voluntarily adopted the 1963 Statement as its statement of faith. Many, if not all, state conventions have followed suit. Many local churches have done likewise. I am aware of only one local church that considered it and refused to adopt it as such. It agreed with the Statement but refused to let anyone outside that congregation tell it what it believed. Three of our seminaries use it as the document of faith signed by all faculty members.

Repeatedly since 1963, the Southern Baptist Convention has refused to change its statement of faith in the inerrant Word of God. For instance, to use the word *infallible* weakens the Statement. Some dictionaries give two meanings of *infallible*: without error; and anything that does what it is supposed to do. You may have a dull knife with gaps in the blade. But if you use it only to cut string, and it does, in that sense, it is infallible, even though it is full of flaws. In that sense, the Bible could be full of errors. But if it is to lead people to salvation in Christ, and if it does, it is infallible.

No, the stronger word is *inerrant*. And this leads me to make three observations about the Bible.

The Bible Is Divinely Inspired

Before me as I write is a leatherbound book. The Greek word for book is *biblos*, whence comes our word "Bible." *Biblia* is the Greek word for "little books." The *Biblos* is made up of sixty-six *Biblia*, thirty-nine in the Old Testament and twenty-seven in the New Testament. These little books were written over a period of fifteen hundred years in places from Babylon to Rome. They had at least forty-five different authors, including kings, prophets, priests, poets, fishermen, a physician, a law-giver, and farmers. None of them knew he was writing what one day would be the Bible.

If one reads the Old Testament without a knowledge of the New Testament, he would ask, "Where is the rest of the story?" Reading the New Testament without a knowledge of the Old, he would ask, "Where is that which preceded it?" Yet when gathered together in the Canon of Scripture, they tell a complete story. The New completes the Old.

This cannot be said about any other set of books. The only logical explanation is that these sixty-six little books had one author—God, through His Holy Spirit.

Evidences of divine inspiration of the Bible are found throughout its pages. Moses wrote at the command of the Lord. "Thus saith the Lord" thunders throughout the prophets.

Second Peter 1:20–21 reads, "No prophecy of the Scripture is of any private interpretation" (v. 20).* This is an unfortunate translation, supporting the idea that only the clergy is qualified to interpret Scripture. Actually it should read "is of private origin." A. T. Robertson says that no prophet is a "self-starter." Instead, "The prophecy came not in old time by the will of man: but holy men of God spake as they were moved by the Holy Ghost [Spirit]" (v. 21). The Greek word for "moved" was used of a ship bearing its cargo along. The authors of the Scripture were picked up and borne along by the Holy Spirit.

In 2 Timothy 3:16 Paul wrote, "All scripture is given by inspiration of God." Literally, "All Scripture is God-breathed." *Inspire* means "to breathe in." The Holy Spirit breathed into the writers the message of God.

Some say that all Scripture is God-breathed, but that all the Bible is not Scripture. That is not what Paul wrote. The Greek word for "all" is without the definite article. "All" without the definite article means every single part of the whole, nothing excepted. So every single part of the whole of Scripture is God-breathed. And a God of truth does not breathe error!

Of course in inspiration there is both a divine and a human side. For instance, in parallel accounts of the Gospels, one uses "kingdom of God" while another used "kingdom of heaven." It is a case of different words but the same meaning. Most interesting is Jesus' mention of a camel going through the eye of a needle. Matthew and Mark used the word for a sewing needle. Luke, a physician, used the one for a surgical needle. Each used the word with which he was familiar. Again, different words but the same meaning.

Among Southern Baptists, two theories are held as to the method of inspiration. The Plenary Theory holds that the Holy Spirit inspired every word in the Bible. The Dynamic Theory holds that the Holy Spirit inspired the message, guarded the authors from error, but left each one free to write it in his own

---

* Unless otherwise noted, all Scripture quotations in this chapter are from the King James Version of the Bible.

way, so that each book bears the imprint of its author's personality. Both views see the Bible as the divinely inspired Word of God.

The Bible Is Historically Accurate

Had efforts to destroy the Bible been made against any other book, it would have disappeared ages ago. But the Bible still remains as the best seller. Through dedicated people, the Holy Spirit, who inspired the Bible, has also preserved it.

One of the most vicious efforts to destroy the Bible has been made by seeking to undermine its historical accuracy. And in this struggle, archaeology has proved to be one of the greatest friends of the Bible. Where this science has thrown light on problems pertaining to the Bible, it has always supported God's Word.

Many years ago Sir William Ramsey, a British archaeologist, went into the Middle East with the expressed purpose of proving that a man named Paul never lived and that Luke (Luke–Acts) was totally unreliable as to historical material. After years of digging, he changed completely. He wrote books about Paul, such as *St. Paul the Traveller and Roman Citizen* and *The Cities of St. Paul.* He also wrote a book on Luke in which he said that Luke was one of the greatest historians. Ramsey found that where Luke did not coincide with known Roman history, our knowledge of Roman history was incomplete. This fact has been enlarged by later discoveries in archaeology. A prime example is the enrollment for taxation mentioned in Luke's account of Jesus' birth. Negative critics questioned and even denied that such was ever taken. Records in the papyri now show that beginning in 8 B.C. such an enrollment was made every fourteen years, reaching into the last quarter of the third century A.D. There are very few gaps in this chain of papyri examples.

Space does not permit an exhaustive set of examples. But let us look at two found respectively in Daniel 5 and John 5.

Daniel 5 gives the account of a banquet given by King Belshazzar. It was on that night that Babylon fell to the Mede-Persians under Darius the Mede. And Belshazzar was slain. Thus, according to Daniel, he was the last king of Babylon.

The negative critics had a field day concerning Belshazzar. They said that the last king of Babylon was Nabonidus. As for Belshazzar, his name did not exist other than in the book of Daniel. They insisted that it was a fictitious name chosen by the author of Daniel as one would do in writing a novel. These critics pointed out that Nabonidus was the last king of Babylon. The friends of the Bible had no definitive answer for that charge.

But once again archaeology came to the rescue. Many years ago archaeologists discovered the ruins of a library in that region. In it they found what is known as the Babylonian Cylinder, which gives the history of the Babylonian empire. Ancient Babylon had many canals, which resulted in the city having a high humidity. This did not agree with Nabonidus's health. So he moved to Tema (a city in the empire), built a palace, and reigned there. He left his son to reign as king in Babylon. And his son's name was—Belshazzar! Daniel had preserved a bit of Babylonian history that was otherwise unknown for centuries and centuries.

John 5 relates the healing of the lame man at the pool of Bethesda. It is said to have had five porches or colonnaded areas and was located near the sheep gate. From the book of Nehemiah we know the location of the sheep gate. Negative critics said that there was no pool there. Instead they suggested the pool of Siloam and Virgin's Fountain. Furthermore, they belittled the idea of five porches. Four, perhaps on the four sides. But not five.

Their argument was based on their contention that the Gospel of John was written in the second century by an Elder John of Ephesus who made a tourist's visit to Palestine and then wrote the gospel. Also they contended that it was a theological treatise with no historical value.

In 1885, a German archaeologist discovered the ruins of a Crusaders' shrine in that area. The Crusaders built shrines at sacred places. Why they did not excavate the site I do not know. But in recent years it has been done. During the time of this "dig," Frances and I made periodic visits to Palestine and followed the progress of the excavation. On our final visit they had completed it. Without doubt this is the pool of Bethesda, exactly, where John said it was. The bases for the columns of the five porches are there. On all four sides and a fifth down the middle, they form two pools.

This authenticates the historical value of the Gospel. It also shows that it was not written by a second-century Elder John with only a tourist's knowledge. It was written by someone who was familiar with the topography of Jerusalem prior to A.D. 70, when the city was destroyed by the Romans. Who else but the apostle John? Thus, once again, the "stones" cried out to show the accuracy of the Bible.

The Bible Is Scientifically Correct

The Bible is not a textbook in science, but when it speaks in that realm, it speaks truth. It does so, not in the technical terminology of modern science, but in the popular language of the people. And truth is truth, no matter in what language it may be recorded.

One area in which the Bible is confronted by the worldly-minded is miracles. Humanism says that what man cannot do, God cannot do. Hence to them, the miraculous is dismissed as contrary to natural law and merely the product of primitive, superstitious minds. But does man know all of God's laws?

Let me define *miracle*. It is an act of God, contrary to natural law as man understands it, but not contrary to natural law as God understands it, and through which He works to accomplish His redemptive will and purpose.

It is true that God has ordained that the natural universe shall operate by laws. Otherwise we would live in a madhouse. But at the same time, God has other laws that are brought into play to accomplish a given end. The law of gravity says that a heavier-than-air object, if suspended in air, will fall to the ground. However, God has another law, the law of aerodynamics, that enables a plane weighing tons and tons to fly through the air. Yet, the law of gravity still works. If the pilot violates the law of aerodynamics, the plane will crash to the ground. The examples could be almost endless. The truth is that all of God's laws have been in God's mind and plan from eternity. Some of them man has discovered and uses. I personally prefer to say that God revealed them rather than that man discovered them.

Take, for instance, the atom bomb. The United States and Nazi Germany were in a race to produce it. Neither side had a corner on mental power. In fact, following World War II some of the greatest minds in the field were German nuclear scientists brought into our nation's nuclear and space programs.

Just suppose that Hitler had had the first nuclear bomb. The consequences are too terrible to imagine!

The major arena of conflict between the Bible and science is as to the origin of the universe and of man. Let me say at the outset that some theologians and scientists may disagree, but between true religion and true science there is no disagreement. For instance, if you take the biblical account of Creation and the facts, not theories, of the various sciences such as geology, botany, biology, and anthropology, and lay them side by side, they are in basic agreement i.e., both the Bible and biology agree that life began in water.

It is when some scientists bring the theory of evolution into the process that conflict ensues. Evolution is a theory, nothing more. There is evidence of development within given species, but there is no evidence that any lower species ever climbed to a higher level. To teach that evolution is a fact, not a theory, is grossly unscientific.

Material science is incapable of determining the cause of the universe and of man. It deals only with observable phenomena. Indeed, it moves backward from effect to cause until it finally comes to the first effect for which there is no observable cause. This requires a leap of faith; therefore, it ceases to be science and becomes religion.

The Bible takes that leap of faith when it says, "In the beginning God" (Gen. 1:1). When we introduce God into the process it involves a Person.

Let us put it another way. We look at a beautiful building. We know that before the architect put pen to paper he saw the finished product in his mind or thought. So we move back from thing to thought. Eventually we come to a thought before which there is no thing. A thought implies a thinker. So again we must take the leap of faith to see the thinker as God. For the scientist to see this, he too must take the leap of faith. It is at that point that he ceases to be a scientist and becomes a man of religion. This was true of Dr. Arthur Compton, noted physicist. In an interview with a Chicago newspaper, he said that the most profound statement ever written is "In the beginning God."

Many years ago a graduate student in physics at Northwestern University came to my office. He was a Christian who had been led to Christ by the head of the physics department of that school. He told me the following story.

The head of the physics department told the graduate student that, by the rule of cause and effect, he had answers to all his questions when he first came to Northwestern. But one day he was studying a specimen under a microscope. On the lens of the microscope there was a speck of dust. There was an effect for which he had no cause. And that speck of dust led him to God!

Did God create the universe and all those in it in six, twenty-four-hour days? Not necessarily. The word "day" *(yom)* is used three different ways in Genesis 1. We use it in various ways. One may interpret it as he sees it. Science sees the creative act involving vast eras of time. If one says millions or billions of years, it does not change one word in the Bible. "In the beginning" can refer to one second or to vast eons. It is not how much time God needed but how much He took. He could have done it in a fraction of a second, or He could have used billions of years. In either case it was "In the beginning."

Does Genesis 1 teach a flat earth? Some so interpret it. But what about Isaiah 40:22 where God is said to sit on the circle of the earth?

Harry Rimmer was a Presbyterian minister. He was also a first-rate scientist, as attested by his membership in leading scientific societies in Europe and the United States. About halfway through his ministry, he left the pastorate to devote the rest of his life to lecturing on university campuses and in churches and to writing books on the harmony of science and the Scriptures. He told me the following story.

When he entered this new phase of work, he deposited one thousand dollars in a bank. Then he placed an ad in papers across the country saying that anyone who could find and prove a scientific error in the Bible could have the one thousand dollars. Through the years he received many letters pointing out supposed biblical errors. But when he replied explaining the cited Scripture and the scientific meaning, they accepted it.

With one exception. A man sued him in a court in New York state. It was called *So-and-So v. the Bible*. The case was tried before a judge and jury, following the rules of evidence as in any legal case. The jury decided in favor of the Bible.

Dr. Rimmer died with the one thousand dollars plus earnings intact. If there are so many scientific errors in the Bible, as some insist, why didn't someone claim the one thousand dollars?

Constant and Unchangeable

The Bible is constant in existence and in meaning. Efforts to destroy it have failed. Its message is as appropriate today as it was in the first century. Man's outer living conditions change from generation to generation, but his spiritual needs remain the same. As Hebrews 13:8 says of God's Living Word, so we may say of His written Word: It is "the same yesterday and today and forever" (NIV).

This is not true of science. Dealing in theories, it changes from day to day, perhaps from hour to hour.

I am told that in a library in Paris are thousands of volumes that once were the latest word in science. Now they merely gather dust.

Some years ago an effort was made to place in high school textbooks the biblical account of Creation alongside evolutionary theories. The evolutionists screamed to high heaven. That fact tells me they are not as secure in their position as they would have us to think. Truth is not afraid to be confronted by error.

When I was still a pastor, I said in a sermon, "Any textbook in science that is ten years old is obsolete." After the service a lady who taught science in high school came to me. "Pastor," she said, "I want to update you on your information." I replied, "I can stand it. What is it?" She continued, "Any textbook in science that is published is obsolete. Science moves so rapidly that between the time the author finishes his manuscript and it appears in published form, scientific research has moved on beyond it. We have students read them [textbooks] as parallel reading. But we teach from mimeographed material that is prepared daily."

Now the question: Are you willing to place your trust in something that is in a constant state of flux? Or will you place it in the Bible, God's solid rock of revealed truth? Your answer bears eternal consequences!

CHAPTER TWO

The Future of Southern Baptist Theology

TIMOTHY GEORGE

Several years ago Will D. Campbell published a fascinating novel entitled *The Glad River*. The chief character was a man named Doops Momber. Actually his real name was Claudy Momber, but everybody called him Doops because Claudy sounded too much like a girl's name. He grew up among the Baptists of Mississippi, attended the revivals, the hayrides, and the Sunday school wiener roasts, but somehow he never got baptized. Later when he was inducted into the army, his sergeant asked, "You a Protestant or a Catholic?" Doops did not answer for a moment. Then he said, "I guess I'm neither. I'm neither Catholic or Protestant. I never joined. But all my people are Baptist." "But there's a P on your dog tag. Why not a C?" "They asked me what I was and I told them the same thing I told you. And the guy stamped a P on it." "Why do you suppose they did that?" the sergeant asked. "Well," said Doops, "I guess in America you have to be something."[1]

The confusion Doops encountered about his own religious identity is symptomatic of many other Baptist Christians who, unlike Doops, have indeed taken the plunge, but who, no more than he, have any solid understanding about what that means in a post-denominational age of generic religion and dog-tag Christianity. Several years ago I published an essay entitled "The Renewal of Baptist Theology" which began with the following lamentation:

> There is a crisis in Baptist life today which cannot be resolved by bigger budgets, better programs, or more sophisticated systems of data processing and mass communication. It is a crisis of identity rooted in a fundamental theological failure of nerve. The two major diseases of the contemporary church are spiritual amnesia (we have forgotten who we are) and ecclesiastical myopia (whoever we are, we are glad we are not like "them"). While these maladies are not unique to the people of God called Baptists, they are perhaps most glaringly present among us.[2]

This article is a sequel to that earlier essay. First of all, I want to point out some of the difficulties in speaking about the theological identity of Baptists. Then, in the heart of the article, I will present a mosaic for the renewal of Baptist theology by identifying five major components for such an agenda.

Diversity and Adversity

The first problem in sorting out the theological identity of Baptists is the sheer diversity of the movement. From the beginning of the Baptist experiment in seventeenth-century England, General (Arminian) and Particular (Calvinistic) Baptists developed diverse, even mutually incompatible, paradigms for what it meant to be a Baptist. The Particulars, who were better educated, better organized, and more successful than the Generals, forged alliances with other mainstream dissenting bodies, denying that they were in any way guilty of "those heterodoxies and fundamental errors" that had been unfairly attributed to them.[3] The Generals, on the other hand, were drawn into the orbit of that "swarm of sectaries and schismatics," as John Taylor put it, that included Levelers, Ranters, Seekers, Quakers, and, at the far end of the Puritan movement, the mysterious Family of Love. It was, as Christopher Hill has called it, a world turned upside down. An anonymous rhymester may well have had the General Baptists in mind when he penned these lines in 1641: "When women preach and cobblers pray, the fiends in hell make holiday."[4]

The diversification of the Baptist tradition that began in England was accelerated in America where the great fact of national life was the frontier—a seemingly endless expanse that offered limitless opportunities for escaping the past. "If you and yours don't agree with me and mine, you can pack your Scofield Bibles in your hip pockets and start your own church!" And so they did. The line stretches from Roger Williams, who left Massachusetts to practice soul-liberty in Rhode Island; to Brigham Young, who carried the Mormons to Utah; to Jim Jones in California and David Koresh in Waco. The frontier was always there.

As for the Baptists, one only has to skim through Mead's *Handbook of Denominations* to appreciate the bewildering variety. Among many others, there are American Baptists, Southern Baptists, National Baptists, United Baptists, Conservative Baptists, General Association of Regular Baptists (GARB), Free Will Baptists, Landmark Baptists, Duck River and Kindred Associations of Baptists, Six Principle Baptists, Primitive Baptists, Seventh Day Baptists, Two-Seed-in-the-Spirit Predestinarian Baptists, and the National Baptist Evangelical Life and Soul-Saving Assembly of the USA, Inc. That's a lot of Baptists! How do you talk about theological identity amidst that kind of variety?

There's a second factor we also need to consider—not only *diversity* within the tradition but *adversity* from the environing culture. While Baptists in America, especially in the South, have long been accustomed to the accoutrements of an established religion, we began as a small, persecuted sect. Long after the 1689 Act of Toleration granted statutory freedom of worship, Baptists, along with other Nonconformists in England, suffered harassment, discrimination, and ridicule. One critic labels them as "miscreants begat in rebellion, born in sedition, and nursed in faction."[5] The struggles for religious liberty continued for Baptists in America. Obadiah Holmes was publicly beaten on the streets of Danvers, Massachusetts, and John Leland was clapped into a Virginia jail.

An example of the low esteem in which Baptist folk were held in the early nineteenth century was recorded by David Benedict, who traveled by horseback through all seventeen states of the new nation collecting historical information and impressions about the Baptists. One person, "a very honest and candid old lady," gave Benedict the following impression she had formed of the Baptists: "There was a company of them in the back part of our town, and an outlandish set of people they certainly were. . . . You could hardly find one among them but what was deformed in some way or other. Some of them were hair-lipped, others were bleary-eyed, or hump-backed, or bow-legged, or clump-footed; hardly any of them looked like other people. But they were all strong for plunging, and let their poor ignorant children run wild, and never had the seal of the covenant put on them."[6]

Despite diversity within and adversity without, by mid-nineteenth century, Baptists in America had developed a remarkable unity of purpose and vision, a theological consensus that even cut across the seismic fault line produced by slavery and the Civil War. Thus Francis Wayland, a Northern Baptist, could write: "I do not believe that any denomination of Christians exists, which, for so long a period as the Baptist, have maintained so invariably the truth of their early confessions. . . . The theological tenets of the Baptists, both in England and America, may be briefly stated as follows: they are emphatically the doctrines of the Reformation, and they have been held with singular unanimity and consistency."[7]

Thus, despite countless splits and some doctrinal defections (for example, the lapse of certain Baptists into Universalism), there emerged among Baptists in the late nineteenth- and early twentieth-century America what might be called an orthodox Baptist consensus, represented in the North by Augustus H. Strong, in the South by E. Y. Mullins.

One knew instinctively when the bounds of this consensus had been transgressed. Thus, in the controversy surrounding the forced departure of Crawford Howell Toy from Southern Seminary in 1879, both Toy and the colleagues who bid him a tearful adieu were all aware that, as Toy himself put it, he "no longer stood where most of his brethren did."[8]

Erosion of Theological Consensus

The history of the Baptist movement in the twentieth century could be largely written as the story of the erosion of that theological consensus that prevailed in most places until the Fundamentalist-Modernism disputes. In the face of the pressures of this era, the Baptist apologetic made a twofold response, neither of which was really adequate to deal with the challenge at hand. The first response was an appeal to "Baptist distinctives." In part, this effort was fueled by old-fashioned denominational braggadocio, as seen in the book *Baptist Why and Why Not* published by Baptist Sunday School Board in 1900. Chapter titles include: "Why Baptist and Not Methodist," "Why Baptist and Not Episcopalian," "Why Immersion and Not Sprinkling," "Why Close Communion and Not Open Communion," etc.[9]

Further emphasis on Baptist distinctives such as the separation of church and state, the nonsacramental character of the ordinances, and the noncreedal character of our confessions appeared as a litany of negative constraints, rather than the positive exposition of an essential doctrinal core. Indeed, for some Baptists these so-called distinctives, often interpreted in an attenuated, reductionistic form, became the essence of the Baptist tradition itself.

This consensus was further eroded by what may be called the privatization of Baptist theology. Historically, Baptist life was shaped by strong communitarian features. The congregation was not merely an aggregate of like-minded individuals, but rather a body of baptized believers gathered in solemn *covenant* with one another and the Lord. Nor were Baptists doctrinal anarchists who boasted of their "right" to believe in anything they wanted to. Instead of flaunting their Christian freedom in this way, Baptists used it to produce and publish *confessions* of faith, both as a means of declaring their own faith to the world and of guarding the theological integrity of their own fellowship.[10] Nor did Baptists want their young children "to think for themselves," as the liberal cliché has it, but instead to be thoroughly grounded in the faith once for all delivered to the saints. Thus they developed Baptist catechisms and used them in both home and church to instruct their children in the rudiments of Christian theology.

The communitarian character of Baptist life, exemplified by covenants, confessions, and catechisms, was undermined by the privatization of Baptist theology and the rising tide of modern, rugged individualism that swept through American culture in the early twentieth century. It should be noted that this movement influenced Baptists at both ends of the religious spectrum. Liberal Baptists followed the theological trajectory of Schleiermacher and Ritschl into revisionist models of theology that denied, in some cases, the most fundamental truths of the gospel.[11] At the other extreme, anti-intellectual pietism and emotion-laden revivalism pitted theology against piety, soul religion against a reflective faith, thus producing a schizophrenic split between sound doctrine and holy living. Although Billy Sunday belonged to another denomination, many Baptists could resonate with his assertion that he did not know any more about theology than a jackrabbit knew about Ping-Pong!

Thus there developed, not least among Southern Baptists, a kind of theological vacuity, a doctrinal numbness, that resulted in a "form of godliness which denied the power thereof," an insipid culture religion cut off from the vital wellsprings of the historic Baptist heritage. Denominational pragmatism became the infallible dogma of Southern Baptist life. In the three decades following World War II, Baptist bureaucrats and denominational elites gradually led the SBC toward alignment with mainline Protestant concerns. For example, as amazing as it seems now, the SBC Christian Life Commission during these years was an ardent supporter of the Religious Coalition for Abortion Rights. Without some kind of conservative resurgence, Southern Baptists would doubtless have followed the same path of spiritual decline and theological erosion evident in many mainline denominations.[12]

It should be stated clearly, however, that the mere replacement of one set of bureaucrats with another doth not a reformation make! The conservative victory in the SBC will prove hollow unless it is accompanied by genuine spiritual and theological renewal. The dawn of a new century is a good occasion to consider a renewed framework of theological integrity for a world that looks very different from that of 1845 when 293 "delegates," as they were then called, met in Augusta, Georgia, and adopted a plan "for eliciting, combining and directing the energies of the whole denomination in one sacred effort, for the propagation of the gospel."[13]

Identity Markers

What are the benchmarks for shaping Baptist theological identity for such a time as this? Rather than put forth subtle speculations or a new methodology, I propose that we look again at five classic principles drawn from our own Baptist heritage. These five affirmations form a cluster of convictions that have seen us through turbulent storms in the past. They are worthy anchors for us to cast into the sea of modernity as we seek not merely to weather the storm but to sail with confidence into the future God has prepared for us.

Orthodox Convictions

In 1994 the Southern Baptist Convention unanimously adopted a resolution acknowledging that "Southern Baptists have historically confessed with all true Christians everywhere belief in the Triune God, Father, Son, and Holy Spirit, the full deity and perfect humanity of Jesus Christ, His virgin birth, His sinless life, His substitutionary atonement for sins, His resurrection from the dead, His exaltation to the right hand of God, and His triumphal return; and we recognize that born again believers in the Lord Jesus Christ may be found in all Christian denominations."

Baptists are orthodox Christians who stand in continuity with the dogmatic consensus of the early church on matters such as the scope of Holy Scripture (canon), the doctrine of God (Trinity), and the person and work of Jesus Christ (Christology). Leon McBeth is correct when he observes that Baptists have "often used confessions not to proclaim 'Baptist distinctives' but instead to show how similar Baptists were to other orthodox Christians."[14] Thus, article 38 of the "Orthodox Confession" of 1678 incorporated the Apostles', Nicene, and Athanasian creeds, declaring that all three "ought thoroughly to be received, and believed. For we believe, that they may be proved, by most undoubted authority of Holy Scripture and are necessary to be understood of all Christians."[15] Reflecting this same impulse, the Baptists who gathered in London for the inaugural meeting of the Baptist World Alliance in 1905 stood in that assembly and recited in unison the Apostles' Creed.

Fundamentalism arose in the early part of this century as a protest against the concessions and denials of liberal theologians on cardinal tenets such as the virgin birth of Christ, the inerrancy of the Bible, and penal substitutionary atonement. This was a valid and necessary protest, and we should be grateful for those worthy forebears who stood with courage and conviction on these matters. However, the problem with fundamentalism as a theological movement was its tendency toward reductionism—not what it affirmed, but what it left out.

In recent years the inspiration and authority of the Bible have again assumed a major role in Baptist polemics. From the drafting of the *Baptist Faith and Message* in 1963 through the adoption of the Presidential Theological Study Committee Report in 1994, Southern Baptists have repeatedly affirmed their confidence in the inerrancy or total truthfulness of Holy Scripture. As the latter report declares, "What the Bible says, God says; what the Bible says happened, really happened; every miracle, every event, in every book of the Old and New Testaments is altogether true and trustworthy." In more recent years, however, the SBC has found it necessary to address other pressing doctrinal issues such as the being of God and the importance of using biblical language to address Him (over against contemporary feminism), and our belief in Jesus Christ as sole and sufficient Savior (over against universalism and soteriological pluralism). Southern Baptists need to cultivate a holistic orthodoxy, based on a high view of the Scriptures and congruent with the trinitarian and christological consensus of the early church. Only in this way will we avoid the dangers of rigid reductionism on the one hand and liberal revisionism on the other.

Evangelical Heritage

Baptists are evangelical Christians who affirm, with Martin Luther and John Calvin, both the formal and material principles of the Reformation: Scripture alone and justification by faith alone. In setting forth these twin peaks of evangelical faith, the Reformers were not introducing new doctrines or novel ideas. They argued like this: If the doctrine of the Trinity really presents us with the true God of Creation and redemption; if Jesus Christ really is what we confess Him to be, that is, God from God, Light from Light, very God, from very God; and if original sin is as pervasive and debilitating as we believe it to be, then the doctrine of justification by faith alone is the only faithful interpretation of the New Testament promise of forgiveness, pardon, and new life in Christ. While not agreeing with everything Luther or Calvin taught, Baptists claim the heritage of the Reformation as their own. We gladly identify ourselves with other evangelical believers who are "not ashamed of the gospel of Christ, for it is the power of God to salvation for everyone who believes" (Rom. 1:16, NKJV).

The word "evangelical" has a myriad of other meanings as well, and Southern Baptists can rightly claim at least two of these. First, we are heirs of the Evangelical Awakening, which swept across the eighteenth century producing Pietism in Germany, Methodism in England, and the First Great Awakening in the American colonies. Many features of Baptist life resonate deeply with this mighty moving of the Spirit of God: our evangelistic witness and missionary vision, our historic emphasis on disciplined church life and godly living, our commitment to a regenerate church membership and Spirit-filled worship, our refusal to divorce the personal and social dimensions of the gospel.

More recently, the word *evangelical* has been associated with the post-fundamentalist resurgence among Bible-believing Christians in North America. Significantly, the two most formative shapers of this movement are both Southern Baptists: Billy Graham and Carl F. H. Henry. While certain moderate Southern Baptists, reflecting an entrenched parochialism, have eschewed the label "evangelical" as a "Yankee word" unworthy for *Southern* Baptists to wear, more and more Southern Baptists are discovering that they have far more in common with conservative, Bible-believing Christians in other denominations than they do with left-leaning Baptists in their own denomination.[16]

Far more important than wearing the label "evangelical," is the substance of the word in the three senses outlined here. Southern Baptists can and should rightly lay claim to the doctrinal legacy of the Reformation, the missionary and evangelistic impulse of the Great Awakening, and a transdenominational fellowship of Bible-believing Christians with whom we share a common commitment to the Word of God and the task of world evangelization.

Reformed Perspective

Despite a persistent Arminian strain within Baptist life, for much of our history most Baptists adhered faithfully to the doctrines of grace as set forth in Pauline-Augustinian-Reformed theology. David Benedict, following his extensive tour of Baptist churches throughout America in the early nineteenth century, gave the following summary of the Baptist theology he encountered:

> Take this denomination at large, I believe the following will be found a pretty correct statement of their views of doctrine. They hold that man in his natural condition is entirely depraved and sinful; but unless he is born again—changed by grace—or made alive unto God—he cannot be fitted for the communion of saints on earth, nor the enjoyment of God in heaven; that where God hath begun a good work, He will carry it on to the end; that there is an election of grace—an effectual calling, etc., and that the happiness of the righteous and the misery of the wicked will both be eternal.[17]

When in 1856 James Petigru Boyce set forth his plan for Southern Baptists' first theological seminary, he warned against the twin errors of Campbellism and Arminianism, the distinctive principles of which "have been engrafted upon many of our churches: and even some of our ministry have not hesitated publicly to avow them."[18]

As late as 1905, F. H. Kerfoot, Boyce's successor as professor of systematic theology at Southern Seminary, could still say, "Nearly all Baptists believe what are usually termed the 'doctrines of grace.'"[19] E. Y. Mullins, who disliked the label "Calvinist" and "Arminian," sought to transcend the controversy altogether. While retaining most of the content of traditional Calvinist soteriology, he gave it a new casting by restating it in terms of his distinctive theology of experience.

For some, the evangelical Calvinism of earlier Baptist generations has been eclipsed by a truncated hyper-Calvinism with its antimissionary, antievangelistic emphasis. Many other factors have also contributed to the blurring of this part of the Reformation heritage that has shaped Baptist identity: the routinization of revivalism, the growth of pragmatism as a denominational strategy, an attenuated doctrine of the Holy Spirit, and a general theological laxity which has resulted in doctrinal apathy. While seeking to restate traditional themes in fresh contemporary ways, Baptists would do well to connect again with the ideas that inform the theology of such great heroes of the past as John Bunyan,

Roger Williams, Andrew Fuller, Adoniram Judson, Luther Rice, and Charles Haddon Spurgeon.

I rejoice in the growing awareness of Reformed theology among Southern Baptists today. I know of nothing that has happened in the history of salvation since the day of James P. Boyce and B. H. Carroll that would make their understanding of God's grace obsolete in the modern world. To the contrary, a renewed commitment to the sovereignty of God in salvation, worship that centers on the glory of God rather than the entertainment of the audience, and a perspective on history and culture that sees Jesus Christ as Lord of time and eternity—all of this can only result in the building up of the Body of Christ.

At the same time, it is imperative for Reformed Southern Baptists to guard against the real dangers of hyper-Calvinism that emphasize divine sovereignty to the exclusion of human responsibility and that deny that the offer of the gospel is to be extended to all peoples everywhere. And, as we call on our fellow Baptist brothers and sisters to return to the rock from which we were hewn, we must learn to live in gracious equipoise with some of them who don't ring all five bells quite the same way we do! In this regard, we do well to heed the following statement by the great missionary statesman Luther Rice: "How absurd it is, therefore, to contend against the doctrine of election, or decrees, or divine sovereignty. Let us not, however, become bitter against those who view this matter in a different light, nor treat them in a super serious manner; rather let us be gentle towards all men. For who has made us to differ from what we once were? Who has removed the scales from our eyes?"[20]

Baptist Distinctives

While Baptists owe much to the great doctrinal legacy of the mainline reformers, our ecclesiology most closely approximates the Anabaptist ideal in its emphasis on the church as an intentional community composed of regenerated and baptized believers who are bound to one another and their Lord by a solemn covenant. One of the most important contributions that Baptists have made to the wider life of the church is the recovery of the early church practice of baptism as an adult right of initiation signifying a committed participation in the life, death, and resurrection of Jesus Christ. In many contemporary Baptist settings, however, baptism is in danger of being divorced from the context of the decisive life commitment. This unfortunate development is reflected both in the liturgical placement of baptism in the worship service—often tacked on at the end as a kind of afterthought—and also in the proper age and preparation of baptismal candidates. This situation muffles the historic Baptist protest against infant baptism, a protest that insisted on the intrinsic connection between biblical baptism and repentance and faith.[21]

We must also guard against a minimalist understanding of the Lord's Supper that reduces this vital ordinance to an empty ritual detached from the spiritual life of believers. Several years ago I experienced a powerful service of the Lord's Supper at the First Baptist Church of Dallas, Texas. During a Sunday morning service, that great congregation was asked to kneel and prayerfully receive the elements while the meaning of the ordinance was carefully explained from the Scriptures. In this kind of setting, the experience of worship is a transforming encounter with the living Christ. We need not fall prey to the lure of sacramentalism or the false doctrine of transubstantiation to reclaim the historic Baptist understanding of the Lord's Supper, which has nowhere been better described than in the Second London Confession of 1689: "Worthy receivers, outwardly partaking of the visible elements in this ordinance, do then also inwardly by faith, really and indeed, yet not carnally and corporally, but spiritually receive, and feed upon Christ crucified and all the benefits of His death: the Body and Blood of Christ, being then not corporally, or carnally, but spiritually present to the faith of believers, in that ordinance, as the elements themselves are to the outward senses."

Confessional Context

As we approach a new century, we would do well to remember and reclaim the confessional character of our common Christian commitment. Baptists are not a creedal people in that we regard no humanly devised statement as equal to the Bible. Nor do we believe that the state has any authority to impose religious beliefs on its subjects. However, Baptists have historically approved and circulated confessions of faith for a threefold purpose: as an expression of our religious liberty, as a statement of our theological convictions, and as a witness of the truths we hold in sacred trust. Our confessions are always accountable to Holy Scripture and revisable in the light of that divine revelation.

Just as a confession declares what we believe, so a church covenant is concerned with how we live. It sets forth in practical terms the ideal of the Christian life: a living faith, working by love, leading to holiness. The congregation's covenant also outlines that process of mutual admonition and responsibility through which fellow believers engage to "watch over" one another through encouragement, correction, and prayer.

Finally, catechisis is concerned with passing on the faith intact to the rising generation. This responsibility is jointly shared by parents and pastors. May God give us again Baptist families and Baptist churches who will take seriously the awesome responsibility of indoctrinating our children in the things of God.

Conclusion

In his *Commentary on Daniel* (9:25), John Calvin compared the work of God among his ancient people with the challenge of his own day. "God still wishes in these days to build His spiritual temple amidst the anxieties of the times. The faithful must still hold the trowel in one hand and the sword in the other, because the building of the church must still be combined with many struggles." That struggle continues today, not against enemies of flesh and blood but against principalities and powers, against lethargy and laziness, against defection and darkness on every hand. Yet God does continue to build His church amidst the anxieties of the times. For more than 150 years He has blessed and used the people of God called Southern Baptists in ways that future historians will record as remarkable beyond belief. As we remember and give thanks for the mighty acts of God in days gone by, let us press forward in the earnest expectation that the Lord, in the words of John Robinson, "hath yet more truth and light to break forth out of His Holy Word." Above all, let us never forget that it is "not by might, nor by power, but by my spirit, saith the LORD" (Zech. 4:6, KJV).

Endnotes

1. Will D. Campbell, *The Glad River* (New York: Holt, Rinehart, and Winston, 1982), 107.
2. Timothy George and David S. Dockery, eds., *Baptist Theologians* (Nashville: Broadman Press, 1990), 13.
3. William L. Lumpkin, ed., *Baptist Confessions of Faith* (Valley Forge: Judson Press, 1959), 244.
4. Michael Watts, *The Dissenters* (Oxford: Clarendon Press, 1978), 83.
5. Henry Sacheverell, *The Perils of False Brethren* (London: 1709), 36.
6. David Benedict, *Fifty Years Among the Baptists* (New York: Sheldon and Co., 1860), 93–94.
7. Francis Wayland, *The Principles and Practices of Baptist Churches* (London: J. Heaton and Son, 1861), 15–16.
8. George H. Shiver, ed., *American Religious Heretics* (Nashville: Abingdon, 1966), 56–88.
9. James M. Frost, ed., *Baptist Why and Why Not* (Nashville: Sunday School Board, 1900).
10. See the classic statement by James P. Boyce in his "Three Changes in Theological Institutions," in *James Petigru Boyce: Selected Writings*, ed. Timothy George (Nashville: Broadman Press, 1989), 48–59.
11. Thus by the end of his life in 1921 A. H. Strong, a moderate throughout his career, had sided with the Fundamentalists in their dispute with Modernism. Lamenting "some common theological trends of our time," Strong warned: "Under the influence of Ritchl and his Kantian relativism, many of our teachers and preachers have swung off into a practical denial of Christ's deity and of His atonement. We seem upon the verge of a second Unitarian defection, that will break up churches and compel secessions, in a worse manner than did that of Channing and Ware a

century ago. American Christianity recovered from that disaster only by vigorously asserting the authority of Christ and the inspiration of the Scriptures. . . . Without a revival of this faith our churches will become secularized, mission enterprise will die out, and the candlestick will be removed out of its place as it was with the seven churches of Asia, and as it has been with the apostate churches of New England." *Systematic Theology* (Valley Forge, Penn.: Judson Press, 1907).

12. For an analysis of the SBC controversy along these lines, see Timothy George, "Toward an Evangelical Future," in *Southern Baptists Observed: Multiple Perspectives of a Changing Denomination*, ed. Nancy T. Ammerman (Knoxville: University of Tennessee Press, 1993), 276–300.

13. Robert A. Baker, ed., *A Baptist Source Book* (Nashville: Broadman Press, 1966), 116.

14. H. Leon McBeth, *The Baptist Heritage* (Nashville: Broadman Press, 1987), 68.

15. W. L. Lumpkin, ed., *Baptist Confessions of Faith* (Valley Forge, Penn.: Judson Press, 1959), 326.

16. Cf. the reaction of an SBC agency head to the press's dubbing of Jimmy Carter as a "Southern Baptist evangelical" during the 1976 presidential campaign: "We are *not* evangelicals. That's a Yankee word. They want to claim us because we are big and successful and growing every year. But we have our own traditions, our own hymns and more students in our seminaries than they have in all of theirs put together." Quoted in Kenneth L. Woodward et al., "Born Again! The Year of the Evangelicals," *Newsweek* 25 October 1976, 76. Early on in the SBC controversy, two Baptist historians, E. Glenn Hinson and James Leo Garrett Jr., engaged in a scholarly debate over the question, "Are Southern Baptists Evangelicals?" Garrett, who answered in the affirmative, presented a much more credible historical analysis than Hinson. It is only fair to admit, however, that Hinson did represent a libertarian subculture within Southern Baptist life whose forebears would not want to be classified as evangelicals. See James Leo Garrett Jr., E. Glenn Hinson, and James E. Tull, *Are Southern Baptists "Evangelicals"?* (Macon: Mercer University Press, 1983).

17. David Benedict, *A General History of the Baptist Denomination in America* (Boston: Lincoln and Edmands, 1813), 2:456.

18. George, ed., *Boyce*, 33.

19. Quoted in Thomas J. Nettles, *By His Grace and for His Glory* (Grand Rapids: Baker, 1986), 50.

20. James B. Taylor, *Memoir of Rev. Luther Rice, One of the First American Missionaries to the East* (Baltimore: Armstrong and Berry, 1840), 332–333.

21. See Timothy George, "The Reformed Doctrine of Believer's Baptism," *Interpretation* 47 (1993), 242–254.

CHAPTER THREE

Back to the Future: An Analysis of Southern Baptist Evangelism

CHUCK KELLEY

At the founding meeting of the Southern Baptist Convention in 1845, one of the first resolutions passed went as follows: "Resolved, That for peace and harmony, and in order to accomplish the greatest amount of good, and for the maintenance of those scriptural principles on which the General Missionary Convention of the Baptist denomination of the United States, was originally formed it is proper that this Convention at once proceed to organize a Society for the propagation."[1]

From their earliest days, Southern Baptists rooted their identity in the task of evangelism. The denomination's initial efforts in the United States focused primarily on church planting through the Board for Domestic Missions, which became the Home Mission Board. From time to time motions were made in the convention calling for a more direct involvement in evangelism by appointing evangelists, but the primary evangelistic strategy of Southern Baptists was church planting.

At the 1904 convention, Len Broughton, a Georgia pastor, made a motion that Southern Baptists form a department of evangelism. One would think that a motion to create a department of evangelism would pass easily. Instead, his motion began a three-year controversy (1904–06).

The source of the controversy was not evangelism but rather an influential theological perspective called Landmarkism. Landmarkism is characterized simplistically as an extreme emphasis on the local church. Those influenced by Landmarkism feared that the formation of an evangelism department would mean the denomination would take over a task the New Testament assigned to the local church. They appeared to assume all churches were involved in effective evangelism and preferred not to assign to a denominational entity the responsibility of assisting and encouraging churches to evangelize.

In the third year of discussion, B. H. Carroll, founder of Southwestern Baptist Theological Seminary, made an eloquent and moving address about the role of the evangelist in the New Testament and the usefulness of the evangelist in the church in his day. He concluded in dramatic fashion: "The bedrock of Scripture underlies it [evangelism]. Experience demonstrates its wisdom and feasibility. If the Home Mission Board may employ any man, it may employ evangelists. Altogether, then, with a ring, let us support this measure. If I were the secretary of this board, I would come before this body in humility and tears and say: 'Brethren, give me evangelists. Deny not fins to things that must swim against the tide, nor wings to things that must fly against the wind.'"[2]

After his stirring address, the convention approved the motion. The messengers decided that assigned responsibility (giving specific assignment to a denominational entity to help churches do evangelism) was more desirable than assumed responsibility (assuming that all churches would do evangelism efficiently and effectively without outside support, encouragement, and help). So began the Home Mission Board Department of Evangelism.

Four Southern Baptist Evangelistic Methods

Four methods of doing evangelism came to characterize Southern Baptist churches.

Evangelism Method 1: Decisional Preaching

Many churches emphasize preaching. Southern Baptists, however, focus not simply on proclamation but on decisional proclamation. They believe that whenever the Word of God is proclaimed, people are obliged to respond. If hearers have an obligation to respond, then they ought to be given an opportunity to respond. The regular use of an invitation following the sermon in Southern Baptist Convention worship services is the result.

Decisional preaching flavors the Southern Baptist approach to worship, and it also helps to create an evangelistic climate. Every worship service is a reminder that people are lost until they respond to the gospel. Thus the church and individual believers must be active in giving people opportunities to be saved. The emphasis on response helps to create a climate in which the value and priority of evangelism are constantly reinforced.

Evangelism Method 2: Personal Evangelism

Christians are to go to people outside the church and share their faith in Jesus Christ. Southern Baptists have done this over the years through various forms of visitation. In its simplest forms, personal evangelism for Southern Baptists includes telling one's friends and family members about Jesus and going out once a week as a church to visit in the homes of prospects for salvation and church membership. The most important aspect of personal evangelism for Southern Baptists, however, has been the development of various forms of training church members to witness.

One of the denomination's great theologians, E. Y. Mullins, was among the first Southern Baptists to write a book on soul-winning.[3] This book was little more than a series of lectures published as a booklet, but it is the earliest personal evangelism training tool found by this researcher. From published lectures, Southern Baptists moved to short, simple study course books. These books were written to be training tools to teach small groups of people about various aspects of evangelism. They were user-friendly for teachers and easy for participants to read. No one has catalogued all such books that the Sunday School Board produced on evangelism, especially in the forties and fifties; but the number is significant. Perhaps the most underrated aspect of Southern Baptist evangelism is the influence of these little books on the rank and file of Southern Baptist lay leadership.

Following these study courses came training programs like the Cultivative Witness Program introduced by C. E. Autrey. This witnessing strategy suggested multiple visits to share Christ with a lost person. After that came the Lay Evangelism School, which intended to make persons comfortable talking about their faith to others. Continuing Witness Training, which taught witnessing skills through Bible study, observation, and actual experience, followed. The current trend is to simplify the training process and emphasize sharing Christ day by day.

The common thread in the Southern Baptist approach to personal evangelism is the recognition that all Christians should speak of Jesus outside church services. Through the years the denomination consistently emphasized the need for the church to go and tell rather than waiting for the lost to come and listen. Through visitation and personal evangelism, Southern Baptists often made their first contact with people who eventually came to Christ.

Evangelism Method 3: Sunday School

In the latter part of the nineteenth century, two men born in England had a similar dream. That dream was to do something to help illiterate children who were overlooked by society. Robert Raikes and William Fox wanted to teach children the basic skills necessary to function in society. Raikes set up a school to teach children on Sunday, because it was the only day many children were not working in the factories or elsewhere. The purpose of the school was to teach them reading, writing, and arithmetic.

Fox also envisioned a school to teach children functional skills needed to succeed in life, but he wanted to use the Bible as a textbook. He began his program as a weekday school. After hearing what Raikes was doing with the Sunday school, however, he switched his school meeting day to Sunday. These two streams merged over time to form what we know today as Sunday school.[4]

Today 97 percent of all Southern Baptist churches have a Sunday school. Though now the most popular program in SBC church, it was not always so. Sunday school began in the United States as an independent movement, not a local church ministry. Two groups promoted it: the publishers that produced the materials and independent Sunday school associations. Often Sunday schools were held apart from a church. In addition, the Sunday school movement was largely lay led. Christian lay leaders were the movers and shakers more than clergy in many instances. Because Sunday school did not emerge from the church and often was not supervised by the church, some clergy were skeptical about its value.

For these and other reasons, Southern Baptists were slow to adopt Sunday school. By 1857, only 25 percent of Southern Baptist churches had a Sunday school. Yet eventually SBC churches adopted the orphan of Sunday school and used it as a tool for reaching people. Today it is hard to imagine a Southern Baptist church without a Sunday school.

The turning point came when Southern Baptists realized that Sunday school was more than a way to reach children or teach the Bible. Sunday school was a way the church could do evangelism. By enrolling people in Sunday school, teaching them the Bible, and helping them to establish relationships with Christians, the lost could be converted. Sunday school became one of the most effective Southern Baptist strategies for evangelism because lost prospects of all ages could be cultivated and nudged toward conversion.

Evangelism Method 4: Revivalism

Revivalism refers to the use of revival meetings for evangelism. It is woven into the heart and soul of the Southern Baptist identity. The decision to create a Department of Evangelism was based upon the effectiveness of revivalism. B. H. Carroll focused his plea to the convention to establish the department upon the need of Southern Baptists to have good, qualified evangelists to lead churches in revival meetings. In fact, the first Department of Evangelism was little more than a "stable of evangelists." Churches contacted the department whenever they needed someone to come and help them plan or do a revival meeting.

Why were Southern Baptists doing revivals? In the discussions about creating the Department of Evangelism, revivalism was emphasized as the best way to reach the cities of our nation.[5] In effect, Southern Baptists chose revivalism as their initial strategy for urban evangelism. In the many years of Southern Baptist history, revival meetings have ebbed and flowed in popularity. In the forties and fifties revivals were the most popular method for doing evangelism. They are less popular today. Still, even to this day, the SBC averages more than one revival per church per year. Revival meetings are deeply woven into the fabric of who Southern Baptists are, and they continue to be a way to reach people for Jesus Christ.

Old McBaptist Had A Farm

The genius of Southern Baptist Evangelism dawned on me while I was working on a book about the history of Southern Baptist evangelism. I had been seeing these four basic methods as separate ways to do evangelism, but then I realized that the integration of the methods was responsible for the tremendous time of growth in our past. In effect, old McBaptist had a farm, for it is the paradigm of a farm that best explains the evangelistic effectiveness of Southern Baptists.

The climate determines the harvest potential of a farm, and the climate or values of a congregation determine the evangelistic potential of a church. Decisional preaching helped Southern Baptists create an atmosphere or climate affirming evangelism and encouraging people to give their lives to Jesus Christ. The constant emphasis upon the necessity of conversion encouraged churches to value highly the work and fruit of evangelism.

In the context of this evangelistic climate, Southern Baptists visited in their communities and planted gospel seeds much as a farmer would sow his field. Through personal evangelism, churches found people outside the church and began explaining the gospel to them. Once contact was made, prospects were enrolled in Sunday school. As the farmer cultivates a field after planting, so Southern Baptists used Sunday school as a tool for cultivating lost people and moving them toward conversion. Bible study made the gospel clearer, and personal relationships with class members made the gospel more desirable. In reality, Sunday school is the original southern Baptist strategy for relational evangelism. Through the bonding of class relationships, people were prepared to give their lives to Christ and to become a part of a church.

In an atmosphere of evangelism, following the planting of personal evangelism and the cultivation of Sunday school, revival meetings provided an appropriate means of harvesting results. With a special emphasis on drawing the net, the revival meeting provided a logical time and place for the lost to begin following Jesus. That is why churches in the past would have as many as 70 percent of their conversions in a year during that time of revival meeting.

The genius of Southern Baptist evangelism is not in the methods used but in the integration of those methods. The paradigm of the farm helped rural Southern Baptists become the largest Protestant denomination in America. As a result Southern Baptists experienced their golden age in the forties and fifties. But the problem with a golden age is: What do you do for an encore?

This is the tension currently facing Southern Baptists who care about evangelism.

Old McBaptist Had a Farm
Climate: Decisional Preaching
Planting: Personal Evangelism
Cultivating: Sunday School
Harvesting: Revivalism

Looking to Tomorrow

For nearly forty years, Southern Baptists have been groping to rediscover the pulse of America's soul. From 1945 to 1955 the SBC moved from baptizing 256,699 persons to baptizing 416,867 persons annually. After baptizing more than 415,000 in 1955, the SBC since then has never reached that number in any one year. In the opinion of this writer, the key for Southern Baptists is to go "back to the future." There are some clues for the present and future to be found in the past.

1. Clue number one is that assigned responsibility is more effective than assumed responsibility. The convention assigned responsibility to the Department of Evangelism to lead Southern Baptists in evangelism. Greater productivity in evangelism followed. Later the convention, under the direction of C. E. Matthews, suggested a director of evangelism for every state convention and an evangelism council in every local church. Our greatest harvest in evangelism followed. Unless the responsibility for doing evangelism is assigned, the work of bringing people to Jesus can get lost in the clutter of everything that Baptists are doing. There is so much going on in ministry today that one assumes evangelism will be done. In reality, often it is not done unless specific responsibility is assigned. Over the years Southern Baptist churches transformed the church evangelism council into the church council. Shifting congregational leadership away from a specific focus on evangelism appears to have lessened congregational involvement in evangelism.

2. The second clue from the past is that Southern Baptists must be willing to adopt some orphans. Sunday school is not a

Southern Baptist phenomenon. They did not conceive it. It was independent of churches and had a life of its own. This orphan could have appeared threatening, but SBC churches finally saw it as a tool for evangelism. They adopted and adapted it, making it one of the most effective evangelistic tools in the Southern Baptist arsenal. God may have other orphans needing a home in our churches today. If God stirred Southern Baptists to adopt an orphan in the past, He probably intends for us to adopt other orphans in the future.

3. The third hint is the significance of church planting. Nearly everyone has heard more than they care to hear about baby boomers. Boomers draw much attention because they are the largest block of the U.S. population, giving them a great influence on our culture and in our churches. A "baby boom" of churches, an explosion in the number of churches, is needed for Southern Baptists to have greater influence on the culture.

4. A fourth clue is to give priorities to the cities. Our SBC forefathers knew they had to reach the cities in order to capture the soul of America. Revivalism was heavily emphasized because it was effective urban evangelism. Methods come and go, but the cities are still the key. Until we make it in the cities, we cannot reach America for Christ.

Adjusting Our Approaches

A final insight comes from the Word of God. C. E. Matthews was a former secretary of evangelism for Southern Baptists (1946–55). During his tenure Southern Baptists experienced their fastest growth. He put innovations in place that are still in use today. His life verse, however, was not a verse about evangelism. You will find it in James 1:5: "If any of you lack wisdom, let him ask of God, that giveth to all men liberally, and upbraideth not; and it shall be given him" (KJV). Matthews recognized that fruitfulness in evangelism is the result of understanding what God wants to do.

Recall for a moment the SBC farming paradigm for evangelism. Those four ways Southern Baptists do evangelism were not developed in a denominational meeting; they emerged in our congregational life by the grace of God. If Southern Baptists are to find the strategies to reach our nation, we will have to look beyond a simple analysis of the demographics. Effectiveness will not come from an intensive study of what is working somewhere else. It will come when we are on our knees before a holy, sovereign God and follow His agenda for how to grow churches.

The issue is not, Is there a way to reach this tough, hard, increasingly secular nation with the gospel of Jesus Christ? The issue is, Are we willing to let God make adjustments in our approaches to fine-tune us for the future? The future of Southern Baptist evangelism depends upon our response to that question.

Endnotes

1. Annual of the Southern Baptist Convention, 1845, 13.
2. *Baptist Standard*, 31 May 1906, 1–2. Readers interested in the full text of Carroll's address may find it in Charles S. Kelley Jr., *How Did They Do It?* (New Orleans, La.: Insight Press, 1992), appendix D.
3. E. Y. Mullins, *Quiet Talks on Soul-Winning* (Nashville: Sunday School Board of the Southern Baptist Convention, 1920).
4. For a thorough discussion of the origins of Sunday school, see Anne M. Boylan, *Sunday School: The Formation of an American Institution 1790–1880* (New Haven: Yale University Press, 1988).
5. See Kelley, *How Did They Do It?* 180–206.

CHAPTER FOUR

Into All the World: Fulfilling the Great Commission

ROBERT E. NAYLOR AND REBEKAH ANN NAYLOR

"And he said unto them, Go ye into all the world, and preach the gospel to every creature" (Mark 16:15).*

"Go ye therefore, and teach all nations, baptizing them in the name of the Father, and of the Son, and of the Holy Ghost: teaching them to observe all things whatsoever I have commanded you; and, lo, I am with you alway, even unto the end of the world. Amen" (Matt. 28:19-20).

---

* Unless otherwise noted all Scripture quotations in this chapter are from the King James Version of the Bible.

Into All The World: Part 1

Robert E. Naylor

The Master's Mandate

Into all the world! What a magnificent finale to the earthly ministry of our risen Lord. Every resurrection moment must have been one of breathless wonder for the disciples. When they came to this final moment, what was His impact? What did they think? Surely, they must have drawn a little closer to each other as the magnitude of the Great Commission broke in upon them. The Commission has never lost that sense of impact upon His disciples, then or now.

They should have been prepared for the new horizons. There had been those wonderful three years. The Twelve had known the personal invitation of the Master and the transforming touch of His presence and forgiveness. They had seen the miracles. True, in that last little while He had begun to tell them that He was to die. This they could not understand. The Sinless was to die for the sinful. The Master, who had manifested His authority over men and over nature, was suddenly to become a dying Servant. The concept must have been most difficult. Peter undertook to remonstrate with Jesus and say, "Not so Lord." Peter counted himself worthy to die, but not the Master. They had faced this.

Then there had been the awful gloom and darkness of the betrayal, of the crucifixion, of those strange words from the cross. They had turned aside in dazed wonder to the little fellowship of the group. Is this all of it? Suddenly, word came that the tomb was empty. Jesus stands among them. The response of each one as given in the Scriptures was an understood excitement.

Perhaps in this last moment Peter was remembering that moment in Caesarea Philippi when Jesus had said, "Upon this rock I will build my church" (Matt. 16:18). There was to be something in this world that had never been there before. Jesus was to institute His church, His New Testament church, into the affairs and lives and needs of a lost world. I believe that Peter must have said many times to himself, "My church," and the wonder and the shock of it was constantly with him.

Now, however, he had heard the Master say as a final parting word, "Into all the world." He had indicated that He was going away. He had promised that He would return. In the meantime, the disciples, these disciples, the five hundred, all disciples, are to "Go into all the world" telling the story about Jesus, preaching the gospel that Paul later defines as, "Christ died for our sins according to the scriptures; and that he was buried and He rose again the third day according to the scriptures" (1 Cor. 15:3–4). Wonderful news indeed—but to be taken to the whole world.

There is no suggestion that the disciples raised a single question. There is no room for doubt as to the personal understanding of the disciples with reference to the command. Every disciple is responsible. All the disciples are responsible. To belong to Jesus is to be sent by Jesus. To be a sharer of His grace is to be responsible for the entire lost world, that they may know that hope is found only in this resurrected Christ.

Commissioned Mission

Only a few nights before, according to John's Gospel, Jesus stood in the midst of these same disciples and said, "Peace be unto you: as my Father hath sent me, even so send I you" (20:21). For any disciple seeking to understand the perimeters of Christian discipleship, he should know that they are to be found in this simple passage. That which brought Jesus to this world "to seek and to save that which was lost" (Luke 19:10) is to take us "into all the world." The qualities that Jesus manifested in the faithful pursuit of His mission His disciples are to manifest. The disciples of our Lord are immediately put into our Lord's business.

There is an underlying truth in the language of this short sentence that we should not miss. When Jesus said, "As my Father hath sent Me," He used the Greek word *apostello*. It is from this word that we derive our word "apostle." This is not to suggest that we are all apostles in the same sense as the eleven, yet when

He finishes the sentence by saying, "so send I you," He uses another Greek word, *pempo*.

Moulton says, "*Apostello* means commission and *pempo* means mission. With the first words, our thoughts turn to the 'special embassy,' with the second to the authority of the 'ambassador' and the obedience of the sent." He even goes so far as to suggest, "The Master's mission is the Great Commission. The disciples' mission is obedience, and the word 'mission' more appropriately applies." Jesus comes with divine authority, with a mission viewed from eternity, with a pure compassionate love that is the hope of our salvation. The disciple, on the other hand, obeys the Master's instruction.

Where this word *pempo* is used, it means "someone to do something." Luke records that John the Baptist summoned two of his disciples and sent them to Jesus saying, "Art thou he that should come? or look we for another?" (Luke 7:19). Matthew describes the fate of John the Baptist when he wrote, "He sent, and beheaded John" (Matt. 14:10).

In the same sense, teachers who come forward by God's command and with His authority are said to be sent by God (See John 1:33). Thayer, in commenting upon this word, said, "*Pempo* is the general term (differing from others in directing attention not to the exit but to the advent). It may even imply accompaniment (as when the sender is God)." Thayer continued, "*Apostello* includes a reference to equipment and suggests official authoritative sending."

No phrase is more familiar among our Baptist people than "the Great Commission"; it is our Lord's mission of mercy from heaven's glory to earth's poverty. Then let our response to His Commission, our sharing in that Commission, be *the mission*—our obedience unto the command of our risen Lord. This is not to say less about our responsibility but to enhance it, to extend it, to move under divine authority.

At the outset, let us continue for a moment the insight given to us by Jesus in those last momentous days. In His great intercessory prayer recorded in the seventeenth chapter of John, Jesus said, "I pray not that thou shouldest take them out of the world, but that thou shouldest keep them from the evil. They are not of the world, even as I am not of the world. Sanctify them through thy truth: thy word is truth. As thou has sent me into the world, even so have I also sent them into the world" (vv. 15–18).

Jesus used the same word that He used later in the text to identify His mission, which we have discussed. This is *apostello*. He identified His sending and the disciples' response with the same glory, the same sense of divine involvement. What did He mean? The clue is in verse 5 of the same chapter: "O Father, glorify thou me with thine own self with the glory which I had with thee before the world was." Then in verse 18 he added, "As thou has sent me into the world, even so have I also sent them into the world." Remember, He already said, "They are not of the world even as I am not of the world."

Jesus affirmed His presence with the Father in glory from eternity. The Father sent Him out of that glory into this world. To the amazement of the heavenly hosts, Jesus walked away from His eternal glory to the poverty of earth.

Now He declares that His disciples are not of this world either. When we are born again—saved, made alive in Christ Jesus, given everlasting life—we enter into His glory. As it is with Jesus, so it is with His disciples—out of that glory and into this world. When the mission is done, it will be back again to glory.

Because every believer is responsible, mission becomes a corporate response. Where you find disciples, you find churches. Jesus insisted, "I will build My church." The new nature involves a fellowship of family, an identity of family, a part of the family of God. These are churches. Occasionally you hear people speak of church as though it were another organization into which they had entered and over which they exercised authority. It is not so with Jesus. Where some believe, they seek each other, need each other, and are responsible with each other to respond to the command of our Lord.

When Saul of Tarsus was on the road to Damascus, he had in his pocket a commission to destroy Christians, to hush their testimony. Yet when he arrived in Damascus, it was another Saul of

Tarsus. The Christians he sought to destroy he now sought for fellowship. There was no indication that it was a matter of personal threat that drove him to the others, rather it was that he had become a part of a believer's fellowship. This is the basic material of a New Testament Church.

We Baptists describe our churches as New Testament churches. By that we mean that the doctrine, the structure, the relationship of discipleship are all to be found in the pages of the New Testament. Who called us Baptists first? We are not sure. It certainly is a name intended to describe us, but it becomes to all of us a badge of honor, a source of gratitude, a description of doctrine, a declaration of obedience, an understanding of priorities that makes for strong, vital churches.

Quickly after receiving the Great Commission, the disciples, scattered by persecution, went everywhere preaching the Word. Where they preached, the people believed. Where people believed, churches came into being. Where churches came into being, they witnessed corporately and individually. And so the gospel is still preached. The commission has become mission, and mission has become life. It is that story that we should tell at this point in our history.

Our History

Who are the Baptists? The late Lynn May, Executive Secretary of the Historical Commission, spoke of our "emergence into history," and it is an apt description. No one really puts a beginning date upon this group. There are those who insist that after the decades of the first century, there were groups identifiable by doctrine with Baptists from the beginning. On the basis of our doctrines, polity, and practices, we Baptists believe that we are following the teachings of Jesus and the patterns of New Testament churches. Throughout our history, Baptists have sought to reproduce the pattern of Christianity and church life found in the New Testament.

May identifies nine distinctive Baptist beliefs. Baptists believe in:

1. The authority and sufficiency of the Scriptures.
2. The priesthood of the believer.
3. Salvation as God's gift of divine grace received by man through repentance and faith in Jesus Christ.
4. A regenerated church membership.
5. Baptism by immersion of believers only.
6. Two ordinances: baptism and the Lord's Supper, viewed primarily as symbols and reminders.
7. Each church as an independent self-governing body, the members possessing equal rights and privileges.
8. Religious liberty for all.
9. Separation of church and state.

What we believe is what we really are. Our doctrines become the fountain of our missionary witness, the evidence of missionary impulse.

Following the 1975 Seminar on Missions Support which met at Lake Yale, Florida, stewardship leaders from the Stewardship Commission of the Southern Baptist Convention and the state conventions asked Morris Ashcraft, then dean of Southeastern Baptist Theological Seminary in Wake Forest, to formulate a summary of the major doctrinal convictions commonly held by Baptists that motivate their missionary enterprise. He wrote the following:

> One, God is one; He is the Lord of our lives and also of all creation and all people. Two, man is the creature of God, made in the image of God but fallen in sin; yet he is redeemable and can be transformed into God's image again. Three, Jesus Christ died on the cross and rose from the dead to save us from sin and to reconcile us to God. Four, the Gospel is the good news about Jesus Christ and His saving work; that Gospel is the Word of God and has power to save. Five, the Holy Spirit attends the preaching of the Word, giving it power and converting sinful persons so they are able to be redeemed. Six, persons reconciled to God through Christ are entrusted with this Good News for the world. Seven, there is "no other name" by which people can

be saved yet this exclusiveness is accompanied by the all-inclusive love of God that desires all people to be saved. Eight, the world is lost, and today is the day of salvation.

Ashcraft summarized this by saying, "The Bible is a missionary book, not because it contains isolated texts with a missionary flavor, but because the main line of argument brings together all its volumes in the expectation, the unfolding, and the gradual execution of a missionary purpose."

Early Baptist Organizations

The seeds of Southern Baptist missions were sown when the Boston Baptist Missionary Society was formed to take over the support of Ann and Adoniram Judson. They commissioned Luther Rice to tour the United States eliciting support for the new missionaries. These three had become Baptists through study of the Scriptures while on their way to India. Rice began to conceive of a denominational organization for the propagation of the gospel. Later Rice, with the encouragement of W. B. Johnson of Georgia, suggested that the Philadelphia Association host a meeting. In May of 1814, the Triennial Convention was organized.

Hortense Woodson, in her book *Giants in the Land*, described the organization of this Triennial Convention. "The organization of this Convention (Triennial Convention) formed an epoch in the history of the Baptists of the United States, that was followed by a most blessed era of successful, benevolent effort in various departments of the Kingdom of Christ, that spread the unspeakable blessings of literature and salvation throughout millions of our race in these and foreign lands."

A few years later, in the name of the Savannah Society for Foreign Missions, W. B. Johnson (who later became the first president of the Southern Baptist Convention) wrote the following significant words:

> Since the succession of our dear brethren, Rice, Judson and lady . . . several missionary societies have been formed by the Baptists of America. These societies have for their object the establishment and support of Foreign Missions; and it is contemplated

> that delegates from them all will convene in some central situation of the United States for the purpose of organizing an efficient and practical plan, on which the energies of the whole Baptist denomination, throughout America, may be elicited, combined and directed, in one sacred effort for sending the Word of life to idolatrous lands."

That is perhaps the first time the words "elicit, combine, direct" were used in connection with Baptist organizations, and they appear recurrently in other compositions that Johnson had a hand in writing.

It is to be noted that it was missions that caused the Baptists of America to be pronounced a denomination. All that we are as Southern Baptists has a missions birth. The purpose of these pages is not history first, but an understanding of the missionary thrust that marked the birth of our Convention. It is from Jesus Himself, always urgent, always inclusive. Success is to be measured only in terms of our obedience.

The Southern Baptist Convention

Lynn May, in discussing the separation of Northern and Southern Baptists, tells us:

> After 30 years of united effort, Baptists in the North and South separated in 1845. Several divisive issues had begun to appear several years before that finally led to the cleavage. One, growing tension over the slavery issue ultimately led in 1844 to the Home Mission Society's refusal to appoint a slave holder as a missionary. This action provided the immediate explosion that produced the separation. Second, emphasis upon decentralization in organized Baptist life had resulted in a separate organization for each phase of work: Home Missions, Foreign Missions, publications and others. Many Southern leaders, however, wanted an all-inclusive convention instead of independent societies. Three, many in the South charged that the Home Mission Society was neglecting the mission fields in the South.

In all of the documents and minutes of the meeting that brought the Southern Baptist Convention into being in May of 1845, there is the evident thrust that missions was the major motivation. The strains upon fellowship had been manifest, but in the midst of that, our forebears demanded that the missionary task be seen as the principle purpose of the organization.

There needs to be an understanding of what we mean when we speak of the Society plan as opposed to the Convention plan. Baptists need to understand the difference between the Society plan and the Convention plan. According to the Society plan, individuals who are interested in a given benevolence come together voluntarily to give money and promote the cause that unites them. A separate Society is organized for each cause. The Societies have no church connection and sometimes divide the churches, even as they hamper the development of the denomination.

In response to the call of their leaders, Southern Baptists sent 293 messengers to Augusta, Georgia, May 8, 1845. The Constitution they adopted on May 10 created the Southern Baptist Convention, a general body organized for the purpose of "eliciting, combining and directing" the work of the whole denomination. Under this plan the Convention would conduct denominational work through various boards that would oversee such tasks as missions, education, and publication. Each board would be elected periodically by the general body, and they would be directly responsible to it. This was quite different from the plan previously followed.

The written proceedings of that first meeting began with this paragraph: "Pursuant to a call by the Board of Managers of the Virginia Foreign Baptist Mission Society, responded to by various other bodies, a large number of delegates assembled in the meeting house of the Baptist church in Augusta."

It is noteworthy that on Friday morning, May 9, the report of the Committee concerning the actual organization of the Convention was received. It said that "after a full, free and harmonious discussion, the Preamble and Resolution were separately adopted, by the unanimous vote of the Convention as follows."

> "The Committee to whom it has been referred to report a Preamble and Resolutions cannot but express their profound sense of the responsibility resting upon your body at the present eventful crisis, as the integrity of the nation, the interest of truth, the

> sacred enterprise of converting the heathen were all involved in your deliberations. That this Convention was imperatively demanded, must be apparent to all."

The Preamble and Constitution of the Convention deserves a proper place in this document:

> We, the delegates of Missionary Societies, churches, and other religious bodies of the Baptist denomination in various parts of the United States, met in Convention, in the city of Augusta, Georgia, for the purpose of carrying into effect the benevolent institutions of our Constituents, by organizing a plan for eliciting, combining and directing the energies of the whole denomination in one sacred effort, for the propagation of the gospel, agree to the following rules or fundamental principles:
>
> • Article One: This body shall be styled the Southern Baptist Convention.
>
> • Article Two: It shall be the design of this convention's remote, foreign and domestic missions and other important objects connected with the Redeemer's kingdom, and to combine for this purpose such a portion of the Baptist denomination in the United States as may desire a general organization for the Christian benevolence, which shall fully respect the independence and equal rights of the churches.

In its inception there were two mission boards established. One was the Board of Managers for Foreign Missions. The other was the Board of Managers for Domestic Missions. The Foreign Mission Board was to be located in Richmond, Virginia, and the Domestic Board of Missions at Marion, Alabama.

The work of both Foreign and Home Missions would be conducted by one Convention, with a separate board for each rather than with a completely independent organization for each. The establishment and direction of the mission boards by the Convention itself identified the work of missions as a basic concern of the Convention. The basic qualifications of missionaries were stated in the original constitution. Much of our attention centers on the Foreign Mission Board, but Southern Baptists have always said, "*All* the world."

The Southern Baptist Convention, having come into being in that 1845 meeting, appointed a committee to set forth the reasons that led to the formation of the Southern Baptist Convention. W. B. Johnson, President of the Convention, opened the committee report with the following statement: "A painful division has taken place in the missionary operations of the American Baptists. Let not the extent of this disunion be exaggerated. At the present time, it involves only the Foreign and Domestic Missions of the denomination. Northern and Southern Baptists are still brethren. They differ in no article of the faith. They are guided by the same principles of gospel order."

Johnson continued,

> Our objects . . . will appear in detail on the face of our Constitution. They are distributed, at present, between two acting boards for Foreign and Domestic Missions. We sympathize with the Macedonian Cry from every part of the heathen world—with the low moan for spiritual aid, the four million of half-stifled Red Men, their hands of supplication held out to the Gospel, to God and to all His people, and have shaken ourselves free from the nightmare of a six years "strife about words to no profit" for the profit of these poor, perishing, precious souls. Our language to all America and to all Christendom, if they will hear us, is "Come over."

When the Convention met for the second time on June 10-15, 1846, in Richmond, Virginia, J. B. Taylor, Executive Secretary of the Foreign Mission Board, reported that three missionaries had already been appointed. They were J. Lewis Shuck of South Carolina, Samuel C. Cloptin, and George Percy. The speakers at this meeting were J. Lewis Shuck, who in 1835 had gone to China as the first Baptist missionary to that country; Young Seen Sang, whom Shuck had brought to America with him; and Brother Simons of the Burman Mission.

For the purposes of this discussion of missionary involvement, this first report of the Board of Foreign Missions is of surpassing interest. With what Christian love they had addressed the questions of transfer of missions, of mutual claims and such! Finances and fields of labor were basic subjects. China and Africa, in particular, were treated as missionary fields. The focus, however, came at last upon the appointment of missionaries.

The name of Brother J. Lewis Shuck was doubtless familiar to all the Southern churches. He was the first American Baptist missionary located in the empire of China. With his wife, Henrietta Hall Shuck, he sailed from this country in September, 1835, and had been engaged at different points with gratifying success in preaching Christ to the Chinese. Following the death of his wife, Brother Lewis Shuck returned to the United States with five motherless children whom he placed under the care of his wife's parents. The Board gladly availed themselves of the opportunity of securing his services as their missionary.

Likewise, the report of the Board of Domestic Missions was positive. Agents had been appointed in the states of Georgia, South Carolina, and Virginia.

William Owen Carver, one of the great Baptist historians and longtime professor of Southern Baptist Theological Seminary, once stated, "The Baptist denomination was the direct product of the missionary interest."

The Convention idea itself was new. A people committed totally to the Scriptures as the Word of our living Lord, unhesitatingly declaring the independence of every believer, declared also that God had made us responsible, one with the other, to go into a whole world with our witness concerning Jesus. The focus of the Convention had been firmly fixed. The missionary fires had been kindled, never to go out in the life of the Convention.

Seven Denominational Milestones

There are moments in the life of a great denomination when the focus is fixed again, the line of march more clearly prescribed. I have chosen simply to choose seven such moments and call them milestones in our march "into all the world." It could have been fewer or more, but these seven, in retrospect, were clearly the works of God in holding us to our basic commitment.

Milestone 1: The War Between the States: 1860-1865

This war became the first test of survival for the Southern Baptist Convention. Arthur Rutledge, in his history of the

Home Mission Board, *Mission America*, wrote: "With the outbreak of the Civil War in 1861, funds declined to the point that the Board was unable to pay the salaries of the missionaries." In three short years, the number of home missionaries declined from 159 in 1860 to 32. Rutledge entitled that chapter "Conflict and Near Collapse."

On the very eve of the war, Southern Baptist Theological Seminary was founded in Greenville, South Carolina. At the close of the war the first faculty—Boyce, Broadus, Manly, and Williams—met at once. Broadus is credited with the following quotation: "Suppose we quietly agree that the Seminary may die, but we'll die first." The Seminary did reopen. There were only seven students, but the line of march resumed.

It is not to be assumed that the previous years had been fruitless. J. B. Taylor began his work as corresponding secretary of the Foreign Mission Board in 1846 with three missionaries under appointment. By 1871 Southern Baptists had eighty-one missionaries serving in China, Liberia, Sierra Leone, Nigeria, and Italy. Following the war, in the midst of poverty, hunger, and death, the march into all the world became a healing hope, even in the South.

Milestone 2: Woman's Missionary Union: 1888

A Southern Baptist Convention Committee on "Women's Work" (1878) recommended to the two mission boards that they organize central committees of women in each state. In 1883, they began to meet quietly at the annual meetings of the Southern Baptist Convention.

In May 1888, Woman's Missionary Union was organized in Richmond, Virginia, and became a dynamic missionary organization of Southern Baptist women. Its purpose was stated thus:

> We, the women of the churches connected with the Southern Baptist Convention, desirous of stimulating the missionary spirit and the grace of giving among women and children of the churches, and aiding in collecting funds for missionary purposes, to be disbursed by the Boards of the Southern Baptist Convention, and disdaining all intention of independent action organize and adopt the following: the twofold object of the Executive

> Committee shall be first, to distribute missionary information and stimulate effort through the state central committees where they may exist; and where they do not, to encourage the organization of new societies. Second, to secure the earnest systematic cooperation of women and children in collecting and raising money for missions.

In the closing months of 1887, Lottie Moon, already a longtime missionary to China, suggested that Southern Baptist women set apart the week before Christmas as a week of prayer and offering for world missions. Later in 1888, Henry Allen Tupper, the Foreign Mission Board secretary, passed on to Woman's Missionary Union a challenge from Miss Moon to make a special offering that Christmas to send two new missionaries to Ping Tu. Annie Armstrong, the corresponding secretary of Woman's Missionary Union, accepted this challenge and sent out handwritten letters to fifteen hundred societies. The offering goal of $2,000 was exceeded, for $3,315.26 was given.

Through the years the results of this Week of Prayer and Lottie Moon Christmas Offering for Foreign Missions have been phenomenal. From the modest beginning of $3,315, the offering has grown to more than $81 million in 1991.

Only eternity will reveal contributions made by Woman's Missionary Union to maintaining the focus upon our Master's mandate "Into all the world." Even during the dark days, the women of our churches have been steadfast in their obedience.

Milestone 3: The Seventy-Five Million Campaign: 1918-1923

The years between 1888 and 1918 were rich years of missionary endeavor. In 1918, the Southern Baptist Convention had given to 24,883 cooperating churches. There were 1,153 home missionaries under the appointment of our Home Mission Board. The Foreign Mission Board itself had appointed 16 new missionaries in 1918, bringing it to a total of 316.

My family identity with the Southern Baptist Convention began in 1897, soon to be a hundred years of Southern Baptist life. My father, George Rufus Naylor, was born in 1869 in Rockwall County, Texas. He was saved in his late twenties in a revival meeting in Ellis County. In 1897, my father was farming in Denton County. God called him to preach. The very next year he attended the associational meeting and the next year was ordained and asked to be the missionary "on trial" in Cook County Association near Gainesville. From the day he came to know Jesus as his personal Savior, Dad was a missionary. His reports from that early missionary responsibility show a tireless commitment. It was a ministry largely on horseback, more than four thousand miles in a single year. Fifty people were saved and baptized.

He and Mother married in 1901 and went to the Indian Territory where he was pastor at Wagoner. He always attended the Convention. Every offering he counted an opportunity, and he led the way. The subsidy a mission church received the first year was always less the next year. Soon they were self-supporting, mission-contributing churches.

Dad became a general missionary for the state of Oklahoma under the Home Mission Board and the Oklahoma Baptist Convention in 1920. He was the last of these missionaries because the work was closed in 1930 by the Depression. He immediately became an associational missionary in Pattawatomie Association.

I was saved in 1918 and became a Southern Baptist. I have been a Southern Baptist in commitment and in actual membership more than half of the life of the Convention, I know from personal experience that the Convention's outlook has always been "into the world, all the world for Jesus." I never heard a note in those early years that was not directly in obedience to the command of our Lord. All of this is inserted at this point simply to recount a single event.

In 1919, the Convention president, J. B. Gambrell, challenged Southern Baptists "to adopt a program of work commensurate with the reasonable demands upon us." Southern Baptists were in the condition of total financial disarray. The Seventy-Five Million Five-Year Campaign was a pledge campaign. Members in every church were asked to sign pledge cards and pay their pledges within the five years from 1919-24. The goal was an amount that staggered and ultimately stretched the imagination of Southern Baptists of that day.

L. R. Scarborough, president of Southwestern Baptist Theological Seminary in Fort Worth, was asked to be chairman of the campaign. The resolution that brought it into being was in May of 1919. It was stated, even in the determination of outline, that Victory Sunday in the campaign would be set for the same year in November. Without radio, without television, with limited telephone communications, traveling almost entirely by railroad, Southern Baptists set out to complete a campaign of unparalleled size in the single period of seven months.

Cecil Ray, in his book on the Cooperative Program, discusses the results under the title "How It Both Failed and Succeeded." The facts are that Southern Baptists pledged in this single campaign \$92,630,923, although they finally paid only \$58,591,713. Frank E. Burkholter, in summarizing the remarkable achievement, said, "The Home Mission Board received \$6,622,725 compared to \$8,188,730 received in its preceding 74 years. The Foreign Mission Board received \$11,615,327 compared to \$12,500,000 in all its previous years." There's no room for failure in that analysis.

Some years ago when I was preaching in the First Baptist Church of San Antonio, I met a woman who was a girl in the days of my own childhood in Heavener, Oklahoma. I remembered the family, the uncle and aunt who reared her, as a faithful Baptist family. The woman invited us into her home. As we sat there, she asked if I would like to see her mother's Bible. When I began to thumb through the Book, well-worn and well-marked, suddenly a paper fell from between the pages. When I picked it up, it was a list of the pledges to the Seventy-Five Million Campaign in 1919 in my father's church in Heavener, Oklahoma. Included in the list were the names of my father, my mother, my four brothers and sisters, and my own name. I like to remember that, at a moment as meaningful as any in Southern Baptist history, God allowed me to have a part.

Cecil Ray, in summarizing the benefits of this remarkable effort, listed these:

> One, it lifted the sights of Baptists. Two, it helped Baptists realize what Robert Baker the historian calls the ambivalence of their

structure, a convention that was supposed to be strong and united, with a weak and fragmented system of support. Three, Baptists recognized the spiritual blessings that sacrificial giving produces. Four, Baptists discovered that a united effort did not rob the churches. Finally, it gave Baptists a pattern for ongoing cooperation between the Southern Baptist Convention and the state conventions.

Scarborough (whose memory for me is a lift into the very presence of our King) described the unification of our people. He spoke of the deepening of spiritual life with revival fires everywhere. The Campaign was marked by indoctrination in the fundamentals of the Baptist faith. There was the calling out of the new and enlarged leadership. Finally he said, "We have just started." He then added "Not a faint heart reached the Promised Land."

Milestone 4: The Cooperative Program: 1925

If there were a subtitle on this quick section, it would be, "Into All the World Together." Cecil Ray, in listing six or seven great decision-moments in the Southern Baptist Convention, puts the Seventy-Five Million Campaign and the Cooperative Program Decision together under the title "The Unity Decision." They are together, both in point of time and in point of significance. Yet each one was so direction-determining that I believe they should have separate discussions.

In Kansas City in 1923, the Southern Baptist Convention Executive Committee reported, "A special committee was appointed to make special recommendations of a general outline of plans for the next forward movement for Southern Baptists." In the 1924 meeting in Atlanta, the Future Program Committee, of which M. E. Dodd was chairman, laid the foundation for the Cooperative Program event of 1925. That 1925 Convention meeting in Memphis heard first of all from this Future Program Committee, "a report of victory." In the year just closing, there had been given for Southwide causes $7,072,244. The report included the phrase "a working plan of our Cooperative Program."

Finally, the report said, "Your committee would further recommend that from the adoption of this report by the Convention, our Cooperative work be known as the 'Cooperative Program of Southern Baptists.' This commission shall be known as the Commission on Cooperative Program of Southern Baptists." Adopted enthusiastically by the Convention, it marked the actual beginning of the program. Later, the Convention assigned to the Executive Committee the responsibility of being the disbursing or distributing agent of the Convention.

An adequate evaluation of the Cooperative Program demands a personal evaluation. As I said before, I was born again in 1918 and had been a member of a Southern Baptist church from that time until the birth of the Cooperative Program in 1925. I have not at any time since been a member of a church that did not actively participate in the Cooperative Program. There has never been a year in my own pilgrimage in which I failed to be a part of the Cooperative Program by my personal stewardship. It is a part of my life.

As a pastor for thirty years, the churches where I was privileged to serve constantly struggled to move forward in their participation in the worldwide mission witness through the Cooperative Program. From 1932 until 1958 in four Southern Baptist State conventions, we did not lose sight of the ultimate objectives.

From 1958 until 1978, as president of Southwestern Baptist Theological Seminary, I was the recipient, both personally and institutionally, of the direct ministry of the Cooperative Program. My salary came from that source.

The Cooperative Program of the Southern Baptist Convention is not an object of worship or a magic wand. It is a clear-cut affirmation that we Southern Baptists believe that God intends for us to work together. In the Seventy-Five Mission Campaign, we discovered the miracle of Spirit-led cooperation. We have constantly affirmed the freedom of the individual, the autonomy of the local church, and just as consistently, that God puts us together in the Cooperative Program.

Milestone 5: The Depression

Every milestone has meant advance. In these shaping moments for Southern Baptists, we have moved forward toward that ultimate goal "into all the world." We need to regard the greatest trials that have come to us as God's shaping, molding, empowering work among us. The years immediately following the 1925 Memphis Convention were years of growth in stewardship and in baptisms.

As Southern Baptists through their history have sought to obey the Master's mandate and move into all the world, there have been memorials along the way. Just as surely as Jacob took the stone that was his pillow and made it a pillar and said, "Surely the LORD is in this place; and I knew it not" (Gen. 28:16), even so we Southern Baptists say of the Depression years.

In 1928, within months, there were statements from our mission boards we had never seen before. The Home Mission Board said, "The defalcation of the treasury of the Home Mission Board was the greatest financial calamity ever to strike the work of the Southern Baptist Convention."

Only months before, the Foreign Mission Board had said, "For the first time in the 82 years of this board's history has there been occasion for it to report the loss of a dollar by an official employee." The defalcation amounted to $103,772.

James Love, executive secretary of the Foreign Mission Board, died suddenly on May 3, 1928. Executive secretary since 1915, he had seen the work grow steadily from 298 missionaries in nine fields in 1915 to 489 missionaries in fifteen fields in 1928.

Also in 1928 it is said, "When T. B. Ray became acting Executive Secretary in 1928, the debt of the Board had already reached the tremendous total of $1,065,791.18." The other institutions of the convention had likewise accumulated debts anticipating income that was not realized, unwisely mortgaging their future.

On a more personal note, God called me to preach in 1928, my senior year in college. Having preached my first sermon and having been licensed by the First Baptist Church of Ada, Oklahoma, I entered Southwestern Seminary in the fall of 1928.

These events might seen unrelated, but the analysis here is a direct result of those difficult years.

In the same year that the Southern Baptist Convention approved the Cooperative Program, the Southwestern Baptist Theological Seminary was received by the Southern Baptist Convention as an agency of the Convention. The Seminary had been founded in 1908 under the leadership of B. H. Carroll and out of the Bible Department of Baylor University. It moved to Fort Worth in 1910 and L. R. Scarborough became president in 1915 upon the death of Carroll. In the four years that I was a student there—the darkest years in Southern Baptist life—I never heard a discouraging word. Southwestern was born with certain missionary emphases that fit well the mandate of "Our Lord into all the world."

There was a Missionary Department for Women from the very beginning of the Seminary. The first Chair of Evangelism, which came to be know as the Chair of Fire, was central in its life. During those four Depression years, there were times, I learned later, when professors did not receive their salaries, sometimes receiving food out of a Seminary commissary. Yet Southwestern was always optimistic, forward looking, soul seeking, and mission emphasizing throughout these years.

It is said that debts "led to retrenchment on the mission fields, with large numbers of missionaries having to remain in the states. Appropriations for the work in 1929 were the lowest in 10 years. During the years 1926-29, 82 missionaries resigned and nine died. During those same years, only 12 new missionaries were appointed." By 1932, the Foreign Mission Board owed four banks in Richmond $1,110,000; and on the several mission fields, missionaries had incurred additional obligations to the extent of $249,000. Charles Maddry said, when he became executive secretary in 1933, "A greater handicap, perhaps, than the debt itself was the low morale and the spirit of defeatism that had gripped the churches."

When I graduated from the Seminary in 1932, I became pastor of the First Baptist Church, Nashville, Arkansas. It was a fine county seat church with an excellent mission history. Early on I discovered that Arkansas Baptists had settled a tremendous debt—thirty-three and one-third cents on the dollar—and the State Secretary was urging the churches to take Honor Offerings so that the principal of the debt might be paid as a matter of honor even though it was not an obligation of law.

This shows that God, in our darkest hours, was bringing the Convention directly into focus again. We were discovering anew that a world was lost, and a spirit of evangelism began to possess the people. At that 1933 convention in Washington, D. C., the Hundred Thousand Club was born. The challenge was to find one hundred thousand Southern Baptists who, beyond their gifts, would give a dollar a month to pay toward the debts that were straining the agencies. I find satisfaction in remembering that we never missed a month being members of the Club. The slogan "Debt Free in 43" became a song of triumph and direction.

Milestone 6: The Foreign Mission Board's Program of Advance: 1948

There can be little doubt that our afflictions work for us. Southern Baptists marched forward, even while emerging from the burdens of debt, in a nation only gradually recovering from its economic devastation, and, finally, in the middle of a great, costly war. In another kind of report, you would hear of missionaries being appointed, of new seminaries being established, of evangelism made central in our Southern Baptist churches. The westward expansion of the Convention, the northeastward expansion of the Convention, the multiplication of state conventions all spoke of a people determined to obey.

When the Southern Baptist Convention met in Memphis in 1948, the Foreign Mission Board, under the leadership of M. Theron Rankin, brought a recommendation for the Foreign Mission Board's Program of Advance. In its briefest form, the program called for the appointment of 1,750 missionaries, an annual budget of $10 million to underwrite their support, and an enlarging program of world missions. The Convention eagerly adopted the program, set goals for the Home Mission Board and the agencies of the Convention, and the Cooperative Program continued its marvelous growth.

In 1954, under the slogan "A Million More in 54," Southern Baptists baptized more people than ever in their history, before or since.

Milestone 7: Bold Mission Thrust: 1976-2000

Amid renewing dissension and economic uncertainties, Southern Baptists rose to their most visionary time. With the adoption of Bold Mission Thrust in 1976 and 1978, they declared their intention not only to enter a new era but to undertake the Christian message as no other generation of Baptists had done. They voted to take on the massive task of seeking to witness of Christ to every person on earth by the year 2000.

Goals set in order to do the job included:

1. Doubling the Cooperative Program by 1982 and doubling it twice more by a.d. 2000.
2. Enlarging the Foreign Mission Program to more than five thousand missionaries serving in 125 countries.
3. Enlisting ten thousand missionary volunteers overseas each year.
4. Increasing home missionaries to five thousand.
5. Starting enough new churches to have fifty thousand Southern Baptist churches by the year 2000.
6. Renewing Sunday School growth by increasing enrollment to eight and a half million by 1985.

Every year since, reports have been made to the Convention that measured our progress towards these goals. Some goals have been achieved or are nearing achievement. At the end of 1992, there were 3,893 foreign missionaries and 4,868 home missionaries. Southern Baptists were represented in 129 countries of the world. Volunteer totals overseas numbered 11,197. There were 43,387 Southern Baptist churches. Though much has happened, much remains to be done.

God brought me to the presidency of Southwestern Seminary in 1958. I have often reflected that it was like taking a human artery into your hands in that the very lifeblood of the kingdom of God flows across this campus. Half of the missionaries appointed by our mission boards have come through Southwestern Baptist Theological Seminary. Week by week through the academic years, students have been challenged to face God's will for their own life "into all the world."

When I became president of the Seminary, I wondered whether thirty years of being a pastor had changed my perspective and what impact one would make upon the other. I quickly discovered that one was part of the other. For Southwestern, the churches are always a priority, and the world is constantly in view. I discovered that Southwestern Seminary was in direct focus with that major thrust of New Testament churches—missions.

I remember that it was that way in my student years. Chapel messages bore a major mission imprint. L. R. Scarborough, in every utterance, in all the facets of leadership, directed our attention to the whole world to which Jesus came and for which He died. The noonday prayer meetings, the mission band, the presence of the missionaries were all evidence remembered. Too, in those depression years I remembered that when the Board could no longer send missionaries due to financial reasons, there were many in our midst who went under the aegis of the Board but were financially supported by fellow students.

The leadership of the Seminary was in direct relationship to the pastoral emphasis to which my ministry had been devoted. The annual Mission Conference in the spring was an affirmation of this major focus. Students from the colleges of our Southern Baptist Convention came to this conference and laid their lives open to the leadership of God. There are many on the mission fields today whose confirmation of call came in the midst of this conference.

There were daily emphases in the classrooms. The Department of Missions had a major impact on the total student body. Evangelism as an academic discipline began in Southwestern Seminary when it was founded. For a week each spring, the Seminary closed and the students scattered out across our Southern Baptist Convention organizing churches, preaching in revivals, and giving living obedience into all the world.

In the academic world, the Seminary pursued the finest academic standards and found in them no conflict with the focus of the Seminary and of our churches—into all the world with the gospel.

The Seminary rapidly became known as the largest theological seminary in the world, and it continues to be that. One encouragement in the present is that a fellowship of common concern bonds our six seminary presidents.

Let it be emphasized that Bold Mission Thrust brought nothing new to Southern Baptists in point of purpose and substance. Our marching orders were plain from the beginning. The heart of all of it appears in the statement of the seminary purpose: "God-called men and women." We have talked about a denomination facing His mandate, but before it was that, it was one person facing the will of God and the purpose of our Savior—that every person in the world shall know Him.

Into All The World: Part 2
Rebekah Ann Naylor

The Witness

One such person, confronted with a lost world and God's call, became a young teenager, Rebekah Naylor, daughter of a Baptist pastor with a long heritage of missionary involvement and mission support. In those early years, as a Sunbeam and a member of Girls' Auxiliary, I received an excellent missions education. The understanding of how we as Southern Baptists supported missions all over the world was coupled with many living examples as missionaries visited our church and our home. They told wonderful stories of people in many lands hearing about Jesus and believing in Him. They testified concerning their own call to mission service and God's continuing work in their lives and ministries. My father, my pastor, preached often of the call to every Christian to be a witness for Jesus. He led our church in financial support of missions through the Cooperative Program and the special offerings for foreign, home, and state missions. There was always a very strong denominational identification. I was privileged to travel in the United States and abroad, seeing firsthand a world different from my own, a world in need physically, and a world without Jesus.

During the Week of Prayer for Foreign Missions in our church in 1957, God spoke very personally to me about my role and responsibility to be His ambassador and representative overseas. Already I had felt God's direction toward a career in medicine. Both then and now I felt a sense of awe that God chose me for this special task and gave me a burden for the physical and spiritual needs of countless millions of people. My response could only be one of obedience and commitment, "Wherever He leads, I'll go."

That initial call and response has been followed by almost forty years of missions involvement and participation. Through the years of education and preparation, God equipped me not only with medical knowledge and skills but also provided churches and individuals who further contributed to my spiritual growth and development. Being involved daily in a secular, mostly non-Christian environment gave opportunities for mission and witness long before my arrival overseas.

It was also a time to consider why I planned to seek appointment as a Southern Baptist missionary. First of all, I am a Baptist, thoroughly convinced of our doctrinal position and our commitment to missions and evangelism. Southern Baptists' priority of the establishment of New Testament churches is one that I share. But almost equally important is our denominational cooperative system of mission support that results not only in adequate financial support, but more importantly, in support through prayer by thousands of churches and millions of individuals. Through these years of missionary service, I remain grateful and proud to be a Southern Baptist missionary.

God ultimately led me to the nation of India, definitely the place of His choosing. As representatives of the Foreign Mission Board talked to me about needs and opportunities, they spoke of the new Bangalore Baptist Hospital soon opening in this populous land. Medical missions was the open door for Southern

Baptists. So it was that in 1974 I arrived as missionary surgeon in Bangalore, India.

India is the world's second most populous nation, with the population expected to cross a billion by the turn of the century. After more than two hundred years of missionary presence, only 2 percent of the people identify themselves as Christian. It is a nation marked by poverty, illiteracy, and disease. There is religious freedom in this democracy, yet there is growing persecution, socially and economically, of Christians. Many of the important changes and situations prominent on today's world-scene are very evident in India. The exploding of technology has brought rapid changes in business, education, and health care to name only a few areas. Urbanization is proceeding at an astounding pace, further increasing poverty. Daily the country is beset by ethnic and communal violence with much loss of life and property, fear, and uncertainty. Though many in India have had exposure to the gospel, yet there are large people groups with no Christian presence or witness.

Even as the nation of India is in many ways representative of our world, so also Southern Baptists' approach to this country has been representative of the changes and new ways of taking the gospel to a lost world. The Bangalore Baptist Hospital provided the avenue for Southern Baptist presence in India. Missionary evangelists in the traditional sense have not been permitted to enter India for a number of years. Since its inception, the hospital's purpose has been to provide, and to train others to provide, care for the whole person in the spirit of Jesus Christ and to provide this care with such compassion that people will be drawn to Jesus. This priority has governed policies, programs, and personnel of the hospital. Thousands and thousands have heard about Jesus in the Bangalore Baptist Hospital, many of them for the first time. Scores of churches have been started as new believers were baptized into Christian fellowship.

My earliest experiences in India vividly taught me that profession and witness are so totally integrated as to be inseparable. I recall going out on Sunday afternoons to slums and villages with other missionary doctors. Access to many communities was open because of the ministry of the hospital. We would tell people that we had come with the story of Jesus, who loved them and died for them.

In the wards of the hospital, the opportunities for witness are unlimited. Nine Baptist chaplains, along with other Christian staff, present Jesus through personal evangelism, through printed materials, through services in the wards and clinic, through films, and through a lifestyle that is unique and different because of Jesus.

During these twenty years in India, I have seen the evolution of national leadership in the churches and in the hospital. We have continually encouraged the churches to be self-supporting and no longer do we support any pastors financially. We have encouraged the churches to be indigenous so far as cultural expression. The hospital, particularly, has been affected by the declining emphasis of the Foreign Mission Board on support of institutions. The result has been a strong partnership between the Foreign Mission Board, the founder and owner and participant, and national entities who manage and direct the work of the hospital. As the only missionary remaining in India, I have assumed the role of supporter, encourager, counselor, and colleague, rather than leader.

To meet the needs and enter the open doors in India, Southern Baptists have also used other means that are representative of new approaches worldwide. India contains a number of unreached people groups—so-called "World A." Non-resident missionaries have developed contacts in these various groups. As information is gained, strategy can be planned. Another approach is to provide leadership training for existing Baptist groups and associations all over India. This is being done by itinerant missionaries who travel place to place equipping local leaders to be more effective in church planting and evangelism. There has been an increase in volunteer efforts and partnership evangelism in recent years. In 1993, at the time of the bicentennial celebration of William Carey's arrival in India, Crossover India was one example of hundreds of volunteers joining hands with local churches in concentrated evangelism across India.

Also in India today, there are growing numbers of local missionaries supported by churches (Baptists and other) and Indian organizations. Indeed, all of these approaches are necessary to achieve the goal that every person should hear about Jesus by the year 2000.

The World

The world with Jesus was not just a first-century world. "Jesus Christ, the same yesterday, today and forever." His world includes all of us—from Adam until the last person is saved and He returns. It includes all the world of sin, of war, of hunger, of human desperation. It reaches out to every race and every place.

With us, the world is, first of all, geographical. How constantly the map has changed from the first century until now. Luke had a geographical view when he wrote "in Jerusalem, and in all Judaea, and in Samaria, and unto the uttermost part of the earth" (Acts 1:8). He did say, "the uttermost." Barriers shut us out from some places. Yet today it is probably not true to label such places as "closed" since new approaches are before us. At the same time, walls crumble, national boundaries change, and all nations become objects of our mission. Perhaps the most striking current example is the falling of the Iron Curtain, opening the vast Soviet Union and Eastern Europe to evangelism and missionary endeavor. While that door is open, thousands of evangelical Christians have gone there to evangelize and train and encourage the national Christians.

It has always seemed to me that beyond geographical definition, basic within such restrictions, is a world of people. As a child, I belonged to the Sunbeam Band. Even then we would sing, "Red and yellow, black and white, they are precious in His sight." Southern Baptists have always been at their best when they were most inclusive. The multiethnic congregations within our churches are not strange anymore. Indeed, every individual is one for whom Christ died.

As we look at this world of people, current writers refer to "World C": Christians now found in some ten thousand different ethnolinguistic peoples. "World B" includes 2.3 billion people who are aware of Christ and the gospel through presence, witness, evangelism, local church outreach, social action, foreign missions, etc. However, "World A" consists of 1.2 billion people who remain untouched by Christian missionaries, mission agencies, or local churches. The awareness of these untouched by the gospel has caused Southern Baptists to seek innovative means and redeploy personnel and other resources to reach these inhabitants of "World A."

Today's world is also one of tremendous changes that are having great effect on the mission enterprise. Communication and transportation have advanced rapidly, almost beyond imagination. Urbanization continues across the world. With the ending of the Cold War, ethnic conflicts have become prominent on the world stage. There is an information revolution sparked by computerization and other technological advances.

Against this brief summary of today's world, Southern Baptists must stand ready to enter open doors. Already we are seeking more involvement with other national Baptist bodies. If every person is to hear the gospel by the year 2000, there must be increasing cooperation with other evangelical Christians. Many countries whose people once comprised a mission field are now sending missionaries to people both inside and outside their national borders. This must be further encouraged.

R. Keith Parks, in a series of articles entitled "World View," has described the need for balance at several points:

- local and global involvement
- evangelism and ministry
- efforts among responsive and resistant people
- effectiveness of career missionaries with distinctive contribution of volunteers
- missionary role and role of indigenous leadership
- stability and change

Parks concludes that keeping our balance is helped by our denominational approach, and balance is achieved in light of Biblical truth and the person of Jesus Christ.

The Way

Jesus said, "I am the way, the truth, and the life" (John 14:6). Amidst all that is taking place in our world today, we are to present a Person, Jesus Christ, the only way that men can be saved. As we are surrounded by change, Jesus remains the same. The Great Commission is the same. The way to salvation is the same. The joy over one sinner who repents is the same.

At first blush, when we think of billions in this world who have not yet heard, just one word comes to mind: *impossible.* It would have been the same word in the mind of God confronted with the lostness of humanity, except that which is impossible with man is possible with God. God sent His Son to do an impossible thing, and the last word said is, "It is finished." There is a wonderful fellowship at the point of the impossible. We have our own thrilling moments in history when the small group agrees to do the impossible.

The world means our world. It is not yesterday's world or the world of the future, but today's world. We, as Southern Baptists are responsible to go into all the world, preaching the Good News, telling that Jesus has come to seek and to save the lost. And as we go, we say with Paul, "I determined to know nothing among you except Jesus Christ, and Him crucified (1 Cor. 2:2, NASB)"—the Way, the Truth, and the Life.

CHAPTER FIVE
Baptists and Higher Education

CARL F. H. HENRY

In the preface to the volume *Baptist Theologians*, the editors remind us that "theology is not an ivory-tower exercise for sturdy academics; it is the serious responsibility of every Christian and every church that seeks to be faithful to its Lord."[1]

In comments in the closing chapter to that volume on representative and yet sometimes quite diverse theologians, Dockery speaks of "the multi-faceted nature of Baptist theology."[2]

That diversity has cast its long shadow over the history of Baptist educational institutions in America. Their story is largely one of flux. For one reason or another, Baptists seem often unable to preserve their academic institutions for the mission for which their founders established them.

Notably the Constitution of the Southern Association of Baptist Colleges and Schools contains no doctrinal statement whatever. Its statement of purpose is "to provide and maintain an organization through which Baptist educational institutions in the territory of the Southern Baptist Convention may cooperate in promoting the interests of Christian education." The separate schools do, of course, have their own charters.

In 1977, Southern Baptists owned, controlled, or had a substantial governing interest in seventy-one schools, some owned by the Southern Baptist Convention and others—mostly academies, Bible schools, and two- or four-year colleges—owned by individual state conventions.[3] Since their founding they had graduated almost four hundred thousand students.[4] Their property value at that time was $882,228,769. Hester concludes his overview with the comment: "Baptist leaders and people have never been more solidly behind their educational institutions."[5] Yet in the years that have followed, the invasion of denominational faculties and classrooms by emphases alien to the biblical heritage has become an increasing source of constituency criticism and controversy.

The Baptist inversion of the view—really an insight also of the Protestant Reformation—that the clergy are a special professional class, to the view that everyone is a minister of Christ, had numerous consequences for denominational schools, some laudatory, some questionable. While it recovered the biblical view of vocation, it also left in doubt the need for special training by a full-time technical ministry.[6] Yet the churches needed full-time leaders, and for their provision a corpus of specialized knowledge and skills was needed, though not a few aspirants continued to rely only on the leading of the Holy Spirit.

Any survey of Baptist involvement in education is complicated by the fact that a considerable number of Baptist movements exist—some fiercely independent, others gathered into unions or conventions, some aggressively ecumenical. Almost a century ago, the index to H. K. Carroll's *The Religious Forces of The United States* already listed twenty-one varieties of Baptists based on the 1890 census.[7] For all that, the Baptist heritage has historically stressed the unbroken authority of the Bible, the priesthood of all believers, the autonomy of the local church, separation of church and state, personal religious freedom, and believer's baptism by immersion.

It cannot be said, however, that Baptists have without exception championed education. The hyper-Calvinistic Primitive or Old-School Baptists opposed Sunday schools as well as missionary societies on the ground that they are "human institutions." But that has hardly been the norm. Not a few English Baptists, influenced by the Keswick movement, notes David W. Bebbington, considered sociopolitical activity a distraction; some, being influenced by dispensational premillenialism in their withdrawal from the cultural arena, could not but influence not only public policymaking but attitudes toward general education as well.[8] English Baptists did, however, promote disestablishment, or at least they urged Anglicans to promote it, while Roman Catholics tended, by contrast, to push for increased state subsidies for their schools.

Yet American Baptists were, as Hester comments, "among the first to realize the necessity of establishing institutions of higher learning."[9] In 1764, they founded Rhode Island College, which later became Brown University. They also founded Vassar, believed to be the first real college in America for the higher education of women. Among other colleges established by Baptists were Bates, Baylor, Bucknall, Chicago, Colby, Columbian College (George Washington University), Colgate, Furman, Mercer, Mississippi, Richmond, Wake Forest, and William Jewell. In his treatise on *The History of Southern Baptist Higher Education*, Leon McBeth notes that before 1825, academic sponsorship by Baptists in the south focused especially on Charleston, Philadelphia, and Washington, D.C.[10]

The motivation for establishing many, if not most, of these schools was the preparation of young men for Christian ministry. Today very few of the denominational colleges show impressive statistics along that line, since the number of nonministerial students now far outnumbers—in some cases by 10 to 1—those going into technical Christian service. Nonetheless, the continuing primary purpose "of the now impressive array of senior colleges, academies, and seminaries" remains, as Spright Dowell writes, "the training of ministers."[11] Yet there is growing emphasis upon "the education of other students, both men and women, to meet the needs of churches, communities, and commonwealths for Christian leadership." Among the oldest Baptist theological seminaries in America was Colgate, organized in 1820 at Hamilton, New York, but by 1839 it was already admitting students not desiring to enter the ministry.

However, the most notable change in Baptist higher education is other than numerical. Baptist seminaries (among the earliest of which was Newton, founded in 1825) were among those that, beginning with the formation of Andover in Massachusetts in 1808, arose in evangelical protest against the inroads of Unitarianism in the universities. But as young professors pursued doctoral studies in German universities, they in turn increasingly questioned the supernatural and miraculous aspects of the Christian religion. The large growth in attendance at emerging conservative seminaries was a consequence, most students envisioning the pastorate or missions as a career, while the liberal seminaries aimed specially to provide teachers and denominational or ecumenical leadership. Curriculums were modified to reflect these interests.

The Baptist Bible Union emerged between 1923 and 1932 as an alliance hostile to modernism and linking fundamentalists in the Northern Baptist Convention—led by W. B. Riley—to Southern fundamentalists, led by J. Frank Norris, and Canadian fundamentalists, led by T. T. Shields. Their focus was on education and missions. The movement purchased Des Moines University in 1927 and projected it as a conservative bastion (much like Jerry Falwell did in 1971 when he founded Liberty Baptist College in Virginia and exuberantly promoted it as a "fundamentalist Harvard"). But questions of control and emphasis in 1929 led to Des Moines University's closure and the rise in 1932 of the General Association of Regular Baptist Churches. Theological tensions over modernism and its impact on denominational and educational bureaucracies entered into the rise of such movements as the American Baptist Association, the Baptist Bible Fellowship, and the Conservative Baptist Association, which operates seminaries in Denver and Portland. The Baptist General Conference had roots in Swedish pietism but has now largely lost this ethnic identity; it operates Bethel college and Bethel Seminary in St. Paul, Minnesota.

Whereas degree-granting institutions in England, such as Oxford and Cambridge, held a monopoly under Parliamentary authority until London University was founded in 1827, no such restriction on higher education existed in America. Religious denominations established Harvard in 1636, William and Mary in 1698, and Yale in 1701. But the real multiplication of religious colleges came with "the Great Awakening" in the mid-eighteenth century. By the time of the American Revolution, Baptists as well as Congregationalists, Presbyterians, Anglicans, Methodists, Lutherans, and other denominations had their own colleges.

With the rise of other types of schools and the classroom emphasis on social and economic goals no less than on theism and the classics, there arose a diversity that, as Sol Cohen notes, questioned, challenged, altered, and discarded almost every aspect of the original collegiate inheritance.[12] The nondenominational common-school system that emerged by 1860 reflected the American faith in education, shaped especially under the influence of Horace Mann, a Unitarian, who looked upon education "as part of the Providence of God by which the human race is to be redeemed."[13] The nonsectarian liberal Protestantism of the public schools soon provoked Roman Catholics to promote their own schools energetically. Mann thought that the public schools were teaching common elements (especially morality) of the Christian religion shared by all denominations. Protestants never anticipated that the Bible might itself be declared sectarian.

In Britain, Baptists had not sponsored denominational schools. Like other nonconformists, they accepted the provisions of the 1944 Education Act supportive of religious education within the academically established curriculum. Baptist leaders and agencies monitored trends and stressed the desirability and importance of a Christian witness by teachers in the school system and the pursuit of teaching as a vocation. For all that, Arthur Jennings observes that "education rarely becomes a major issue" either in the Baptist Union of Great Britain or in the local churches, although a small number of independent churches have established private schools for children of members that inculcate biblical learning in contrast to mainly secular education.[14]

At midcentury, comments Brenda Watson, "it would have been taken for granted that the Bible should occupy a central place in Religious Education." But this activity has more recently become a highly contentious area of study. "Now," Watson observes, the Bible "is frequently bypassed altogether."[15] Watson thinks, however, that the reasons often given for this—"misleading and deficient Bible teaching" and the "explosion of interest" in world religions and in contemporary priorities that regard the Scriptures as "old-fashioned"—are not as decisive for the Bible's relevance or irrelevance as is the quality of classroom teaching.[16] Education is paying the price of displacing the importance of transmitting fixed truth and norms in education by an emphasis instead on self-expression of one's inner capacities. The educator may at times have little of permanent value to transmit, yet he or she is championed nonetheless as a guide to one's self-discovery.

It is no longer merely a few rancid naturalists or outspoken atheists who tell us that Western society would be better off had it never heard of Jesus and the Bible, but rather a growing movement of confused common people who are products of technological societies that accommodate a barbaric way of life. It is less and less the case that society transmits a culture that distinguishes contemporary mankind essentially from primitive humanity. The neomodern teenager professes an outlook on morality, music, literature, and art alien to that of most adults. Alienated from the supernatural and from history, youth are plagued by anxiety in an age of comparative affluence and technological brilliance.

The controversy over education extends from the discussion of its foundation to its goals, and embraces at its core the questions of the legitimacy of the role of the supernatural and of the nature of values. Sidney Hook, no advocate of theism, commented that "the history of education, especially American education, leads one to the generalization that educational institutions respond more to social needs and pressures than to first principles."[17] This adverse verdict, sad to say, is applicable to the religious colleges and universities also, and even more sadly, in view of the special interest of this survey, to much Baptist higher education also. The plans projected by educators for the reform of academia tend to concentrate on curriculum changes, restructuring of levels of learning, classroom teaching techniques, tuition costs, the role of vocational preparation, and so on. It has taken a volume like Alan Bloom's *The Closing of the American Mind*[18] to shock the academic community into a reconsideration of the fact that ideas and truth are what genuine education is really about.

Ironically, it is the "professors of theology," as Soren Kierkegaard warned, who reduced God and the gospel to educational irrelevance. The New Testament has a role for bishops, presbyters, and deacons (still somewhat obscurely preserved) but, Kierkegaard comments, "'The professor is a later Christian invention . . . made about the time when Christianity began to go backward, and the culminating point of the Professor's ascent coincides exactly with our age when Christianity is entirely abolished."[19]

As John A. Stoops observes, "The God of the Judeo-Christian tradition is denied his full presence in the free market of ideas" to which the younger generation turns for its "lessons about life and values."[20] Stoops adds, moreover, that "Luther and Aquinas are both indispensable spirits in any school which educates its children in humanity."[21]

As secularism increasingly impacts public education, churches are more and more emphasizing the importance of family training, rather than expecting churches and schools to act as surrogate parents. The education of children involves a public promise to instruct and encourage them in the Christian way. In our time, education—especially for senior adults—has gained increased attention.

In evangelical Protestant circles, the sermon has probably least of all attained its immense educational possibilities. The reason is not reducible to the flimsy wants of the congregation as much as to the minister's lack of serious study and preparation. Too many pastors are ready to settle for some cute comment on the prevalent secular outlook instead of earnestly wrestling the false gods of our time and consistently expounding the biblical worldview and the life-changing demands it imposes on believers. God has not called Baptists to be intellectually stunted priests, but to serve Him spiritually and vocationally outside as well as inside church buildings.

Religious education has many facets, ranging from pulpit instruction, inquirers' classes for potential church members, and formal church school classes, to special training courses that may focus on biblical teaching, historical origins and growth of the Christian movement, or contemporary issues. Some churches seek these objectives in conjunction with midweek prayer meeting, correlating them with an appropriate Scripture lesson. More specialized are courses that prepare Sunday school teachers, ready college students for academic dialogue, or instruct lay leaders in the application of Christian principles in their respective vocations. Some of the larger groups issue certificates or diplomas upon completion of a prescribed course of studies.

In 1959, Gerald E. Knoff of the National Council of Churches estimated that almost one-third—or 14,190,000—of the movement's thirty-seven Protestant and Eastern Orthodox denominations were enrolled in adult church school departments.[22] Much of this lay participation has been squandered by ecumenically-aligned denominations that neglected biblical instruction and evangelism, and reduced Christian education to socialistic motifs and political theology. The significance of Christian theology for adult education was evaporated in the very places that were intended to provide it. The modernist pulpit shunned a defense of the supernatural miraculous and focused instead on scientific relativities and social revolution. Basic truths of the Christian faith were blurred beyond recognition. Remarkably, it was the recovery of world evangelism as an irreducible imperative by laymen who were finding Christ on the outer fringes of ecumenism that contributed so largely to evangelical church growth, although it unfortunately lacked comparable enthusiasm for Christian education.

Baptists have long emphasized the importance of parental instruction of children in accord with biblical emphases (e.g., Deut. 6:4–6) and have viewed the Great Commission as a mandate to win followers of Christ (Matt. 28:19–20), who in turn will love God with the entire self, the mind included (Matt. 22:37 ff.). Their emphasis on biblical authority and shunning of denominational creedal diversity is sometimes misunderstood as disdain for cognitive principles. But Sunday school instructional emphases suggest otherwise. Still, many Baptists view formal education as corruptive, especially because of its uncritical indoctrination in evolution and its resistance to biblical doctrine. In consequence, many approve Christian day schools.

Yet daily family reading of the Bible has vanished from many homes, topical preaching has displaced expository preaching in many churches, and in worship services classic hymnbooks often give way to projections of light contemporary ditties. Students are sent to Baptist colleges in the expectation that faculty members will function as surrogate parents. But as the parent generation itself reflects the tawdry values of the 1960s, and as professors as well increasingly reflect that era, a much diluted form of Christianity prevails, and colleges and universities are lost to authentic Christian faith.

The notion that a durable philosophy of education requires the reversibility of all intellectual judgments has gained the status of academic formality and orthodoxy. Albert J. Taylor insists that "all positions" are adjustable positions and nothing more: "None are final, absolute, unalterable, and unquestionable truths."[23] Each person, suggests Kingsley Price, must probe for himself or herself what significance the competing philosophies of education may have for our age.[24] It is the case, of course, that nobody can make life's ultimate commitment for us. But if no commitments have universal validity, it is scarce worth the effort to probe everchanging options.

So biblical theism sounds ever more irrelevant and antiquated. Almost a generation ago, Robert Ulich of Harvard boldly and uncritically claimed that "millions of Christians profess what they no longer believe," and Christianity has for them "become nothing but a respectable convention which they do not leave because they are mentally too indifferent or because they do not know where to go."[25]

Timothy George, dean of Beeson Divinity School of Samford University, has called attention to great theological themes that press for clarification as Baptists approach the twenty-first century: the authority of Scripture, the doctrine of God, the person and work of Jesus Christ, the ministry of the Holy Spirit, and the church. The restoration of such cardinal doctrines to a place of importance in the academic curriculum will help to revitalize collegiate education. If Baptist higher education is to fulfill the intention of the founders by whose sacrifices these schools of learning became a reality, the truly learned graduate will have no difficulty affirming the full authority and reliability of the Bible, the self-revelation of the Creator-Redeemer God whose final judgment will embrace all men and nations, the deity and salvific life, the death and resurrection of Jesus Christ, the Holy Spirit's regeneration of penitent sinners, and the divinely given mission of the church as the new society in an otherwise doomed and ill-fated world.

The economics of education is now routinely discussed more than its content. Even when it runs from the nursery through doctoral studies two decades later, education in recent modern times has been often justified as a sound investment. Under this economic umbrella, education has in the last half of the twentieth century become almost universal. Financial expectations have overshadowed the pursuit of knowledge for recreational enjoyment or social status, let alone its truth. Not surprisingly, educational policymakers promote cost-benefit analysis as much as do the recipients of learning. The now prevalent "doctor of ministries" degree offered by seminaries has been widely criticized as a program less justified by academic priorities than by financial considerations. While for many in developing countries higher education remains a prerogative only of children of the elite, the recognition that illiteracy is a devastating liability now accelerates a universal demand for primary education, which the Universal Declaration of Human Rights espouses.

A dramatic value-transformation is involved in this development. An educational process that concentrates exclusively on worldly concerns and promotes a sensate culture that devalues the invisible moral world, by its neglect of enduring truth and of unchanging moral imperatives, contrasts starkly with the spiritual and cultural offerings of the noblest earlier human societies and cultures. Previous civilizations recognized the distinction between good and evil to be an objective one, irreducible to personal or social preference. In virtually all ancient civilizations, education included an awareness of the transcendent divine, except for China, although even the Confucianism tradition had an essentially moral character. It is no exaggeration to say that religion saturated education in the ancient world.

Once in Palestine, the ancient Hebrews developed education of a distinctive type. Alongside the Phoenician, they placed writing by scribes who, as servants of the king, copied and taught the sacred law, thereby instilling high wisdom and promoting character training. The synagogue was not only a house of spiritual assembly and of prayer, but as Henri-Irenee Marrov remarks, it was "also a school with a 'house of the book' and a 'house of instruction' corresponding roughly to elementary or secondary or advanced levels of education."[26]

Christians took quite a different attitude toward classical Greco-Roman education. They did not perpetuate education solely along the lines of the rabbinical school. Aware though they were of classical education's connection with the pagan past, they held the family and the church responsible for religious education, and set up catechetical schools for candidates for baptism. While they barred themselves from teaching in the classical schools, they sent their children to them. The question of compatibility or incompatibility of Greco-Roman thought and Christian truth remained, therefore, ongoingly relevant. Aware of the idolatry and immorality promoted by study of the classics, Christians gradually "assimilated and took over classical education" and by the fourth century occupied "teaching positions at all levels from schoolmasters and grammarians to the highest chairs of eloquence."[27] Without participation in the culturally established education, the Christian life would have lacked a disciplined comprehension of the deeper philosophical issues or of the essential uniqueness of the gospel. The Bible was increasingly stressed as the moral sourcebook.

For all that, once infant baptism prevailed, not even religious education was required. Only children in training to become clergy or monks, or children of the upper classes were regularly educated. With the Protestant Reformation and the translation of the Bible into the language of the people came a notable extension of elementary and other education. The Christian mandate to proclaim the gospel and make disciples worldwide challenged the notion of education reserved only for the privileged. Elemental education was no longer anybody's sole privilege, not even the clergy's, and it was considered as necessary in rural areas as in the cities. John Wycliffe stressed that everyone should be a theologian. Martin Luther's translation of Scripture made available to children attending school a reading of original sources.

The recent loss of the Bible by Western academic institutions of higher learning would have astounded the Reformers. It provides a sad commentary on the spiritual lethargy of modernity. It was none other than John Baillie, a churchman often leagued with modernist colleagues, who recalled nonetheless that he was but five years old when he learned that "man's chief end is to glorify God, and to enjoy Him forever" and then commented pointedly that our civilization is "doomed to swift integration and decay, if it should cease to be aware of itself as standing within that context."[28]

It is increasingly recognized in Baptist circles today that trustees are in the final instance the responsible academic policymaking bodies. It is their duty to articulate carefully and clearly the Christian purpose of their institutions and to publish these openly to faculty, staff, students, and alumni, and then to honor these active goals of the educational program. Execution of the educational policy is the task primarily of the president. In carrying out the board's stated policy, the president must have the full cooperation and understanding of the trustees.[29]

The great overarching vision of a Christian university, more specifically a Baptist university, that would prepare a new generation of evangelical clergy and churchgoers devoted to the Christian world-life view was a grand prospect a century ago. But it flourished only to perish as mediating scholars gradually attenuated the original vision. In 1897 the Scottish Presbyterian apologist James Orr delivered his Kerr Lectures on "The Christian View of God and the World" at Lake Forest in the suburban Chicago area. Orr pointedly noted that the religion of Jesus Christ "exalts the teaching office" and does so precisely in view of an emphasis on doctrine that ancient paganism lacked.[30] The New Testament bases true religion on knowledge, on definite teaching that it considers normatively true. The recovery of cognitive truth is an indispensable condition for virile Christian education.

Chicago-area Baptists gradually lost the golden opportunity for an institution solidly committed to biblical norms. The University of Chicago experiment retains its somber warning over the high price of compromise. It was, in its early discussions, projected as an academic enterprise set against faddish trends, spiritual relativism, and theological radicalism as these existed in that day; but more than that, it was to bring to the world of learning the best Christian minds of that day. It foreshadowed an opportunity that remains to be recovered in our day as revitalized Southern Baptists work toward a new academic consensus in implementing the historical evangelical mission. Instead of accommodating the frontier fashions of political correctness, multiculturalism and contextualization, revolutionary theology, and radical feminism, it would stand tall in our time for Christ and the Bible.

The initial Chicago vision was of a great Baptist seminary on the way to becoming a Baptist university. In 1867, the Baptist Theological Union Seminary was moved from suburban Morgan Park to Chicago's Midway to meet a condition stipulated by the philanthropist John D. Rockefeller as a condition for founding the university. It was the divinity school that birthed the university in 1891–92.

Initially, the case for a Baptist college in the Chicago area, ultimately to become a great university, was promoted by noting to the clergy that hundreds of Baptist ministerial candidates lacked training, not because of Baptist apathy or nonsupport of education, but because most of the denomination's schools were located in small towns removed from wealthy churchmen. The grand vision that now gripped the Chicago-area clergy was relayed by President James Taylor of Vassar College and by William Rainey Harper, professor at Yale, to Rockefeller, who was a prominent member of the Baptist church in Cleveland, where the Baptist theologian A. H. Strong ministered.[31] Rockefeller chose Harper, a brilliant Hebraist who insisted on a critical approach to the Bible and on faculty freedom to teach whatever professors considered true and right, as first president. Rockefeller's contribution was $30 million.

The university was projected as a Baptist university by A. H. Strong, the Northern Baptist theologian, in early conversations with Rockefeller. This vision was finally altered to a Christian university with a Baptist divinity school (which swallowed up what had been Swedish and Danish-Norwegian seminaries located at Morgan Park). Step by step the university projection became nonsectarian. By 1915 the divinity school had become so modernist in its emphasis that Northern Baptist Theological Seminary was founded in the basement of Chicago's Second Baptist Church as an evangelical alternative. Within two decades, the fledgling conservative campus attracted the largest enrollment of any of the denomination's seminaries, until after midcentury it too fell victim to some of the critical theories it was initially formed to combat.

The university-based Chicago School of Theology was at first broadly modernist. Increasingly empirical in stance, it tended to define God in terms of cosmic support for theism, and viewed the development of Christian doctrine critically. It became a center for emerging humanist thought and still later for process theology, until in the 1960s diversity overtook even this commitment. In 1993 the University of Chicago was prominent in the Parliament of the World's Religions, with participating religious personalities from almost all the living modern faiths. The vision of a distinctly Baptist academic witness to a nation in spiritual need had yielded to interreligious dialogue in a society now deeply confused by the very pluralism that Chicago's founders had hoped to surmount.

Endnotes

1. Timothy George and David S. Dockery, ed., (Nashville: Broadman Press, 1990), x.

2. Ibid. 692.

3. H. I. Hester, *Partners in Purpose and Progress: A Brief History of the Education Commission of the Southern Baptist Convention* (Nashville: Southern Baptist Convention, Education Commission, c. 1977), 9.

4. Ibid., 93.

5. Ibid., 99.

6. Hugh Hartshorne and Milton C. Froyd, *Theological in the Northern Baptist Convention* (Philadelphia: The Judson Press, 1945), 21 ff.

7. (New York: Charles Scribner's Sons, 1912), 480.

8. K. W. Clements, ed., *Baptists in the Twentieth Century*, (London: Baptist Historical Society, 1983), 82.

9. *Southern Baptists in Christian Education*, (Murfreesboro, N.C.: 1968), 4.

10. Leon McBeth, (Nashville: Education Commission of the Southern Baptist Convention, 1966), 6.

11. Introduction to Charles P. Johnson, *Higher Education of Southern Baptists: An Institutional History 1826–1954*, (Waco, Tex.: Baylor University Press, 1955), vii.

12. George F. Kneller, ed., *Foundations of Education* (New York:

John Wiley & Sons, Inc., 1971), 12.

13. Quoted by Cohen, Ibid., 18.

14. John M. Sutcliffe, ed., *A Dictionary of Religious Education*, (London: SCM Press Ltd., 1984), 40.

15. Brenda Watson, *Education for Belief* (Oxford: Basil Blackwell Ltd., 1987), 151.

16. Ibid., 152.

17. *Education and the Taming of Power* (London: Alcove Press, 1974), 291.

18. (New York: A Touchstone Book, Simon & Schuster, 1987).

19. *Christian Discourses*, quoted by Walter Lowrie, *Kierkegaard*, vol. 2 (New York: Harper and Brothers, 1962), 508.

20. *Religious Values In Education* (Danville, Ill.: The Interstate, 1967), 105.

21. Ibid., 146.

22. Lawrence C. Little, ed., *The Future Course of Christian Adult Education* (Pittsburgh: University of Pittsburgh Press, 1959), 12.

23. *An Introduction to the Philosophy of Education* (New York: University Press of America, 1983) 190.

24. *Education and Philosophical Thought* (Boston: Allyn and Bacon, Inc., 1962), 503.

25. *Philosophy of Education* (New York: American Book Company, 1961), 20.

26. *Encyclopedia Britannica*, 15th ed., s.v. "history of education."

27. Ibid., 329.

28. "Education for the Service of God," *His Magazine*, February 1958, 3.

29. Ben C. Fisher, *An Orientation Manual For Trustees of Church Related Colleges* (Nashville, Tenn.: Education Commission, SBC, 1980), 21f.; 70ff.

30. Ibid., 20.

31. Richard J. Storr, *Harper's University: The Beginnings* (Chicago and London: The University of Chicago Press, 1966), 16ff.

CHAPTER SIX

The Church in the Twenty-First Century

PAIGE PATTERSON

"Baptists are not a creedal people." Those words have been employed in recent years as a smoke screen to justify just about any departure from the faith of the New Testament that one could imagine. But as J. M. Frost poignantly stipulated in the 1900 introduction to *Baptist Why and Why Not*, Baptists, of necessity, are a "confessional" people. Frost said that a confession is "only a declaration of faith showing who we are, somewhat as a flag floating above the steamer at sea shows its nationality. By this declaration of principles, and in the name of our God, we set up the banner that it may be displayed because of the truth."[1]

In the same volume, R. M. Dudley, in his chapter "The Distinctive Baptist Why," recognized, as well as Frost, that Baptists were in general agreement with many of the churches of other denominations regarding the inerrancy of Scripture, the deity and humanity of Christ, the substitutionary sacrifice of our Lord, and other doctrines. Both writers are forced then to ask why there should be a Baptist denomination at all? Implicit in the query is the confidence that the Christology of Baptist people was essentially Nicaean and Chalcedonian, even if these creeds were seldom formally invoked. Almost no Baptist in 1900 questioned the Reformation's soteriological principles of *sola gratia* and *sola fide*, constructed as they were on the firm epistemological foundation of *sola scriptura*.

Why, then, should there be Baptist churches? Why have a Baptist denomination? What prompted the Anabaptists of the sixteenth century to hazard their lives? Was it not enough to risk the ire of the Roman Church? What led them to tweak the whiskers of the lions of Wittenburg, Geneva, and Zurich? In 1952, Franklin H. Littell identified the unique discovery of the Anabaptist vision, a discovery passed along to and treasured by Baptists of every generation.[2] This was the rediscovery of the New Testament principle of a church consisting only of believers, those who had experienced the new birth and given witness of that regeneration through baptism. To the Anabaptist mind, the Magisterial Reformers were correct in what they professed about salvation but totally inconsistent in the application of those truths, particularly as they related to the church. While professing to believe that people were saved by faith alone, the Magisterial Reformers never parted with the *Volkskirche*, that is the concept of a regional or nationally established church into which infants were added by baptism shortly after birth. William A. Mueller captures Luther's thinking regarding this *Volkskirche*: "Luther's advocacy of the 'Volkskirche' is closely related to his rejection of the sectarian ideal of the 'pure church.' This donatist error Luther believed to be the error of the Anabaptists of his day, whose real genius, I am bold to say, the reformer unfortunately failed to realize. To Luther, it was colossal pride to venture forth towards the formation of a church composed of believers only."[3]

In contradistinction to this *Volkskirche*, the Anabaptists and modern Baptists have insisted on a restoration of the New Testament pattern, which included a church consisting only of born-again, baptized believers. The Anabaptists of the sixteenth century did not view themselves as "reformers" of existing ecclesiastical structures that they considered hopelessly compromised. Rather, they couched their purpose in terms of "restoration." They intended to rediscover and implement the New Testament pattern for the church. Contemporary Baptists remain committed restorationists. The distinctive contribution of Anabaptist and Baptist thought is in the arena of ecclesiology. J. M. Pendleton focused on the essence of Baptist thought about the church in this definition.

> A church is a congregation of Christ's baptized disciples, acknowledging Him as their Head, relying on His atoning sacrifice for justification before God, and depending on the Holy Spirit for sanctification, united in the belief of the Gospel, agreeing to maintain its ordinances and obey its precepts, meeting together for worship, and cooperating for the extension of Christ's kingdom in the world. If any prefer an abridgment of the definition it may be given thus: A church is a congregation of Christ's baptized disciples, united in the belief of what He has said, and covenanting to do what He has commanded.[4]

Here it is clear that it means something to be a Baptist. Those in the present milieu who would urge that the essence of the Baptist way is freedom to believe anything or nothing at all are unfaithful to this Baptist heritage. Baptist rejection of creeds occurred because Baptists almost universally believed that creeds suffered at two points. First, they were penned by mortal, error-prone men, laboring without the protective intervention of direct inspiration, and, therefore, must always to be distinguished from the perfect, inerrant creed—the inspired Word of God. Second, since the Bible was the perfect creed, by definition, any man-made creed would be incomplete. Hans Küng is correct when he says, "All commentaries and interpretations, all explanations and applications must always be measured against and legitimized by the message contained in Holy Scripture with its original force, concentrated actuality, and supreme relevance. Sacred Scripture is thus the 'norma normans' of the Church's tradition, and tradition must be seen as the 'norma normata.'"[5] Nevertheless, confessions, distillations of those common beliefs that united Baptists, were deemed essential as a matter of public witness. And no portion of those confessions was more critical than the concept of the believer's church.

R. M. Dudley appealed to Armitage in his chapter in *Baptist Why and Why Not* to establish the same point: "I demur to the statement of the venerable Dr. Armitage in the North American Review for March, 1887, that the distinguishing difference of the Baptists is 'in the demand for a positive moral change wrought in the soul by the direct agency of the Holy Spirit as an indispensable qualification for membership in the church.'"[6] To further underscore the maintenance of this continued distinctive witness, Dudley added:

> I am not a Baptist because Baptists practice restricted communion, or immersion, or refuse infant baptism. I am a Baptist because by the fundamental principle of Protestantism I am bound by the Word of God in all matters of faith and practice. I believe in immersion not because I believe in one act above another but because the Bible teaches it; so of closed communion; and so of the rejection of infant baptism. For these peculiarities as peculiarities I care nothing at all. Indeed I am sorry that we are peculiar in these matters. But these peculiarities embody an underlying principle in religion that is more important than reputation or life itself. And to surrender these peculiarities is to surrender that principle. And if an honest adherence to it and an honest endeavor to practice it bring odium upon us let us have the manliness to bear it. To seek odium is detestable; to run from the post of conscience or of duty to avoid it, is cowardly and traitorous.[7]

We can only conclude that insistence upon the idea of the church as a regenerate body of believers who by baptism have provided a public profession of that faith and who engage in self-discipline so as to remain a holy and sanctified body is a New Testament principle eminently worthy of propagation and defense. Indeed, it is this lofty concept that has been the impetus behind the growth of Baptists across the years.

The Concept of "Church" in the New Testament

Almost nothing in the study of ecclesiology has been immune to debate. The very Greek word utilized by the authors of the New Testament is no exception. The problem is that the Greek term *ekklesia* was borrowed from Greco-Roman political culture and baptized into service to describe this new creation of God. However, the problem is exacerbated by the fact that Jesus most likely spoke Aramaic, and there, in the principle text where "church" is found on Jesus's lips, it is apparently a translation of an Aramaic word. Add to this the fact that the Septuagint translators also employed *ekklesia* to translate the important Hebrew words *qahal* and *edah*, both of which mean "congregation" or "assembly."

K. L. Schmidt speculates that *ekklesia* may have been chosen by Jews as a translation of *qahal* in part because of similarity in sound.[8] However that may be, the word was clearly an excellent choice for early Christians. Originally *ekklesia* denoted a popular assembly. In most Greco-Roman cities, the word referred to the citizens summoned by a herald to assemble for the purpose of the execution of legal acts. Interestingly, religious overtones were sometimes associated with the word as a result of prayers often offered by the herald and by individual speakers in the assembly.[9]

Baptist authors of yesteryear emphasized two aspects of *ekklesia*. First, they noted the etymology and drew a conclusion about the significance of that etymology. The word derives from the Greek verb *kaleo* (literally, "to all") with the preposition *ek* (literally, "out") prefixed. Hence, it was argued that the church consisted of men and women "called out" from the world and into the service of Christ. Second, the church was an "assembled" group of these called out of worldliness.

Earl Radmacher and others have contested the etymological conclusions about the word *ekklesia*. Radmacher argues that words change from their etymological origins and that this is a case in point. By the time the word is used in the New Testament, it references only the idea of "assembly."[10] While there is little doubt that Radmacher's conclusion is the overwhelming majority persuasion and that the concept of "assembly" is doubtless the essential connotation of the word, it is, nonetheless, unlikely that the sense derived from the etymology was entirely overlooked by the early church. Calling to salvation, a call to abandon sin and assemble with God's people, was a vivid and conscious soteriological motif in the New Testament (Rom. 8:30; 9:11; 9:24; Gal. 2:12; 1 Peter 2:9). That the Christian assemblies were congregations of God-called, twice-born men and women is evident. Erickson calls attention to the fact that *qahal*, the Hebrew word for "assembly," is probably derived from the word for "voice" and referred to a summons to assemble as well as to the act of assembly.[11] As R. W. Kicklighter said, "'Ekklesia,' from the compound verb 'ek kaleo' meaning 'to call out,' is a fitting term of designation for this 'separate' community."[12]

Robert Saucy has tracked 114 occurrences of *ekklesia* in the New Testament. Five have no reference to the church. The 109 remaining uses employ the word mostly for local churches but also for the universal church of the unity of all true believers in Christ. As he says, "Ekklesia in this sense is not the assembly itself but rather those constituting it; they are the church whether actually assembled or not."[13] He adds, however, that the New Testament says nothing of an invisible church: "As for membership in an invisible church without fellowship with any local assembly, this concept is never contemplated in the New Testament. The universal church was the universal fellowship of believers who met visibly in local assemblies."[14]

Another way to picture the church and comprehend its nature is to examine the descriptive metaphors found in the New Testament. Dale Moody lists three such images. First, the church is said to be the people of God. Next, it is the body of Christ.

Finally, the church is the fellowship of the Holy Spirit.[15] However, there are more than just these three images and variations of images. The New Testament also pictures church, for example, as a priesthood, as the bride of Christ, and elsewhere as the temple of the Holy Spirit. These images are interspersed throughout the New Testament with no single passage serving as a "locus classicus" for the doctrine of the church.

The People of God

In 2 Corinthians 6:16, Paul speaks of God's pledge to be God over the church while making the people "my people."* In 1 Peter 2:9, the church is declared to be a "peculiar people," which more literally translated means "a people for a possession." This analogy emphasizes the church as God's unique possession. All people are the artistic masterpieces of the Creator (Gen. 1:26; 5:1; 9:6; Ps. 8:5; Heb. 2:7–8), but only those redeemed persons who compose the church carry God's providential mark of ownership and, hence, protection.

The Body of Christ

This rich analogy is cogently employed in the New Testament. Initially, every true believer is immersed into the body of Christ at the moment of conversion (1 Cor. 12:13). Christ is the head of the body (Col. 1:18). In this relationship, believers are nourished through Christ (Eph. 4:15–16). The result is that the body of Christ then cooperates together, ministering the gifts of the Spirit thus supplied one to another (1 Cor. 12:13–31). This is a metaphor that focuses on the visible aspect of the church.

The Fellowship of the Spirit

The appealing New Testament term *koinonia* refers to that which is held in common or that which is shared. For example, the New Testament is written in *koine* Greek, that is, the common parlance of the agora rather than the literary Greek of the

---

* Unless otherwise indicated, all Scripture quotations in this chapter are from the King James Version of the Bible.

Hellenistic classics. In order to grasp the significance of this metaphor for the church, one must ask about the nature of that which is shared. The answer to this question is as notable for what it omits as it is for what it includes. For example, common social distinctions were ignored by the early church in that the same fellowship included male and female, slave and free, Jew and Greek (Gal. 3:28). Issues of gender or ethnic background, educational attainment, political prominence, or prosperity were not to exclude any from a genuinely classless fellowship of the redeemed (Acts 10:28; 34–35; 1 Cor. 1:26–31; Phil. 4:22; James 2:1–5).

What binds these diverse elements together in the church is a common revelation, calling, ministry, and commitment. First, Paul speaks of "the fellowship of the mystery" which was hidden with God but is now revealed in Jesus Christ (Eph. 3:9–10). Associated with this revelation of God's purpose in the world is the fellowship of a common efficacious call into that fellowship of Christ (1 Cor. 1:8). This calling to salvation then works itself out in a fellowship of ministering to the saints (2 Cor. 8:4) in various ways. Not infrequently this fellowship of the Spirit demands a commitment even to the extent of embracing the fellowship of Christ's sufferings (Phil. 3:10). This fellowship was symbolized by a warm grasping of hand and arm which is called the "right hand of fellowship" (Gal. 2:9).

The Temple of God

Usually, the individual believer is presented as the temple of God (1 Cor. 3:16; 6:19). However, in 2 Corinthians 6:16–18, it is possible that the church is referred to as the temple of the living God. And certainly this is the metaphor being employed for the church in Ephesians 2:19–22. In the latter crucial passage, the church also is presented as the "household of God" of which all true believers are members. This edifice is constructed on the foundation of the apostles and prophets, with Jesus, Himself, being the chief cornerstone. This "holy temple" should be in a constant state of development, growing into a magnificent holy temple, a dwelling place for God. This process is accomplished through the dynamic of the Holy Spirit.

The Function of the Church

Discussions of the purpose and function of a New Testament church often degenerate into partisan efforts to capture the "major work" of the church. For some, evangelism is the great assignment, while others cast a ballot for worship or for bringing glory to God. This misses the point that everything the church does in response to the mandate of Christ is an act of worship designed to glorify God. A safe place to begin defining the work of the church is, therefore, the commandment of Jesus our Lord.

Three imperatives may be identified in the "Great Commission" of Christ in Matthew 28:16–20, even though only one of the three verbs is actually in the imperative mood. The disciples are told to make disciples, baptize these disciples, and finally, instruct these disciples in all that Jesus had taught. The one imperative verb *(matheteusata)* is clear enough in the Greek Testament but is subject to some confusion in the modern context. Confusion arises from the tendency in the contemporary church to separate evangelization and discipling. But in Matthew 28:19 the word *(matheteusata)* surely means "to evangelize." In fact, the nature of the term will even throw some light on the recent controversy over "Lordship Salvation." To lead someone to Christ is to make him a disciple of Christ or a "learner," implying unadulterated commitment, which is then publicly witnessed by baptism. The new believer, having thus declared himself as a disciple of Christ, is then to be instructed in all that Jesus taught. He has committed himself to the Lord—now he must learn precisely what is involved in the discipleship to which he is committed.

Consequently, the work of evangelizing, carrying to fruition the "Great Commission," is one of the most important ways in which the church worships God and recognizes the lordship of Christ. The church is also responsible for baptism as the public profession of the new believer's faith as well as for the administration of the Lord's table. Associated with the Lord's Supper is the responsibility for the discipline of its own members (1 Cor. 5, 11).

Public reading of the Scriptures, fervent congregational prayer, the singing of hymns, and the exposition of the Word of God were the essential activities of worship in the early church. The communal meal often provided the occasion for the celebration of the Lord's Supper as well as an opportunity for fellowship and worship for the believers (Acts 2:42–47; Eph. 5:19–20). Recovery of these exercises in local assemblies today might very well mark the beginning of revival in our era.

Another aspect of the work of the church includes the ministry of the church to its own members. To this end, the grace gifts *(charismata)* or spiritual gifts *(pneumatikon)* are sovereignly distributed by the Holy Spirit (1 Cor. 12:11, 18) for the profit or edification of the entire body (1 Cor. 12:7; 14:26). Under no circumstances are these gifts to be employed for personal profit or blessing but only in behalf of the body of Christ. At least twenty-one of these gifts are listed (Rom. 12:6–8; 1 Cor. 7:7; 12:8–10, 28–30; Eph. 4:11; 1 Peter 4:10–11). Though these listings defy most efforts to classify them neatly, the purpose for which they are given to the church could not be more obvious.

By way of summary, the work of the church is to worship God and bring glory to His name through the process of making disciples, baptizing and instructing those disciples, and leading them in all of those acts of public and private worship such as adoration, praise, and intercession. These acts employ the vehicles of hymnody, prayer, teaching, preaching, and the observance of the ordinances of baptism and the Lord's Supper.

The Public Witnesses of the Church

The few vignettes of worship in the early church which are available to us suggest nothing of formality and complicated liturgy characteristic of much contemporary worship. Apparently the early assemblies followed the pattern of the Jewish synagogue, a worship consisting of prayer, hymns, and the reading and exposition of the Word of God. In such a liturgy, rituals had little place. Nevertheless, two symbolic rituals or "witnesses" were practiced in obedience to the command of Christ.[16] Together, these two poignantly portrayed the nature of the gospel. The Lord's Supper was a vivid reminder of the body and blood of Christ given for our redemption, whereas baptism pointed to the consequent burial of Christ and His triumphant resurrection on the third day. Some churches have added footwashing as an ordinance. But while this is commanded as an act of humble service, it does not picture the atonement as do the Lord's Supper and baptism.

Baptism was the rite of initiation, the public profession of faith in Jesus and His sacrifice. Modern Baptists have erred in construing a public response to an invitation as a "public profession of faith." The early church asked newly regenerate believers to bear witness to their faith in baptism. This was administered immediately upon conversion, the early church thus expressing confidence in its converts.[17] The mode of baptism in the early church was certainly immersion. Jesus was immersed by John the Baptist, and extensive lexical studies have demonstrated beyond doubt that the Greek word *baptizo* meant "to envelope one substance in another" or "to immerse."[18] Even so, these facts do not constitute the major reasons for immersion as proper mode. The real purpose of immersion is to picture a burial and a resurrection. Regardless of whether Romans 6:1–14 refers to baptism by the Spirit, baptism in water, or both, the imagery is clear. In baptism, the believer rehearses the death, burial, and resurrection of Jesus as the sole basis for his own salvation. Further, he professes through baptism the death of the old man and a resurrection to walk in a new life with Christ.

In turn, this understanding of the purpose and mode of baptism defines the appropriate subject for baptism. Only someone who has by faith received Christ is a proper candidate for baptism. Not only is the New Testament without example of infant baptism for any reason, but also the only persons baptized in the New Testament are those of sufficient age and understanding to have exercised personal faith in Jesus. This concept of a believer's church consisting of regenerate persons who have borne public witness to their faith in Christ is the heart of the Baptist witness to the world.[19]

The second ordinance enjoined on the church is the fellowship meal, the Lord's Supper. The earliest account of the Supper is possibly that of Paul in 1 Corinthians 11:23–34 with additional accounts in the synoptic Gospels. The Lord Himself inaugurated this memorial feast at the Passover meal celebrated with His disciples just prior to the crucifixion. In each account of the Supper, its memorial significance receives the major emphasis. The church assembled is to employ the moment to reflect on the significance of the atoning sacrifice of Christ. The bread, originally from a common loaf, represented the body of Christ. The fruit of the vine memorialized His blood shed for the sins of the world and called to mind Leviticus 17:11, the Passover, and the Day of Atonement.

The question of the presence of Christ in the Supper is variously answered. Generally, Baptists have not only rejected transubstantiation (the idea that the elements of the Supper are transformed into the actual body and blood of Christ) but also any concept of the "Real Presence" of Christ in favor of a symbolic view. The Anabaptist idea of the ordinances as *zeugnis* or "witness" seems to capture the intent of the New Testament authors. Christ, of course, is present in every legitimate witness given, whether in ordinance, preaching, worship or other.

Another important aspect of the Lord's Table is that the Supper apparently served the early church as an expression of the fellowship of the body and, consequently, as the appropriate locus for the exercise of church discipline. In the event that an erring brother refused the initial overtures of the church (Matt. 18:15–17; Gal. 6:1), then the matter was brought before the church. The church then acted to exclude him from the fellowship of the Lord's Table (see 1 Cor. 5:9–13). The church at Corinth was apparently not being asked to erase a name from a church roll (which probably was nonexistent anyway) or even to avoid the presence of an unrepentant member, but rather to act in such a way as to demonstrate that the offending party had breached his fellowship with the body of Christ. Evidently, this last step in the disciplining process was exclusion from the fellowship meal, the Lord's Supper.

The Organized Life of the Church

The organized life of the church includes the governance in the church as well as the officials who provide leadership for the church. Forms of governance practiced among various denominations include hierarchical, episcopal, presbyterial, and congregational.[20] By carefully selecting proof texts, a case can be made for each of these forms of government in the New Testament. This probably suggests a somewhat fluid state in the early church, which was still subject to the extraordinary authority granted to and exercised by the apostles. Nevertheless, the seeds of responsible congregationalism, both exegetically and theologically, are obvious in the documents of the New Testament.

The doctrine of the priesthood of believers, the responsibility for witness and ministry incumbent upon every believer, and the doctrine of the permanent indwelling of the Holy Spirit in every genuine believer provide the theological underpinning for congregationalism. Exegetical evidence may be deduced from such sources as 1 and 2 Corinthians, in which even Paul's apostolic authority is not employed coercively. Paul made every appeal, but in the final analysis, the Corinthian assembly was apparently at liberty to make its own decisions, even in the gravest matters. In Acts 13, the church at Antioch laid hands on Paul and Barnabas and sent them forth on the first mission; they reported upon return to the entire gathered assembly (Acts 14:27). Unworthy elders were to be rebuked before the whole church (1 Tim. 5:20). Apostles, prophets, evangelists, and teachers were all charged with a ministry of "equipping" which would make it possible for the saints to do "the work of the ministry" (Eph. 4:12).

Congregationalism does not, however, grant absolute autonomy to local churches or establish a "democratic" rule in the assemblies. Authentic New Testament churches will recognize and heartily endorse the absolute lordship of Christ. This recognition of the lordship of Christ includes the recognition that the

Scriptures are the very Word of God and, therefore, constitute a perfect and inerrant written code of conduct and mission that carries with it the authority of Christ. Consequently, "congregationalism," properly understood, entitles the local church to practice or proclaim nothing other than what is given by Jesus and His Word, the Bible, in all of those matters that are directly addressed. In all matters not directly addressed, "congregationalism" places responsibility upon the local church corporately to seek the mind of the Holy Spirit within the parameters established by the great principles of the faith; and, having sought the mind of the Spirit through study of biblical principles and fervent prayer, to agree together on a direction, solution, or action. In other words, genuine congregationalism makes the whole body of believers directly accountable to God rather than placing total accountability with a group of elders or bishops.

Churches, then, are autonomous to the extent that no other ecclesiastical body is responsible for their doctrine or practice. But in true New Testament churches this autonomy is never interpreted as the right to believe or to do whatever is desired regardless of the will of God as expressed through Jesus and in the Holy Scriptures. And even though in some ways New Testament churches are the most thoroughgoing democracies in the world, this democratic process is limited to each member's fervent pursuit of the leadership of the Spirit of God. Overemphasis on this democratic process and on autonomy will lead to the prioritizing of rugged individualism over reverent submission to God, to the exercise of business affairs over ministry, and to the rise of human carnality over humble service to the kingdom.

The most important officer of the church is the priest. Unlike the Old Testament priesthood where only sons of Levi were permitted thus to serve, the church presents to the world a priesthood of all believers. Hans Küng begins his discussion of the offices of the church with an extensive affirmation of the priesthood of believers and argues convincingly that such a position is the logical outcome of all soteriology and ecclesiology in the New Testament.[21] Küng states:

> The fundamental error of ecclesiologies which turned out, in fact, to be no more than hierarchologies (where "ecclesia" = "hierarchia") was that they failed to realize that all who hold office are primarily (both temporally and factually speaking) not dignitaries but believers, members of the fellowship of believers; and that compared with this fundamental Christian fact any office they may hold is of secondary if not tertiary importance. Bluntly put: the believer who holds no office is a Christian and member of the Church of Christ; a man who holds office without faith is no Christian and not a member of the Church. The Church must be seen first and foremost as a fellowship of faith, and only in this light can ecclesiastical office be properly understood.[22]

This cherished office is an office of privilege and of responsibility. But the nature of the "privilege" has frequently been totally misunderstood. The priesthood of believers is not a license for invoking whatever one may wish to believe. Those parameters of doctrine are already established through the lordship of Christ and the codification of God's Word in the Bible. Not infrequently, two honored Baptist principles are confused. Baptists do believe in freedom and liberty of conscience. No one should be coerced in any religious belief. But this is very different from the doctrine of the priesthood of believers.

The nature of this priesthood is elucidated only in 1 Peter 2:5 and 9, though the fact of it is mentioned and implied elsewhere. The "privilege" in the doctrine is individual accessibility to God. The "responsibility" of the doctrine includes the "offering of spiritual sacrifices to God through Jesus Christ" and "proclaiming the promises of Him who called you out of darkness into His marvelous light."

The work of the church is to proceed under the guidance of appointed ministers called pastors and deacons. Some attempt has been made to argue for a third level of ministry, by separating "pastors" from "elders." However, the New Testament does not seem to support this idea. First, when qualifications are given for the officers of the church, no separate list is provided for elders. In 1 Timothy 3, for example, bishops and deacons are represented; whereas, in Titus 1 only bishops or pastors are mentioned. Furthermore, the terminology for pastor, bishop, and elder is interchangeably employed in the New Testament to speak of the same person(s). For example, in 1 Peter 5 all three words (Gk. *presbuteroi*, *episcopeo*, and *poimaino* occur) two of them in verbal form, but all describing the work of the same person. While the words seem to be interchangeable in application, each word probably emphasizes a distinct aspect of ministry. "Elder" is a term of respect, which initially has obvious ties to "age." The idea is that a pastor is to be accorded the same level of respect as that due a senior adult. "Bishop" or "overseer" places the emphasis on administrative and organizational aspects of ministry. "Pastor" or "shepherd" focuses attention on the spiritual leadership role of the minister. He is to lead, feed, and protect the flock as well as see to the growth of the flock (evangelism).

Is there a case to be made for "elder rule" on the basis of such passages as 1 Timothy 5:17 ("elders that rule well") and Hebrews 13:7 and 17, where some are said to have the rule over others? These passages do attest to the plurality of elders in at least some of the growing first-century assemblies, and they do suggest a clear level of "pastoral authority." However, paramount in importance is the understanding of the nature of "pastoral authority." The fact that an elder who is sinning is to be rebuked before the entire congregation (1 Tim. 5:20) and that even apostolic or angelic proclamation of a false gospel should be rejected (Gal. 1:6–9) is evidence enough that "elder rule" was not absolute. In fact, the appropriate posture for an elder is that of a "servant." In this servant's role of humble ministry to the church, the elder will eventually experience a kind of "moral and spiritual ascendancy" that will cede to him spiritual leadership in the church. "Rule" should be understood in the sense of God-anointed leadership.

"Deacon" is a word belonging to a treasury of Greek words for servant or slave. This word usually refers to a table-waiter or a butler. Hence, the deacon is not a part of a ruling board or even, for that matter, a part of the decision-making leadership in the church. If Acts 6:1–7 is interpreted as the establishment of the first diaconate, then the venue for deacons is clear. These godly servants were to see to the physical ministries of the church in order that the disciples could devote themselves to prayer and to the ministry of the Word (Acts 6:3–4). The subtle shift in contemporary churches from deacons who watch for the physical needs of the flock to deacons who exercise authority over the flock has been a disaster for churches in most places.

The final question that must be addressed is that of gender as it relates to leadership in the church. Several truths are self-evident in the Scriptures.

1. Women are made in the "imago Dei" just as surely as are men; they can and do experience God just as men do and, hence, are fully equal with men in every way.
2. Under certain conditions, women may pray and prophesy in the church (1 Cor. 11:5).
3. Women are identified in the New Testament as "prophetesses" (Acts 21:8–9) and in many other ways make substantive and even pivotal contributions to New Testament Christianity (Luke 2:36; Acts 18:26; 21:9; Titus 2:3–5).

Nevertheless, the New Testament provides no precedent for women serving as elders or in pastoral positions. Jesus selected only men for His disciples, and there is no case in the New Testament in which women are mentioned with reference to pastoral ministry. Furthermore, 1 Timothy 2:12–15 certainly appears to be a direct prohibition of women serving in any capacity in the church that would place them in authority over men or in authoritative teaching roles. This limitation would exclude women from a calling as pastor.[23]

Those who disagree with this limitation almost always appeal to Galatians 3:28 and argue that in Christ such distinctions are passé. But the problem of precedent and text remains. One of two approaches will then be ventured. Some admit that the text says what it seems to say and respond that Jesus bowed to cultural convention on the point while Paul was simply in error. The other approach is to attempt some form of explanation to attempt to emancipate the verse from its surface significance. As often as not, this explanation will appeal to the culture of the day and suggest that Paul, like Jesus, temporarily accommodated himself to such ignorance or else that the verses in Timothy were intended only for the abusive situation in which Timothy was laboring when he received the epistle.

This argument fails, however, since historical and theological reasons are supplied by the text as rationale for the requirement that women not serve in pastoral capacities. Three reasons are cited.

1. Adam was created first.
2. Adam also sinned knowingly and, therefore, must assume spiritual responsibility.
3. The woman is to find her greatest spiritual impact through the "office" of motherhood.

Worth noting is the fact that since men are clearly assigned spiritual leadership in the home, it would be unlikely for this not to be the case in the church also.

Special Issues for the Church

There are a few additional issues mostly associated with modernity which must be addressed briefly.

Means of Evangelistic Outreach

The first of these issues is the question of the use of "means" in the evangelistic outreach of the church. Two opposite poles vie for the loyalty of the churches. One insists that the use of almost any means other than the preaching of the gospel is unworthy of the church since those who come to Christ do so as a result of the sovereign acts of God. Challenging this today is the "user-friendly" approach that is concerned with "marketing" the church and meeting the "felt needs" of the social order.

A word of caution is appropriate for advocates of both positions. First, Jesus observed that often "the sons of this world are wiser in their own generation than the sons of light" (Luke 16:8, RSV). There is nothing inherently wrong with "marketing" the church or with participatory forms of worship that involve the congregation as more than spectators observing the performance of the ministers. What is disastrous for the church is when such methodologies become ends within themselves or in any way compromise or dilute the message of the gospel, the call to repentance and brokenness, and a commitment to the abandonment of worldliness in exchange for faith in Christ.

On the other hand, those who emphasize the sovereignty of God in the soteriological process are correct when they point to passages such as 1 Corinthians 1:17–31, which assigns relative insignificance to just about everything the world considers significant, placing over against the "wisdom of this world" (v. 20) the "foolishness of preaching" (v. 21). The message of the Bible is that God's work cannot be done in the world's way. Yet, a word of caution to those who focus on divine sovereignty is also necessary. Any doctrine of the sovereignty of God that truncates aggressive personal witnessing, evangelistic preaching, call for decision, or fervent prayer for the salvation of the lost is also foreign to the New Testament.[24]

Associations of Churches and Denominations

Another question that must be faced is the question of the association of churches and denominations. The thesis of this chapter has been that local churches are the primary focus of the New Testament. But we have also acknowledged that the New Testament occasionally employs the word "church" to speak of "the general assembly of the firstborn" (Heb. 12:23) or the "universal church." The very fact that such a reality exists provides the basis for associations with other believers so long as such associations do not involve local churches in compromise. Thus, churches of "like faith and order," since the Jerusalem conference of Acts 15, have cooperated together to accomplish the work of the kingdom. Sometimes these relationships have been informal, while at other times they have taken a more organized form, such as those of associations or conventions. Occasionally, churches that differ rather radically in "faith and order" may even associate together temporarily for some purpose, such as an evangelistic crusade or for some community or national moral concern.

However, Baptist churches have always been wary of "connectionalism." "Connectionalism" is the forming of any organization that results in a local assembly's automatic relationship to still another level of organization. Hence, one local church may voluntarily belong to a local association of churches, to a statewide association, and to a national association such as the Southern Baptist Convention. However, there should never be an automatic "connection" among these, so that, for example, the local church is relating to the state association through the local association and so forth. Such "connectionalism" tends to create an hierarchical or at least episcopal form of church government. Furthermore, each local assembly must bear in mind that the success of all such associations is dependent upon discovering churches of "like faith and order."

Church Constitutions and Bylaws

Another question faced by local churches in the contemporary context is that of the preparation and authority of church constitutions and their attendant bylaws. The early churches managed quite well without constitutions. Furthermore, the New Testament is an accurate and adequate rule for any church. Nevertheless, local, state, and national laws often make it necessary for churches to adopt such constitutions in order to function. In such cases caution needs to be exercised at several points.

First, nothing should be included in the constitution that violates the faith and rule of the New Testament. Second, some statement similar to the following should be adopted as a part of the document.

> The First Baptist Church hereby adopts three documents which shall serve as the governing documents for the faith and order of the Church. These are the New Testament, *The Baptist Faith and Message* of 1963, and this constitution and its bylaws. Their relative importance is according to the order given, and the last document shall be understood to be subservient to the first two. The ultimate standard for adjudication of the faith and order of the church will be the New Testament.

Finally, Baptists have always insisted on the separation of church and state. This vital Baptist tenet is enshrined in the Constitution of the United States in the First Amendment which says:

> Congress shall make no law respecting an establishment of religion, or prohibiting the free exercise thereof; or abridging the freedom of speech, or of the press, or the right of the people peaceably to assemble, and to petition the government for a redress of grievances.

The two important mandates of this amendment are:

- Congress shall make no law to establish a state religion, and
- Congress shall pass no law prohibiting the free exercise of religious conviction.

It should be noted that both mandates are addressed to government—not to the churches! The traditional Baptist insistence on separation of church and states does not

1. prohibit the church from addressing the state,
2. squelch political activism on the part of individual believers or church groups, or
3. limit Christians from serving in government positions.

Christians must be salt and light in society (Matt. 5:13–16), and the isolationism of local churches from the moral and social order has often been a prelude to tragedy.

On the other hand, the church must remember that it is to be in but not of the world (John 17:13–17). The greatest change that the church can effect upon society will be the result of the church's witness to Christ and His regenerating grace. Social activism and political involvement then must always be regulated by the priority assignments of the church.

In conclusion, articles 6 and 7 of *The Baptist Faith and Message* of 1963, printed below, summarize the nature and work of the church, capturing the heart of the New Testament doctrine of the church.

VI. The Church

A New Testament church of the Lord Jesus Christ is a local body of baptized believers who are associated by covenant in the faith and fellowship of the gospel, observing the two ordinances of Christ, committed to His teachings, exercising the gifts, rights, and privileges invested in them by His Word, and seeking to extend the gospel to the ends of the earth.

This church is an autonomous body, operating through democratic processes under the Lordship of Jesus Christ. In such a congregation, members are equally responsible. Its Scriptural officers are pastors and deacons.

The New Testament speaks also of the church as the body of Christ which includes all of the redeemed of all the ages.

VII. Baptism and the Lord's Supper

Christian baptism is the immersion of a believer in water in the name of the Father, the Son, and the Holy Spirit. It is an act of obedience symbolizing the believer's faith in a crucified, buried, and risen Saviour, the believer's death to sin, the burial of the old life, and the resurrection to walk in newness of life in Christ Jesus. It is a testimony to his faith in the final resurrection of the dead. Being a church ordinance, it is prerequisite to the privileges of church membership and to the Lord's Supper.

The Lord's Supper is a symbolic act of obedience whereby members of the church, through partaking of the bread and the fruit of the vine, memorialize the death of the Redeemer and anticipate His second coming.[25]

Endnotes:

1. J. M. Frost, ed., *Baptist Why And Why Not* (Nashville: Sunday School Board of the Southern Baptist Convention, 1900), 13.
2. Franklin H. Littell, *The Anabaptist View of the Church* (Boston: Star King Press, 1952).
3. William A. Mueller, *Church and State in Luther and Calvin* (Nashville: Broadman Press, 1956), 15. If one is inclined to doubt that this remains a substantive issue, consider these words from Wolfhart Pannenberg: "From time to time Christians are

shocked by reports in the secular press about the decline in church attendance, reports that seem to indicate that Christianity is going downhill in our society. Only 15 percent of West German Protestants regularly attend Sunday worship, and at present in the major cities only 25 percent of the Catholics go to church every Sunday. Such reports lend encouragement to those voices which consider that the status of our churches as national churches, supported by taxes and administering infant baptism, is unjustifiable. They demand that the churches become voluntary organizations, to which only truly committed Christians would belong. Such demands overlook the fact that the 75 to 85 percent of Christians who do not attend church regularly still have their children baptized and confirmed, plan church weddings, and expect Christian burial, as well as bear the burden of paying their church taxes. Nothing warrants our assuming that these Christians are inwardly alienated from Christianity." Wolfhart Pannenberg, *The Church* (Philadelphia: The Westminster Press, 1983), 9.

4. J. M. Pendleton, *Baptist Church Manual, Revised* (Nashville: Broadman Press, 1966), 7.

5. Hans Küng, *The Church* (London: Sheed and Ward, 1967), 16.

6. Frost, Baptist Why and Why Not, 25.

7. Ibid., 33.

8. Gerhard Kittel, ed., *Theological Dictionary of the New Testament*, vol. 3, (Grand Rapids: William B. Eerdmans, 1965), 517.

9. Ibid., 513–514.

10. Earl D. Radmacher, *The Nature of the Church* (Portland, Ore.: Western Baptist Press, 1972), 110–113.

11. Millard Erickson, *Christian Theology* (Grand Rapids: Baker, 1985), 1031.

12. Duke N. McCall, ed., *What Is the Church?* (Nashville: Broadman Press, 1958), 34. See also Hans Küng's excellent discussion of *ekklesia* in *The Church*, 84–85. Here Küng emphasizes not only the nature of the church as an entity called together by God but also the fact that "the local 'ekklesia' is not a 'section' or a 'promise' of the whole 'ekklesia,'" but rather that in each local church the church is "wholly present in every place, endowed with the entire promise of the Gospel and the entire faith, recipient of the undivided grace of the Father, having present in it an

undivided Christ and enriched by the undivided Holy Spirit." One of the best discussions on all facets of the doctrine of the church from a Baptist perspective is J. L. Dagg, *A Treatise on Church Order* (Charleston: Southern Baptist Publication Society, 1858). Especially helpful is Dagg's assessment of the doctrine of baptism.

13. Robert L. Saucy, *The Church in God's Program* (Chicago: Moody Press, 1972), 17.

14. Ibid. An incident in the ministry of the far-famed R. G. Lee may or may not be apocryphal. Ostensibly, a woman presented herself to sing in Lee's choir. He inquired about her church affiliation and was informed that she was a member of "the invisible church." Lee purportedly replied, "Fine, sing in their choir." If the incident did not occur, it should have occurred, for it illustrates the simple truth that the "invisible church," "the church triumphant," or "the universal church," while taught in Scripture, has little applicability in the present era beyond the expression that it finds through the ministry of local congregations. On the other hand, E. Y. Mullins was right when he cited Ephesians 5:25–27 as an example of the connection that exists between the local assembly and the universal church. "In this passage the church is viewed as existing in time and in eternity and the continuity of the church which exists in time with that which exists in eternity is made indisputably clear. In time it is a church with spots and wrinkles; in eternity it is without spot or wrinkle. In time it needed cleansing by the washing of water, that is, it was an impure church not yet free from sin. In eternity this same church stands before Christ holy and without blemish. Now if the church here existing in time refers to the local church, then it means the same when it becomes holy and without blemish in eternity, and we have the local church with pastors, deacons and ordinances carried over into eternity. I know of no one who holds this view." E. Y. Mullins, *Baptist Beliefs* (Philadelphia: Judson Press, 1912), 62–63.

15. Dale Moody, *The Word of Truth* (Grand Rapids: William B. Eerdmans, 1981), 42–446.

16. The Anabaptists preferred to use the German term *zeugnis* or "witness" to describe the purpose of the ordinances. Pilgram Marpeck, the lay-theologian of Strasbourg and Augsburg, developed this concept of baptism as "witness" in his *Taufbuchlein* (Lit-

tle Baptism Book) of 1542. See William Klassen, *Covenant and Community: The Life, Writings and Hermeneutics of Pilgram Marpeck* (Grand Rapids: William B. Eerdmans, 1968). Also William Klassen and Walter Klassen, eds., *The Writings of Pilgram Marpeck* (Scottsdale: Herald Press, 1978).

17. In various parts of the world, baptism is often postponed for a period of time, up to as much as two years, in order for the candidate for baptism to prove himself. The rationale for this is (1) that the context or milieu from which new converts are coming is so alien to the Christian faith, and (2) this way a better effort can be made to maintain a regenerate church membership. On three points the argument founders. First, there is no pattern for postponement in the New Testament. To the contrary, Acts 10:47 is Peter's argument for promptness in the baptism of Cornelius. (See also the prompt baptism of the Ethiopian eunuch (Acts 8:26–40). Second, from what kind of background were most gentile converts emerging? Certainly some "God-fearers" were among them, but most came from total paganism and were still baptized immediately. Third, the problem of a pure church is the purpose of church discipline and, I will later argue, belongs to the Lord's table rather than to baptism. Balthasar Hubmaier spoke eloquently and sometimes even sarcastically to this issue. In 1525 in a booklet entitled "On the Christian Baptism of Believers," Hubmaier wrote: "Now do you ask in solemn earnestness. What must I know, or how much must I know, if I want to be baptized? The answer: This much you must know of the Word of God, before you may be baptized: that you are a miserable sinner, and confess it, also, that you believe in the forgiveness of your sins through Christ Jesus, and you desire to begin a new life with the purpose of amending your life in conformity with the will of Christ in the power of God, the Father, the Son, and the Holy Spirit. And you must know that if you go astray therein, you will, according to the rule of Christ in Matt. 18, permit yourself to be chastised, whereby from day to day you may grow in faith just as a mustard seed reaches the heavens." William R. Estep Jr., *Anabaptist Beginnings (1523–1533)* (Nieuwkoop: B. DeGraaf, 1976), 82.

18. See T. J. Counts, The Meaning and Use of Baptizein (Grand Rapids: Kregel, 1977); *Review and Expositor*, 65, no. 1, winter 1968, a superb issue on baptism, especially the articles by William E. Hull, Dale Moody, and Wayne E. Ward. For an ex-

tensive argument against the Baptist position, see James W. Dale's two volumes *Judaic Baptism* and *Classic Baptism* (1867; reprint Bolchazy: Carducci Publishers, 1989).

19. Balthasar Hubmaier argued his point against infant baptism during the Reformation in the following words: "But do you say that there are nowhere in the Scriptures a clear word to the effect that one must not baptize infants? Answer: it is clear enough for him who has eyes to see it, but it is not expressed in so many words, literally: 'do not baptize young children.' May one then baptize them? To that I answer, if so, I may baptize my dog or my donkey, or I may circumcise girls, I may say masses and hold vigils for the dead, I may make idols out of St. Paul and St. Peter, I may bring infants to the Lord's Supper, bless palm leaves, vegetables, salt, land, water, and sell the mass for an offering. For it is nowhere said in so many words that we should not do these things. Is it not true, what a twofold papacy we would set up again if we juggle such things concerning God and the souls of men leaving out the Word of God. You say: 'It is forbidden to baptize donkeys, for Christ calls men to baptism.' Well then, let us also baptize Jews and Turks. You say: 'Yes, only believing men should one baptize.' Answer: why do you then baptize infants?" Estep, *Anabaptist Beginnings*, 91.

20. For a more extended discussion of this issue, see Paige Patterson's "The Meaning of Authority in the Local Church," in John Piper and Wayne Grudem, eds., *Recovering Biblical Manhood and Womanhood* (Wheaton: Crossway Books, 1991), 248–259. See also the discussions of F. J. A. Hort, *The Christian Ecclesia* (London: Macmillan and Co., 1914), and H. E. Dana, *A Manual of Ecclesiology* (Kansas City: Central Seminary Press, 1944).

21. Hans Küng, *The Church*, 363ff. For the best discussion of the history and significance of the doctrine of the priesthood of believers, see Timothy George, "The Priesthood of All Believers," Paul Basden and David S. Dockery, eds., *The People of God* (Nashville: Broadman Press, 1991), 85f.

22. Ibid.

23. Often women object to this prohibition by arguing that they must be true to their "calling." The problem with this kind of argument is that it suggests that God has called the woman to do something that He forbids in Scripture. When the experience of the individual is primary and is not regulated by any authoritative

word from God, then anyone's experience must be accepted as authoritative. When two "authoritative experiences" clash, how is the church to adjudicate the matter?

24. There is, in my estimation, an almost perfect paradigm in the New Testament to address this problem. In Paul's sermon to intellectuals on Mars Hill (Acts 17:16–34), the apostle made use of well-known, even erroneous popular religion (the altar to the unknown God) and appealed to Aratus of Soli, a Greek poet, in the process of presenting his message. However, his blunt and undiluted warning of impending judgment is a clear call for repentance (vv. 30–31) and would probably not be considered "user-friendly" marketing today.

25. *The Baptist Faith and Message* (Nashville: Sunday School Board of the Southern Baptist Convention, 1963), 12–13.

CHAPTER SEVEN

Worship

DAVID S. DOCKERY

The phrase *worship service* creates a variety of images and reactions. Some think, *That's the eleven o'clock hour on Sunday morning*. Others think of "church" as distinguished from the "Sunday school" hours. Some differentiate the Sunday morning service in general from other church meetings.

Does the phrase *worship service* prompt images of preaching? Praise? Singing? Fellowship?

The diversity of worship practices in today's Southern Baptist churches makes any attempt to discuss this subject a big challenge. The variety of hymns, choruses, and gospel songs in the *Baptist Hymnal* (1991) underscores this observation. Some Southern Baptist worship practices reflect high church styles with an emphasis on the liturgy; others concentrate on teaching the Word of God; for others Free Church frontier styles of worship see revivalistic preaching as primary; still others utilize praise/celebration styles; and newer "seeker oriented" services are coming into greater use. This chapter does not advocate any particular style. Instead, it simply issues a call for renewal in Southern Baptist worship that focuses on exalting God and reaching people.

Early Christian Worship

Worship is the foundational activity of the Christian church. It defines the life-giving functions of the people of the new covenant and the new age. Worship is a joyful experience for the believing community and is as necessary for spiritual life as air and food are for physical well-being.

The church that meets us in the pages of the New Testament is a worshiping community of believing men and women (Acts 1:14; 2:42–47; 4:31; 5:12, 42; 20:7–12; 1 Cor. 10–14). Christian worship arose directly out of the matrix of the Jewish traditions in the temple and synagogue. Some distinctly new elements were, however, added from the beginning. Many of the Jewish forms, such as the blessing of God as Creator and Sustainer of life (the *berakah*), were taken over and can be clearly seen in New Testament statements that open with "Blessed be God" (2 Cor. 1:3; Eph. 1:3; 1 Peter 1:3) and "Amens" (1 Cor. 14:16). But the New Testament forms are filled with new content that belongs to the new situation in the history of God's saving purposes for the world. Christians of the apostolic era were conscious of living in days of eschatological fulfillment that flowed from the Incarnation and redeeming cross-work of Jesus of Nazareth in whom they recognized Israel's Messiah and the world's Savior. It was this conviction that stamped itself on their worship in every aspect and gave it a distinctiveness that is unique.

Tokens of that distinctively Christian pattern may be set down. Standing high in the list of features that marked out Christian worship from its antecedents in the Old Testament and Rabbinic Judaism and from the contemporary world of

Greco-Roman religion is the *christological* reality of the risen Christ whose promise to be with His people who assembled in His name (Matt. 18:20; 28:20) was claimed and known. While there is a verbal parallel to the thought of worshipers meeting together in accord and being promised the divine presence, the personal presence of the living Lord speaks of what we may judge to be the structure of early Christian assemblies and can be explained only on the basis of Christ's coming to meet his people.

Worship was a vertical movement, that is, the praise of humanity to God. But there was also a horizontal movement because worship was celebrated with others. Therefore worship was a community act, and the relationships between the members of the worshiping community were of the highest importance.

Genuine community existed in face-to-face relationships, and for Christians this meant that the members of the community were persons bound together by faith and love. This was grounded in Jesus Christ, the *yes* response to the Father (1 Cor. 1:30). Through Christ, the people of God, the community of Christ, responded in thanksgiving and remembrance (*anamnesis*) for the atonement He offered in love to His Father and for the salvation of humankind. One with Christ, as members of His body, a body that was visibly existing in space and time, the church made present the reality of His redeeming work to men and women of succeeding generations.

Worship of Jesus Christ during New Testament times was born in the crucible of events that were recognized as the fulfillment of the Old Testament. Initially, the early church worshiped in a continuity with the past. But a growing conflict between those who accepted Jesus as Messiah and those who did not, created a gradual separation of the different groups. In this context, the church developed characteristics in continuity with and distinct from Jewish worship. In many ways, following the pattern of Jesus Himself, the early church assumed the right to reinterpret the customs of Jewish worship in light of the Christian mission.

The early church developed out of three different groups. These groups represented the backgrounds of the people who were populating the early Christian community.

The first group, identified as Jewish Christians, was characterized by a continuity with temple worship (Acts 2:46; 3:11–26). These Christians were caught in the tension between being Jewish and Christian, as suggested by the additional worship practices in houses (Acts 2:42–47).

The second group we can refer to as Hellenistic Christians. The worship of this group was characterized by the renunciation of Jewish ritualism (Acts 6:1–7:50). Jewish rituals were reinterpreted as having been fulfilled in Christ (Heb. 7–10).

The third and largest group by the end of the first century was comprised of gentile Christians. Gentile Christian worship was exhorted to be orderly (1 Cor. 14:40; 1 Tim. 3:15) since it had developed out of pagan origins. Worship became Christocentric and content oriented (1 Cor. 14:6–26) as preaching and the Lord's Supper characterized its major aspects. Also, worship became more organized and structured as the community developed.

By the end of the first century, the church's worship was commonly Christocentric in that the church worshiped the Father, in and through the work of the Son, by the Holy Spirit, in praise and thanksgiving for the work of redemption. The work of Christ is central to Christian worship. Not only was the Christ-event central to Christian worship, but it formed its meaning as well. Worship was more than an exercise in memory or a matter of simply recounting past events. It dynamically enabled the church to experience the presence of Christ in a specific and decided way.

The Definition of Worship

Important for us at this stage is a careful understanding of the biblical terms used for worship. The English word *worship* comes from the Anglo-Saxon *weorthscipe*, which developed into *worthship* and finally *worship*. As can be seen from the word's derivation, *worship is the act of giving honor to someone of worth*. Thus, to worship God is to ascribe to Him the supreme worth that He alone is worthy to receive.

The Bible does not give a formal definition of worship, but its meaning may be determined from several terms used in Scripture.

The primary New Testament word for worship is *proskyneo*, which literally means "to kiss the hand of one." The verb form occurs fifty-nine times in the New Testament. The word emphasizes exclusive worship addressed to the Lord. Where this verb is used absolutely, it means to share in public worship, to offer prayers of adoration (see Rev. 4:11; 5:9; 7:12; 19:1, 3, 4).

The next most frequently used term is *sebomai* and its various cognates. The word has "fear" as its root meaning and involves reverence that stresses the feeling of awe. The term is used frequently to express a sense of worship (see Acts 18:7, 13; 1 Tim. 2:10; 5:4; 2 Pet. 1:3; 3:11).

A third term, *latreuo*, is a general term for worship denoting prayer (see Acts 13:2–3), giving (see Rom. 15:27; 2 Cor. 9:12) or the ministry of the gospel (see Rom. 15:16). The word *liturgy* is derived from this word. Basically, *latreuo* describes the total manner of life pleasing to God.

The Essence of Worship

The essence of Christian worship is grounded in the Old Testament revelation, though there are two new elements that are at the heart of the New Testament.

First, Christian worship is the active response to God the Father through the Son. The worshiper stands in a personal relation of sonship to God on the basis of adoption in Christ. Praise, prayer, preaching, the celebration of ordinances, confession, and giving are all Christ-centered actions. The focus of the church's worship on the exalted Christ gives a new depth and content that could not be achieved in the Old Testament period.

The second new factor is that the worship of God through the Son is in and by the Holy Spirit. Fitting and acceptable worship can only be offered by and through the enabling ministry of the Holy Spirit.

Varieties in Baptist Worship Yesterday and Today

Just as the early church's worship had aspects of unity and variety, so we can point to similar patterns of unity and variety, as well as continuity and discontinuity, as we observe worship patterns in contemporary Baptist churches.

Worship in Southern Baptist churches reflects the principal types of worship that were transferred from European soil to the American colonies. First, there were those churches that retained a fixed liturgy, such as had been known in the Anglican church. A second type was characteristic of those churches that stemmed from what might be termed radical Puritanism. This form of worship rejected traditionalism and opened the door to American revivalism. A third type of worship reflecting many aspects of American culture de-emphasized the ordinances and highlighted other forms of ministry. Often in this third type, people became more and more adjusted to being spectators rather than participants in their worship services. These three patterns—which we can identify as (1) Charleston, (2) Sandy Creek, (3) and Contemporary—dominate different streams of Southern Baptist life in the 1990s. Let's take a look at these three different practices.

Traditional "Charleston" Worship

Baptists as a whole are not strict traditionalists, but many congregations greatly value this style, which finds its roots in what is called the "Charleston Pattern" of Baptist practices. This traditional worship emphasizes the aesthetic and, at other times, the rational. Most church members who practice traditional worship have a previous background in this style. Some traditional churches follow liturgical patterns and order their worship around the church year.

Prescribed order in traditional worship insures a balanced concentration on scriptural selections and themes. Worship services in these churches are characterized by public Scripture readings, congregational responses, hymns, anthems, the offering, and preaching. Music in general emphasizes the classical, but this is not always the case. There is a variety even in traditional worship that incorporates aspects of the revivalistic and the creative. The major characteristic of traditional services is order or structure. Traditionalists seek to keep the historical significance of worship through the ages. They are aware that they are not the first generation to preach the sermons, sing the hymns, and gather as a corporate community to worship God. Thus, their practices benefit from a continuity with Christians in past times.

Revivalistic "Sandy Creek" Worship

A number of different aspects influenced early Baptist worship. Many Baptist churches began without church buildings, so worship took on the informality of the schoolhouse or the home and reflected the freedom and flexibility of the frontier. Revivalistic worship was characterized by a very simple pattern of unskilled singing, extemporaneous prayer, and evangelistic preaching, patterns rooted in the "Sandy Creek" Baptist tradition.

As the frontier was pushed westward, traditional worship became more and more influenced by revivalism as it spread to new parts of America. Many Southern Baptist churches have their roots in the American revival tradition. The revival meeting began with a song service of many songs chosen to raise the emotional pitch of the congregation. Prayers were offered, and they were intensely personal. Special music, usually a solo, was prepared to enable the congregation to hear and respond to the evangelistic sermon, which was always followed by some form of altar call. At times, strong revivalistic and judgmental preaching tended to overshadow the experience of corporate worship. The evangelistic sermon became the all-important part of the service. The current pattern influenced by the Billy Graham Crusades has greatly shaped Baptist churches during the last decades.

"Contemporary" Worship

In the past decade, creative worship styles, sometimes known as "seeker sensitive" worship, has gained ascendency among

Southern Baptists. Particularly, this is the case in large metropolitan areas and on the west coast. This worship both informs and entertains the congregation. The personality and ability of the preacher is vitally important. Churches are built like theaters with banked seats so that what is taking place in the pulpit area and the choir loft can be more readily observed.

Similarly, seeker sensitive worship patterns follow portions of this model, primarily reaching people twenty-five to forty-five years old, many with little or no church background. Proponents of this style of worship believe that some aspects of both traditional and revivalistic church services repel rather than attract modern people.

These services are creative and intentionally "non-churchy." A major goal of the service is to enable the participant to feel comfortable in worship. Sermons are generally topical, focusing on application. Music, characterized by choruses rather than by hymnody, is a match for the upbeat, popular music that the twenty-five- to forty-five-year-old generation has digested during its lifetime. Many contemporary churches limit the use of choirs and hymnals and highlight small vocal ensembles. Video clips and drama also help to focus the attention of the audience on the issue of the day.

Ordinances are sometimes de-emphasized, and proclamation in the form of sermons, drama, and multimedia presentations is emphasized. These services are adapted to appeal to young Americans living in modern America. Seeker worship does not generally emphasize congregational participation. Perhaps that is the main difference between this approach and that of the early church. New Testament worshipers came to worship expecting to participate fully in the act of giving of themselves (Heb. 13:15–16).

While no form of worship can be said to be inherently better than another, we should always seek to ground our worship practices in the teaching of the New Testament. Perhaps, learning from the early church models, we should expect variety. However, we must never neglect the content of the Christian gospel. In our attempts to renew worship in Baptist life, it is important that we do not neglect to proclaim the whole counsel of God (Acts 20:27) and recover the primacy of expository preaching. Nor in our attempt to identify with the modern world can we even hint that we are ashamed of the gospel (Rom. 1:16). We must find creative ways to touch the lives of the unbelieving and unchurched while creating worship services that simultaneously exalt the trinitarian God and edify the people of God. Anything less fails to be faithful to the New Testament teaching and the early church's pattern.

Why Worship Renewal Is Needed

The preceding overview shows that worship must be God-centered. Our worship needs renewal because our church services tend to be human-centered. The biblical view of worship tells us worship is not primarily for people but for God, as we recognize His glory and exalt His name.

Renewal in our worship will be characterized by at least three things: (1) a significant emphasis on reading and hearing the preached Word; (2) a high degree of congregational involvement in praise, prayer, singing, giving, and confession; and (3) a view of the ordinances that affirm their mystery and value for spiritual formation.

By contrast, much of Baptist worship tends: (1) to be confused about the purpose and order of worship; (2) to evidence a minimal use of the Bible, especially its public reading; (3) to be passive; and (4) to have an inadequate view of the church ordinances.

A variety of circumstances has contributed to our present low view of worship. At least four matters can be identified.

1. The current shift toward an entertainment mentality has created an atmosphere in which church leaders and members come to church expecting to be entertained.
2. The result of the Enlightenment has created over-emphasis in some quarters on the rational element of worship.
3. The rise of revivalism has in other sectors created an unbalanced emotional appeal aimed at unbelievers.

4. The general trend toward secularization and adaption of our culture has diminished the difference between the Christian community and the world.

Each of these forces has had a different impact on our worship practices, but the combination has created an unwelcome situation. Worship, which should stand at the heart of our Christian experience, is unable to form, shape, challenge, inspire, enhance, motivate, nourish, or feed us.

How Worship Can Be Improved

The first step in rediscovering the missing jewel of worship is simply to help the redeemed community recognize that the worship of God is a primary function of the church.

Second, we must help people learn that worship is not passive, but active. Worship is the work of the people directed toward God. We gather on the Lord's Day not so much to receive but to offer sacrifices of praise (see Heb. 13:15–16). We acknowledge what God has done for us and is doing for us. Thus, we bless Him, hymn Him, and offer our gifts to Him, as well as our praise and adoration. We learn to see worship as active participation.

This stance helps us overcome our misconception that the hymns, Scripture reading, and the offering are merely the preliminaries before the preaching or that the ordinances are something we tack on at the beginning or ending of the service.

Third, we need to understand that Christian worship is primarily rooted in an event, the Christ-event in which God revealed Himself as our loving and compassionate Creator and Redeemer. Worship is a response to the birth, ministry, death, and resurrection of Christ.

Fourth, we need to emphasize that worship is primarily spiritual and symbolic. Worship is only possible in and by the Holy Spirit, who prompts our love and praise of God. At the same time, we need to rediscover the wealth of resources available to help us highlight those symbols handed down to us by Christ, the apostles, and the experiences of the saints of the ages. Much that is dismissed as form and tradition can be rebaptized by the Spirit to shape our congregational worship.

Fifth, we must rediscover the significance and importance of the Lord's Supper. If the central act of worship in the New Testament is the corporate celebration of the Lord's Supper, should we not give it greater attention? If indeed the regular observance will enhance our love for our Lord, is it not possible that this is how we would answer that question? Will not greater love for the Lord form the foundation for reaching the world for Him? Should our practice of the Supper not be more than a mere appendage to the preaching service?

Baptists need to establish a special time for the observance so that it is no longer an infrequent practice or a hurried appendage to a lengthy sermon. We must not give up our evangelistic zeal or our growing sense of the importance of edification. We must seek balance. We must place the Lord's Supper in the center of our worship, for nothing is able to help us celebrate the work of Christ in our behalf or enable us to experience His presence among us as does the regular observance of the Supper. It enables the Word to become visible. Also, potential for pastoral care can be expanded. It can also help us emphasize unity in our churches and in our denomination when we recognize that the apostle's words in 1 Corinthians 10:17 call us to unity around the ordinance.

Many are ready to admit that a regular observance of the Lord's Supper was the practice of the early church and the patristic period as well. The usual objection is that when the Supper is observed too frequently, its meaning is lost. Could the same objection not be raised concerning Bible reading, singing, preaching, and praying? If the meaning is lost, the problem is not with the ordinance itself but with the heart of the individual. The testimony of one of the great Baptist preachers in history maintains that, contrary to the previous objection, the opposite can be found true. C. H. Spurgeon concluded:

> My witness is, and I think I speak the mind of many of God's people now present, that coming as some of us do, weekly to the Lord's Table, we do not find the breaking of bread to have lost its

> significance—it is always fresh to us. I have often remarked on Lord's Day evening whatever the subject may have been, whether Sinai has thundered over our heads, or the plaintive notes of Calvary have pierced our hearts, it always seems equally appropriate to come to the breaking of bread. Shame on the church that she should put it off to once a month and mar the first day of the week by depriving it of its glory in the meeting together for fellowship and breaking of bread, and showing forth the death of Christ till He comes. They who once know the sweetness of each Lord's Day celebrating His supper will not be content, I am sure, to put it off to less frequent seasons.[1]

Last, we must help people realize the need to prepare for worship. Worship leaders need to structure services to have coherent movement that is theologically, biblically, and thematically informed. Worshipers will gather not just to sit, listen, and be informed, but to exalt God and to affirm their faith.

The Effects of Renewal on Worship

Renewal in our churches will refocus an emphasis on the importance of all things being done for the glory of God (see 1 Cor. 10:31). We will move away from our individualistic and secular emphases to concentrate on the whole body so that all things will be done for mutual edification (see 1 Cor. 14:26). This mutual upbuilding of the body involves the development of mutual relationships (see 1 Cor. 12:7; 14:3ff). This takes place as each member, enhanced by congregational participation, ministers the gift bestowed to him or her by the Holy Spirit. Edification takes place in sharing with, and thus mutually receiving from, others. True worship produces such interaction and freedom of the Holy Spirit.

When genuine worship takes place, not only is the entire body enhanced and built up, but the mission and outreach of the church is strengthened. Notice that in Isaiah 6:1–8, after the prophet had authentically encountered God, three things resulted: (1) a recognition of who God is; (2) a realization of the need for repentance and forgiveness; and (3) a renewed desire for mission.

The people of God who have worshiped their God and who have been mutually strengthened are prepared to enter the world to touch lives, meet needs, counsel hurts, speak to injustices, and by life and witness, proclaim the saving message of the gospel. Reaching people and exalting God are hardly in conflict. As a matter of fact, real outreach is prefaced upon genuine worship.

As we enter the twenty-first century, may the Spirit of God enable Southern Baptists to recover the significance and vitality of authentic biblical worship for our individual lives and for the corporate church.

Endnotes

1. C. H. Spurgeon, *Treasury of the Old Testament* (London: Marshall, Morgan and Scott, n.d.), 1:543. See the helpful comments by C. F. D. Moule, *Worship in the New Testament* (London: Lutterworth, 1961), 29, who said, "We must be content to say that it is likely enough to have been a weekly practice" in apostolic times. W. B. Johnson, *The Gospel Developed*, (1846), the first president of the Southern Baptist Convention, discussed the approach to Baptist worship that included seven main points, including the regular reception of the Lord's Supper. He said that he did not see why the reception could not be done weekly, even though he chose to practice the ordinance on a monthly basis.

CHAPTER EIGHT

A Church Prayer Ministry

T. W. HUNT

The purpose of the Intercessory Prayer Ministry in the local church is to pray before God for the causes that touch the church. Certain large churches can maintain prayer during the entire 168 hours of the week; some small churches may be able to maintain prayer for only one hour each day of the week.

If a small church has only six prayer warriors willing to give themselves to this ministry, they should be assigned on consecutive days because the purpose is to maintain prayer before God throughout the week. Prayer requests come into the church, and it is there that prayer warriors will obtain the latest information needed to pray spiritually and effectively. Therefore, prayer should be spread throughout the week, ideally with some prayer going on every day of the week.

The Intercessory Prayer Ministry is church-centered and should be headquartered in the church building. Prayer warriors will always have the latest prayer requests. This is not to say that shut-ins and the elderly cannot participate; often they are our most effective prayer warriors. The coordinator can send them regular updates on important prayer requests, and they should remain active in praying for the concerns of the church. However, the ministry exists for the church, and every measure should be taken to emphasize its purpose to church members. One of these measures is centering the work in the church building.

If a church develops a successful Intercessory Prayer Ministry, other programs of the church will be blessed. Baptisms will go up, Sunday school attendance will increase, Discipleship Training will take on a new importance, and all programs will be enhanced. The church will discover that God blesses a ministry that comes from Him and depends upon Him. A vital prayer ministry should pray for all church programs, and in turn, every church activity will benefit from the spiritual impetus that prayer gives.

Praying as Children of the King

If you knew that you would be able to spend thirty minutes with the president of the United States, you might feel emotions you do not normally feel. You probably might approach the president with dread and nervousness. Excitement would grip you, and you would tell others what you were going to do. When the time came to enter into his presence, you would know to restrain your tongue. As a matter of fact, every spoken word would be valuable, and you would probably want to please him. You would measure your words to make sure that each was appropriate.

Why this anxiety? You know that few persons have spent time with the president. He is unavailable to most people. You would have this privilege only once, and your time with him would be limited. Your relationship probably would not continue, and you would have to observe a certain protocol.

When we approach God, we are approaching the highest office in the universe. We can look to many presidents, prime ministers, and kings, but we can come to only one God. He is King of kings and Lord of lords. Only one Person ultimately dispenses the fate of all men and nations. Surely God should command more respect than any earthly monarch!

Why should God command this special respect:

1. His office is heavenly. It is outside the sphere of inherited office; He has always been and always will be eternal and sovereign.
2. His office is spiritual. The spiritual is greater than the material.

The reasons for fearing to come into the presence of important persons do not apply to our relationship with God. God is available. He invites, even commands, us to ask. We do not need an appointment; His availability is limitless. We are related to Him. He undertook terrible measures at painful cost to make us His children. He wants His children to spend time with Him.

As His children, we are royal. We are children of the King—princes and princesses of the realm, destined one day to reign with Christ (Rev. 5:10). And beyond all question, the manner in which we speak to Him should be sensitive. He is the High King, and we are not only His children, we are His subjects. We may address Him, but we also owe Him fierce dread and awe. The rank He has bestowed on us means that we should temper our prayers with nobility of thought. We cannot be petty or small, and our nobility means that we will put Kingdom purposes ahead of personal desires.

The Bible indicates that God expects us to come into His presence, conscious of who He is. As Moses approached the burning bush, God spoke to him: "Do not come any closer. . . . Take off your sandals, for the place where you are standing is holy ground" (Exod. 3:5).* This passage teaches us that God takes the initiative in prayer. It was God who ignited the flaming

* Unless otherwise noted, all Scripture quotations in this chapter are from the New International Version of the Bible.

bush to attract Moses. Moses certainly experienced terror, for he hid his face (v. 6).

Meditating on the Attributes of God

Every morning when I begin my quiet time, I always take several minutes to think about what God is. I meditate on the attributes of God.

The attribute God called to Moses' attention was holiness. We would not find it strange, then, that this was the first thing God introduced into the mind of Isaiah in his encounter with God (Isa. 6:3). Isaiah's desperate cry, "Woe is me!" (Isa. 6:5, KJV) was a response to the holiness of God. When Simon Peter first began to perceive the identity of Jesus, he cried, "Go away from me, Lord; I am a sinful man!" (Luke 5:8). The Bible indicates that holiness is the first attribute of God we should be attentive to.

God has many other characteristics. He is omnipotent. If you think about that for a few minutes, you will understand why our asking is not limited by human possibilities. In John 15:7, Jesus said, "Ask whatever you wish." John repeats the idea in 1 John 3:21–22, "We . . . receive from him anything we ask." Later he says that God hears us "whatever we ask" (1 John 5:15). Our asking is limited by God's will, not by His power.

God is omnipresent. No place in the universe is beyond the reach of prayer. He is omniscient. I know that His answer will take aspects of each situation into consideration that I could not know about. He is transcendent, or other than what we are. We must never forget that we cannot understand the perfection of God. All that He does will bear the mark of His character.

Some days I concentrate on the infinity of God. Finiteness cannot understand infinity, but we can appreciate the fact that it places Him beyond our understanding. God is immortal. At least one consequence of this fact is that He has been working throughout history, and "His story" in the past will reveal something about what He might do in the future. He is immutable. He is always consistent. He is absolute wisdom. His decisions are irrevocable because they demonstrate a perfect understanding of a very large canvas. He is absolute love, as the story of Jesus reveals perfectly.

We should not only think about what God is (the attributes above) but also about *who* He is. He is a Person—a Father who cares and a Master who directs His own work. It is scripturally legitimate to pray to Jesus (Stephen did in Acts 7:59–60), and we can pray to Him as Brother (Heb. 2:11) or as Bridegroom (Matt. 9:15; 25:1–13).

Preparing to Pray

We prepare to pray by concentrating on the Person to whom we are praying. Prayer must be on God's basis—His attributes and His Person. It is for His purposes, not for ours. Answers will demonstrate His character and intention.

In view of the fact that we approach God from His point of view, what are the attitudes or qualities we should seek for ourselves?

First, we should obviously cultivate *fear* of the Lord. Fear is not only the beginning of wisdom (Prov. 9:10), it is the beginning of prayer and of worship. Because God is holy, we must confess our sins before we are compatible with Him. Failure to confess indicates a lack of reverence for God's holiness. Spend time asking God to reveal your conscious and unconscious sins as a response to His holiness.

Second, we should cultivate *humility* in preparing to pray. Only humility can really know the will of God. Presumption indicates self-centeredness. Because of who God is, we approach Him with lowliness.

Third, we should cultivate *purity.* Part of God's purpose in leading us to pray is to make us like Himself. Not only must we confess all our sin, we must deal with it. Prayer warriors, especially, must actively fight against sin. The quality of purity must also include unmixed motives (James 4:1–3). Remember, though, that even our purity is not our own. It is a borrowed or imputed purity. We have the mind of Christ Himself (1 Cor. 2:16).

Fourth, we should cultivate *sincerity.* God pays attention only to what is real. Remember that God knows everything, even the secrets of our hearts. "The Lord searches every heart and understands every motive behind the thoughts" (1 Chron. 28:9).

Finally, we must approach the Lord in *faith*. When you have faith, you know you have made a real transaction with God. Jesus told the blind men that their healing depended on their faith (Matt. 9:29). Having faith is probably harder in the twentieth century than it has ever been. Ask God to increase your faith. Spend time with believing people. Often we can "catch" faith more easily than we can learn it.

In coming to God we must first determine that we really know to whom we are speaking. Consider His Person and His attributes. Then confess all your sins and enter into prayer with the purity of the Lord Jesus that has been imputed to us. Prayerfully cultivate the qualities that should precede an entrance to the holy ground of prayer. God loves us and is waiting for us to come to Him in prayer. But we must come to Him on His terms.

Why Intercession Works

In prayer, God wants us to identify with Him in two ways:

1. He wants us to identify with Him by becoming like His perfect Son. As we talk to Him, God leads us to know Him and His ways so that we can become like Him.
2. He wants us to identify with His purposes. The world is God's work area for bringing His kingdom to fruition. In prayer He leads us to know His purposes, and He wants us to cooperate in accomplishing them by asking for those things that will further His kingdom.

God gave us different kinds of prayer to use to establish these two patterns of identification with Him. Many of our prayers will indeed be a response to God as a Person. Prayers in response to God include confession, worship, praise, and thanksgiving.

In all prayer, God takes the initiative. He prompts us to pray. He has certain ends He wants to accomplish, and at different times His Spirit leads us to pray according to the purpose He has in mind. Sometimes He reveals things about Himself because

He wants us to become like Him. From this revelation He expects that we will respond appropriately.

Confession

The first attribute of God that people in the Bible became aware of was His holiness. The attribute of holiness produces dread, but even as we fear God's holiness, we praise it. God's holiness is glorious. When we are walking in fellowship with God, we glorify Him in His holiness.

But sometimes we are not holy; we sin. Because we are related to God, our sin is an affront to His holiness. God the Spirit convicts us of the sin, and God gives us a kind of prayer to reverse the process of alienation. Confession is the corrective measure for our sin. Confession is saying the same thing God says or agreeing with God. This is the whole point of prayer—to agree with God. If we are like Him, our viewpoints are the same. So confession is a response to God's holiness.

Worship and Praise

Worship and praise are not the same. Worship is adoring or loving God. Praise is elevating the attributes of God; it is lifting up all that God is. As you grow in knowledge of God, you learn His qualities or traits—His attributes. Worship relates to God as a Person; praise exalts God in His divine office. Worship and praise are the proper response to the Holy Person of God.

When we love someone, we fix our attention on that person; that is part of the process of becoming like God. Praise also fixes attention. People imitate what they praise. God wants us to imitate Him. In knowing God, we know what we ought to be like. In elevating His attributes, we fix our eyes on all the worthy attributes we need in our own lives. Worship is response to God's glory. Praise is response to God's attributes.

Thanksgiving

Thanksgiving is response to God's bounty and generosity. Paul tells us to always give thanks for everything (Eph. 5:20), for it is God's will for us in Christ Jesus that we give thanks in all circumstances (1 Thess. 5:18). Paul insisted on this because most of us do not appreciate our blessings. In a world of plenty, we often take for granted the blessings of God. No gift of God should be taken for granted. The daily supply of our lives is a bountiful gift from our heavenly Father—the air we breathe, the water we drink, the food we eat, the marvelous ability of our bodies to process all these things. They indicate that God is constantly in a process of giving; therefore, we ought to be in a constant process of acknowledging that God is our bountiful source of all things. Proper thanksgiving recognizes the greatness of God, as seen in His neverending bounty.

Asking

Asking is one type of prayer that is not in direct response to the Person of God. Throughout His ministry, Jesus constantly emphasized the importance of asking. At the beginning of His career, in the Sermon on the Mount, He taught about asking. He also taught it in the Model Prayer (Matt. 6:9–13) and specifically told us that asking will be rewarded with answers (Matt. 7:7). Later, as a specific encouragement to ask, He told the parable of the friend coming at midnight to borrow bread (Luke 11:5–13). Jesus then told the story of a widow whose persistence secured her protection (Luke 18:1–8). Even at the end of His earthly life He was still stressing the importance of asking. In His Last Discourse, He returned to His ministry-long emphasis on asking (John 14:14; 15:7; 16:24). For the sake of what God wants to do in His kingdom, it is important that we learn to ask properly.

The Bible teaches two kinds of asking—petition and intercession. *Petition* is asking for yourself or for your own group. *Intercession* is asking for others. Prayers for the work of the kingdom are intercession. It would seem that petition should not characterize the great prayer warriors of the Bible, but repeatedly we find them making personal petition. In Genesis 15:2, Abraham asked God for a son. In 1 Samuel 1:10, Hannah prayed for a son. Hezekiah was mortally ill, and he prayed to live (2 Kings 20:1–

3). Zechariah and Elizabeth prayed for a child (Luke 1:13). God heard all of these personal petitions.

God's purpose in encouraging petition is to make us a certain kind of person. In each of the previous biblical petitions, the petitioner was in a process of becoming a greater person. Abraham became a patriarch. Hannah was becoming a certain kind of person when she prayed for a son. Hezekiah became one of Israel's greatest kings.

God functions as Father, a Father who wants greatness in His children. He cares what we become. We are to reign with Christ (Rev. 5:10), and God does not want us to be petty. We are royal. We pray personal prayers to accomplish something that is already in the mind of God, and our personal petitions should be under the leadership of the Holy Spirit as He indicates the kind of person we are to become—a witness, a kingdom worker, a giver, or even a praise for His answer.

In each case of petition mentioned, not only did the person asking become a greater person, but God's work and kingdom were benefited and enhanced. Abraham's prayer resulted in the chosen race that would prepare the way for Christ. Hannah's prayer gave Israel the last of the judges and the first of the prophets. That nation's history pivoted on the hinge that was the answer to Hannah's prayer. Because he did not die, Hezekiah lived to father Manasseh, and in so doing he preserved the Messianic line of David.

We see that the Bible treats petition as legitimate prayer. Of the asking prayers in the Bible that found answers, two-ninths are prayers of petition and seven-ninths are prayers of intercession. We do not know the reason why this is true. We find the same pattern in Jesus' great high priestly prayer of John 17. In that prayer, roughly two-ninths of His asking is for Himself and seven-ninths is for His followers.

Intercession is the greater kind of asking. The biblical pattern is that God did His work through the prayers of great intercessors. When God wanted to deliver the children of Israel from Egyptian bondage, He raised up Moses to pray for them. When God wanted to deliver them from the murderous plot of Haman,

He raised up Esther to fast for them. To rebuild the Jerusalem wall and to review the covenant, He used the prayers of Nehemiah and Ezra. He started the missionary movement through the prayers of the church in Antioch (Acts 13:2–3). Paul's ministry was aided by the church in Corinth (2 Cor. 1:11). The biblical pattern tells us that God does not normally work unilaterally; He prefers to work through the prayers of His saints. Intercession is God's basic method for bringing His will among men.

Establishing and Maintaining the Prayer Ministry

Jesus called the temple a "house of prayer" (Matt. 21:13) from Isaiah's name for it in Isaiah 56:7. The New Testament church was born in prayer (Acts 1:14, 24) and continued in prayer after Pentecost (Acts 2:42; 4:24, 31; 6:4; 12:5). Paul asked prayer of his churches (Col. 4:3; 1 Thess. 5:25; 2 Thess. 3:1) and believed that the Lord blessed his work because of their prayers (2 Cor. 1:11). Jesus' promises indicate that He thought the work of the church would be based on prayer (Matt. 18:19–20; John 14:13–14; 15:7; 16:23–27). Clearly, the New Testament indicates that the church of Jesus Christ should be a "house of prayer."

Intercessory prayer will be at the center of the church's prayer ministry, but it will also have many other expressions—times of prayer, prayer meetings, prayer chains, "prayer walls," prayer groups, and others. A comprehensive prayer ministry is primarily the responsibility of the pastor, so early in his awareness he should begin praying for direction. The first expression of the wider ministry that should occur in the church is some form of Intercessory Prayer Ministry.

The pastor and prayer committee (if the church has a prayer committee) should devote much prayer to preparing the church for a ministry of prayer. It should be a major part of the pastor's work before involving others. He should lead prayer warriors to pray that their church will become a house of prayer (Matt. 21:13). The prayer ministry should be prayed for in the midweek service, and the church should be asked to pray about it. Prior to the prelaunch period, the ministry should be saturated in prayer.

An effective church prayer ministry will require a budget determined by the size of the church. The coordinator and the pastor should convince the finance committee, as well as the church at large, of the importance of prayer. This ministry must be part of the budget. We will invest in what we believe in.

Expenses can vary greatly. A small church will not need a great outlay of money. They will need printed forms, a room, a table, a lock, several chairs, and a sign. The prayer room may be a Sunday school room or other small room set aside for this purpose.

A large church may spend considerably more. To get an outside entrance or an easily accessible entrance, the building may need to be altered. One way is to take a Sunday school room, close in the inside entrance and cut a door on the outside. Some churches have built an extra chapel. Other churches have purchased neighboring houses and used them for the prayer ministry. Still another solution is to use a mobile home.

The furnishings should be simple. Desks may be built to serve as altars; a separate altar may be used also. Furniture should be somewhat stark. Cushioned chairs are acceptable so long as they are not deeply cushioned. The prayer room is a workroom and should not suggest drowsiness or relaxation. An expanded prayer ministry should have a special phone for the prayer room. Usually you can secure an easy-to-memorize number, such as one whose last four digits spell P-R-A-Y. Prayer warriors should be well informed, so it is good to mount one or more bulletin boards.

An expanded prayer ministry will need a volunteer prayer secretary. There will be many forms to maintain, often on a daily basis. In a basic prayer ministry, the church secretary can handle most of the paperwork.

Pre-launch Period

The main goal of the pre-launch period is to acquaint the church with the purpose of the Intercessory Prayer Ministry. It should include preaching and/or teaching to convince Christians that their church urgently needs prayer. It should continue for a month, or even longer. During this time, the pastor should preach often on prayer and encourage the prayer ministry in his column in the church bulletin. The prayer coordinator may write several articles on prayer for the bulletin. A churchwide prayer conference would be excellent at this time. In addition, officers in the prayer ministry may use many other means of publicizing the upcoming launch—memos, postcards, and posters placed about the church. The church should enter the prayer ministry well convinced of the urgency of prayer.

The pre-launch period can be a time of recruiting prayer warriors. Like all offices in the church, the office of prayer warrior is strictly voluntary. The prayer coordinator and the pastor cannot do the work of the Holy Spirit, but they can be used as the Holy Spirit's mouthpiece. We cannot persuade people to come to the prayer room, but we can inform them of God's work. The Holy Spirit does the convincing. The pastor should mention the need for prayer warriors in the media available to him. He should write a general letter to church members explaining the Church Prayer Ministry and asking them to pray about being an intercessor. Also, he should be prepared to answer questions and be enthusiastic about God's work of prayer.

Launch Day/Commitment Sunday

Launch Day can be on a Sunday or on another set church occasion. If the launch is at an annual prayer banquet, the pastor or another person should speak or preach on prayer, giving emphasis to the beginning of the Church Prayer Ministry. Obviously, if it is on Sunday morning, the sermon should be on prayer. Conclude the sermon with an opportunity for persons to commit for the daily prayer hours. The easiest way to do this is to prepare a large, erasable grid, marked off in permanent ink to show all the hours of the week. Prayer warriors then select an hour and enter their names in the appropriate blank spaces. If some persons have flexible hours, they should indicate when they can come to the prayer room, and the prayer coordinator may assign them an available time (perhaps when no one else can pray).

Once the program is underway, the prayer coordinator will have the responsibility of maintaining interest in two groups—the prayer warriors who labor in the prayer room and the congregation at large. Both are important if the church is to become a house of prayer.

In successful prayer ministries that have maintained interest and participation, the prayer coordinator has been a dynamic person of great faith. He or she has passionately believed in the power of prayer and has communicated that continuously. Enthusiasm and faith are both contagious and complementary. To have one without the other is difficult.

Every growing church has a pastor of great faith. This is not to say that the ministry depends on a personality; rather, it is to say that no one prays who does not believe in prayer. Where there is more belief, there is more prayer. Without a burning, consuming desire to bring about the kingdom through prayer, a prayer coordinator will let a prayer ministry die. The same is true of the pastor. Both prayer coordinator and pastor must see the ministry as a way to bring about the kingdom of God.

The pastor should preach occasionally on prayer, mentioning the Church Prayer Ministry. The prayer coordinator should have regular or periodic articles in the church bulletin. He or she should make regular reports at the monthly church business meeting. On other occasions, a report on outstanding answers to prayer will bring excitement. Make occasional announcements about the church prayer ministry in the Sunday worship services. The prayer coordinator should also send periodic letters to the prayer warriors, encouraging them in the work of the Spirit. The pastor or other staff members may do the same thing. The prayer coordinator may send a periodic newsletter sharing answers to prayer, new books or prayer resources, an updated list of substitutes, and encouraging words about prayer. An occasional meeting with intercessors, led by the prayer coordinator, will provide inspiration. Many churches print brochures or pamphlets about their own church prayer ministries. There are many excellent prayer tracts available.

A creative prayer coordinator will find many ways of keeping the program before the people, but always the emphasis should be on the spiritual. Only the Lord can maintain the interest as it should be, and all persons in the prayer room should occasionally pray for the ministry of prayer itself.

A Prayer Ministry for a Small Church

All the work of God should be based on prayer, regardless of church size. Prayer is just as essential to the work of a small church as it is to a larger one. Except for the dimensions of the work, the prayer ministry of a small church will not differ essentially from that of a large church.

God asks, in Zechariah 4:10, "Who despises the day of small things?" With God, size is of no consequence. Dimensions do not matter. He started the Hebrew race with one man, Abraham. One hundred and twenty believers became three thousand at Pentecost. The small church can have a very effective prayer ministry.

All the work of God should be based on prayer, whether the church is large or small. Many churches have made it their goal to be known as a "house of prayer." This title has nothing to do with size.

Size also has nothing to do with quality, or power, or authority in prayer. These depend on your prayer warriors. The most powerful prayer warrior I know personally is a member of a very small church. Some of the most powerful leaders in Christian life today grew up in rural or small-town churches. Furthermore, skill in prayer can be learned. It is available to all Christians, regardless of the size of their church.

In ancient Jewish practice, after the synagogue became established as an institution for local worship (as opposed to the centralized worship in the temple), all that was necessary to establish a local congregation was ten men. It is evident that many of the synagogues in which Paul preached were small. Although the churches in Jerusalem and Antioch were larger, most New Testament churches had very small beginnings.

Small churches have inherent advantages and disadvantages. Sometimes minor aggravations can become major disruptions in the small church. But at the same time, the intimacy of a smaller group makes it easier to agree in prayer. God honors greatly the prayer of unity between Christians. It is possible for a small church to see phenomenal works of prayer because of the possible unity.

The pastor's role as prayer leader is vital. This is just as true of the small church as the medium-sized or large church. No prayer ministry in any church will function without the prayer leadership of the pastor. The small-church pastor may have extra responsibilities that the leader of a larger church will not have. Although the daily operation of the prayer ministry is primarily the responsibility of the prayer coordinator, the pastor of any size church should be actively involved in the ministry. He will need to encourage the prayer coordinator and the prayer warriors. If there is daily prayer in a prayer room, the pastor should be one of the prayer warriors. Occasionally he should speak on prayer from the pulpit; and he should mention it in his articles if the church has a newsletter or a weekly bulletin. His role is crucial.

Praying churches are growing churches; churches that do not pray do not grow. This is also true of individuals. Prayer is basic to all Christian growth, and the small church can no more afford to neglect prayer than can the large church.

A Total Prayer Ministry

Prayer sets in motion the mighty hand of the Lord. If we believe that God moves in answer to our prayers and that prayer is one means of discerning the will of God, then we should spend more time in prayer. The weekly prayer meeting should take on new importance.

Midweek Prayer Services

A church should hold a variety of prayer services. The most important of these, of course, is the midweek prayer service. The midweek service should receive at least as much attention from the pastor as the Sunday sermons, for it secures God's work for us, rather than our work for God.

One problem of the midweek prayer service is that those prayers offered are concerned almost exclusively with local members who are sick or homebound. The pastor should be concerned that his people learn to pray for a multitude of needs.

On occasion it would be appropriate to have a time of confession. This should be preceded by teaching on appropriate confession. Periodically the congregation might even engage in corporate confession. Members might suggest possible corporate sins on slips of paper. Leaders prayerfully evaluate them. Those that are agreed on are printed on a prayer sheet. A period of repentance and public prayer should follow.

The prayer coordinator could select one item each week from the church's program to pray about—the visitation or evangelistic ministry, boys' and girls' missionary organizations, the Bible drill teams, the benevolence program (and its evangelistic outreach), the various choirs, and other weekly activities. The congregation should pray about the depth of worship in the Sunday services and the pastor's messages.

The church occasionally will want to observe other prayer services. An evening prayer service, or vespers, is an appropriate conclusion to any day. Churches also may want to observe a morning prayer service. Special prayer services may be held at any time.

Family Altars

A major responsibility of the church is to encourage prayer in homes. This is the basic link in what should be the unified praying of the entire church. The primary responsibility for this leadership lies with the pastor, although the prayer coordinator also can encourage men to lead their homes in prayer. The family altar need not be elaborate. The period begins with the reading of a daily Bible passage. It may be read by any member of the family, and that privilege should be passed around. Some families like to read through the Bible together. Others use devotionals.

Then each member of the family prays. These prayers may be brief.

The family altar may be brief, never pretentious. Many families have difficulty finding a time for the family altar. It need not require much time—often it may be only fifteen minutes. Some families worship together early in the morning and expect every family member to rise early. Others have it following one of the meals. It may be the last event of the day, just before bedtime. We do find time to do what we think is important.

Prayer Groups

Because prayer links people together so closely, a praying church may develop a number of prayer groups, such as a men's group on Saturday morning, a deacon's group before Sunday morning worship service, or a women's group one evening during the week.

Prayer Chains

A prayer chain is effective for emergency situations that demand sudden and urgent prayer. The ideal plan is to have approximately four or more groups with four persons in each group and a group leader. When emergency prayer is needed, the prayer coordinator calls Group Leader 1, who then calls two persons. He calls the first person in his or her own group who calls the second, the second calls the third, and so on. Group Leader 1 calls Group Leader 2, who begins the process in his or her group and then calls Group Leader 3, and so on. The number of groups can be extended indefinitely, and the number of persons in each group also can be extended.

Prayer requests for the prayer chain should be given to the church prayer coordinator, who records the request for the prayer room, if appropriate, and calls the group leaders with the request. The church can have one prayer chain or several, with one being designated the Emergency Prayer Chain. Members of a prayer chain should be given the list of persons in their own chain, including telephone numbers. Immediately upon receipt of a call, the member calls the next person on the list. If that person does not answer, the member should call the next person on the list to keep the prayer request going. The member may try again later to reach persons who do not answer. Members should pray immediately for the phoned prayer request and later as occasion permits. The last person on the list should call the group leader to verify that the call went through the entire chain. Again, the prayer coordinator should emphasize strongly the importance of confidentiality in all prayer requests.

Prayer Meals

The church may observe regular prayer meals, such as a prayer breakfast, brunch, or luncheon. In addition, the Church Prayer Ministry should sponsor an annual prayer banquet. This is for the entire church, not just the persons who work in the Church Prayer Ministry, although it also should have the purpose of encouraging them. It should be a report to the church on the activities and answers to prayer in the previous year and may have an inspirational speaker. Also, the prayer coordinator can use the occasion as an appeal for additional prayer warriors.

Special Projects Prayer Teams

The pastor, the prayer coordinator, and the prayer committee also may want to appoint special project prayer teams to pray for specified objects. For example, the pastor would certainly want a team to pray for him during the time he preaches. It is assumed, of course, that the prayer room maintains daily prayer for the pastor and his ministry, but the special prayer during the worship hours is quite effective. Prayer leaders also may organize special teams to pray around certain events (such as a revival or a mission trip) or projects (such as a building project). The prayer coordinator may work with the church evangelism director to build a team focusing prayer on members participating in church visitation, especially during the designated visitation time.

One way to involve more persons in the Church Prayer Ministry is to build a "prayer wall" around the church. Intercessors are enlisted who live geographically on the four sides of the church. Their duty is to surround the church with prayer on each of its physical sides. The prayer coordinator will give them instruction in prayer and furnish them with information on prayer needs of the church and staff. These members then pray daily during their own prayer time and at other times for the needs given them by the church prayer coordinator.

Another project involves members in the spiritual needs of their city or community. This project might be called "Prayer Infiltration." The prayer coordinator divides the city into sections and attempts to station "pray-ers" in each of the sections. It is important that all parts of the city be included. These intercessors may pray for many kinds of needs. Their first concern will be the winning of the city for Christ, and they will pray for the lost in their part of the city. As various community needs surface (such as a vote on gambling or the needs of the homeless and poor of the city), the prayer coordinator will inform those who are praying. This work also involves more people in the prayer ministry and helps the church in its effort to become a "house of prayer."

This does not exhaust all the possibilities for ongoing prayer in the church. A creative prayer coordinator will find hundreds of ways to emphasize or maintain prayer. A pastor will want to capitalize on all available means to secure the work of the Holy Spirit in his ministry. We are limited only by our imagination and willingness to follow the Holy Spirit, who is Himself totally creative. God wants to lead, and we can expect His blessing on the ministry of prayer because He Himself thought of it.

CHAPTER NINE

The Preaching Event: A True Baptist Distinctive

O.S. HAWKINS

It is my privilege and challenge to preach each Sunday behind one of, if not, the most famous twentieth-century pulpits. For forty-seven years (1897–1944) the incomparable Dr. George W. Truett thundered the gospel message from that sacred desk. Then, for fifty years (1944–94) Dr. W. A. Criswell, the true prince of modern preachers, expounded the "unsearchable riches" with conviction, clarity, and compassion from the same pulpit.

Our pulpit, like many in Baptist life, is rich in history and heritage. When I was a boy, my mother cooked every meal in our home in the same old cast-iron skillet. Someone once gave her a new Teflon skillet, but she never used it. She continued to cook breakfast, lunch, and dinner in the same old skillet; things just seemed to taste better when they were cooked in it. I am convinced it was because that old skillet had years of "build up" in it. There is a sense in which our pulpit, and most every other Baptist pulpit, is like that old skillet: it has years of "build up."

The Centrality of Preaching

The pulpit in a Baptist church is most always on center stage. It is there to make the statement that central to Baptist worship is the preaching of the book of God to the people of God. One can walk into the auditorium of a Baptist church anywhere in the world and the pulpit is there, signifying the centrality of gospel preaching in the Baptist tradition.

As we enter the new millennium, preaching faces its greatest challenge. We are the "prefix generation." We describe many things in our contemporary culture with the use of prefixes. For example, we use the prefix "mega" repeatedly. We have megabytes, megabucks, megachurches, and even megadittos. Another prominent and popular prefix of today is "eco," as in ecotone or ecosystem. An ecotone is a technological word from the field of biology that describes a particular place where two ecosystems merge and blend together. I first heard of the word while living in Fort Lauderdale, Florida. There is a particular place there where the intercostal waterway and the New River come together and form an ecotone. The salt water from the Atlantic Ocean flows into Port Everglades and into the intercostal waterway. From the Everglades just west of the city the fresh water flows through the river making its way toward the ocean. At the particular place where the salt water and fresh water merge, an ecotone develops. Ecotones are places of tremendous possibilities. Often fish nestle there to lay their eggs. However, ecotones can also be very problematic to those who engage themselves in the battles of ecology.

As we enter the new millennium, our culture is in the midst of its own ecotonic stage. Two worlds are merging and blending at the same time. One is a modern world and the other is a postmodern world. The world in which most of us have been educated is history. The cumulative knowledge of world history will double in the next five years. We are in a postmodern area which in itself can be a time of tremendous possibility for the church of the Lord Jesus Christ. It can also be a time of tremendous problems for those who allow the contemporary culture to dictate their approach to the truths of the gospel message.

The Lure of Market-Driven Preaching

The preaching experience is in the midst of its own ecotonic period. It remains to be seen whether this situation will help or hurt the proclamation of the gospel message. Meanwhile, a new wave of preaching enthusiasts have arisen who advocate an approach to proclamation that is foreign to the apostolic model. They have done their research, written their books, advanced their newsletters, promoted their tapes and seminars, and a new generation of young preachers seem to be influenced by their "findings" and persuasions. These modern church growth gurus have done their "marketing" and have returned to tell us that if we have any hope of penetrating the minds and hearts of our contemporary culture, we must give our listeners what they "want" to hear. Therefore, this modern approach to preaching is one of accommodation with a subtle, yet strong, emphasis on avoiding four specific distinctives that have been historically central to the Baptist preaching event.

There is a blatant emphasis today to *avoid context.* Many young preachers are instructed to preach "topical" sermons on felt needs or wants and to avoid paragraph-by-paragraph, verse-by-verse exposition. That is, one should select a topic related to a felt need and, if possible, find a Scripture to support it. This approach encourages the implementation of not only the latest secular communication principles but also success motivational techniques as well.

Secondly, this new generation of preachers is subtly being influenced to *avoid confessions,* that is, doctrinal truth. We are being told that the men and women we are trying to reach do not want to hear of Bible doctrines and that making much of them will stunt church growth. Being dogmatic on matters of doctrine is "out" in contemporary preaching technique.

Not only is there a subtle emphasis in our day to avoid context and to avoid confessions but we are also being encouraged to *avoid controversy* from our pulpits. This accompanies a kinder, gentler approach to preaching that is tolerant of other people's views so as not to be offensive to them. Thus we find fewer and fewer pulpits taking clear biblical stands on the social and moral issues such as abortion and homosexuality that plague our contemporary culture. The salt seems to be losing its savor, and tragically, the pulpit is to blame.

Finally, a generation of young preachers are being encouraged to *avoid confrontation.* Fewer and fewer pulpits in the Western world are calling for men and women to take personal responsibility for their sin and make a public pledge of their faith to the One who said, "Confess me before men" (Matt. 10:32, KJV). There is little emphasis upon confrontation evangelism today, whether it is personal in the parlor or public from the pulpit. This particular and, unfortunately, popular approach to nonconfrontational proclamation of the gospel is what has led many churches to cease the public invitation and has led to only superficial mission involvement around the world.

One young Baptist pastor is quoted in a Baptist Press news release saying, "We have done one walk-the-aisle public invitation, and some of our folks were very uncomfortable with it because we promoted ourselves as being a church that is non-threatening. I don't think we will ever do it again."[1] Can anyone imagine Peter, James, Paul, or any of the apostolic pastors advertising their church as being "non-threatening"? Simon Peter preached the church's inaugural sermon. In the body of his message he cried out, "You, with the help of wicked men, put him to death by nailing him to the cross" (Acts 2:23, NIV). Then at the end of the message he pleaded "with many other words" (v. 40)[*] for them to come openly and unashamedly to identify with the

* Unless otherwise noted, all Scripture quotations in this chapter are from the New King James Version.

Lord Jesus Christ. The same Baptist Press release cited above carried the words of a young North Carolinian pastor who also boasted about his nonconfrontational approach, saying, "We don't violate their emotion by singing four verses of 'Just As I Am' and trying to manipulate them."[2] The multiplied hundreds of thousands of men and women who will be in heaven because of the preaching and confrontational ministry of Billy Graham are certainly thankful he concluded his messages with an appeal to come to Christ as the choir sang "Just As I Am."

The Biblical Pattern of Preaching

The biblical pattern of proclamation and church growth diametrically opposes these modern philosophies. One says we are to "market the church" by finding out the "wants" of the people and then tailoring our church programs to meet these "wants." We are to avoid context, confessions, controversies, and confrontation in our preaching so as not to appear offensive to our hearers. Yet the biblical pattern is plain. We are to "church the market," that is, to take the gospel into the marketplace itself with an apostolic pattern of confrontational, confessional, contextual, and sometimes controversial preaching that seeks to meet the "needs" of the human heart and not its "wants." In the Book of Acts we find that Bible preaching was central to the task of evangelizing and congregationalizing through the local church. When the church's emphasis centers upon the "wants" of the human heart, it turns inward. However, when it follows a New Testament pattern and centers on the "needs" of the human heart, it turns outward, and the preaching event takes its proper place of priority.

One of the primary reasons the blessing of God has rested upon Baptist churches in the past century is the priority they have placed upon the preaching experience. Baptist churches and Bible preaching have, in the past, been synonymous. We have emphasized the apostolic pattern found in Peter's first recorded sermon on the temple mount on the day of Pentecost (see Acts 2:14–40) and in Paul's first recorded sermon at Pisidian Antioch (See Acts 13:16–41). A careful analysis of each of these

Bible messages reveals a balance in their preaching. They both followed a pattern that Paul later outlined to his young preacher understudy, Timothy. Paul instructed Timothy, and us, saying, "All Scripture is given by inspiration of God, and is profitable for doctrine, for reproof, for correction, for instruction in righteousness, that the man of God may be complete, thoroughly equipped for every good work" (2 Tim. 3:16-17).

Striving for Biblical Balance

Paul's instructions highlight four characteristics that should be applied to every gospel message in a balanced way. A Bible sermon should have in it an element of doctrine, that is, it should not shy away from the great truths of the Bible. It should reprove sin. It should correct false paths. And, it should have an element of instruction in righteousness that helps the hearer to apply to his or her life the Bible truths they have absorbed. Balanced preaching of God's Word provides a road map for men and women journeying through life. The *doctrine* of salvation found in the Lord Jesus Christ enables us to get started on the right road. Along the way we may get off the path by rebellious acts of our own will. It is then that the Bible offers *reproof* for our sin. However, it does not leave us in reproof. It is also profitable for *correction.* It serves to correct our way so that we will not get off on the same side street again. Finally, it is profitable for *instruction in righteousness* so that, once on the right road and headed toward our final destination, we may be being conformed to the image of Christ along the way. An effective and balanced ministry of the Word of God does all four of these things Paul mentions to his young understudy, Timothy.

The appeal is for a balanced ministry of God's Word. Some pulpit ministries go to seed on doctrine. Even though they are orthodox in their beliefs and doctrinally sound, they seldom reprove sin, correct false paths, or instruct in righteous, Spirit-filled living. Consequently, such churches are dead and dying. Others tend to go to seed on reproof. They think their primary God-given call is to reprove everyone in their sin with a self-righteous pointed finger of accusation. They never teach Bible doctrine or instruct in righteousness and are puzzled as to why their churches continue to dwindle in number. Still others go to seed on correction, to the virtual exclusion of training in righteousness and Spirit-filled living. They busy themselves in their attempt to correct everyone else. Finally, there are those pulpit ministries who have gone to seed on "instructing in righteousness." They immerse themselves in contemporary worship forms to the extent that praise often takes priority over proclamation. They speak continually about the Spirit-filled life to the virtual exclusion of teaching and preaching sound doctrine and then wonder why their churches often split and follow "every new wind of doctrine" that comes to town. The apostolic preaching model in the New Testament was one of balance. The apostles incorporated doctrine, reproof, correction, and instruction in righteousness into their messages in a winsome, warm, and balanced manner.

A careful analysis of the Pentecostal proclamation as well as the one at Pisidian Antioch reveals that both Peter and Paul incorporated all four of these elements into the preaching experience. Simon Peter's Pentecostal proclamation, recorded for all posterity in the second chapter of Acts, is a perfect example. He taught doctrine. He pontificated about the doctrine of the deity of the Lord Jesus Christ. Peter proclaimed, "God has made this Jesus, whom you crucified, both Lord and Christ" (Acts 2:36). He reproved sin in the same message when he said, "You, with the help of wicked men, put Him to death by nailing Him to the cross" (Acts 2:23, NIV). He corrected false paths by calling the people to change their minds and "repent" (Acts 2:38). Then he trained them in righteousness by encouraging his hearers to be baptized, to get into God's Word, to break bread together, and to grow in the grace and knowledge of our Lord Jesus Christ (Acts 2:38–46). Peter's sermon contained all four elements of an effective ministry of the Word of God. One finds the same thing in the apostle Paul's first sermon at Antioch of Pisidia (Acts 13:13–41).

The apostolic preaching model is a balanced pattern to be emulated. Paul continued throughout his life to emphasize the necessity of balance in these four areas. He wrote the Book of Romans to emphasize the need of doctrine. He wrote 1 Corinthians to reveal the need of reproof. He wrote Galatians in an attempt to show the importance of the preacher's task of correction. He wrote Ephesians primarily to "instruct in righteousness." The faithful Bible preacher does not avoid context, confessions, controversy, or confrontation but in a balanced manner follows the apostolic pattern in preaching "doctrine, reproof, correction, and instruction in righteousness."

Paul's Example

One of the preacher's most effective patterns is found in Paul's ministry among the Thessalonians, recorded for us in Acts 17. Unlike many modern "preachers" today, he did not go to Thessalonica, take several marketing surveys in an attempt to find out what the people of the city "wanted" to hear, and then develop his ministry among them in order to cater to their wants. It is said in the context of his ministry there that he and these early believers "turned their world upside down" (Acts 17:6). How did this come about?

Paul did four things at Thessalonica that are in diametric opposition to the four modern principles of proclamation being espoused today. In place of avoiding context, he was expository. In place of avoiding confessions, he was explanatory. In place of avoiding controversy, he was explicit. In place of avoiding confrontation, he was expeditious. Herein lies the biblical pattern for Bible preaching that carries with it the blessing of God, which enables the church of the Lord Jesus Christ to "turn its world upside down."

Be Expository

While some modern preaching techniques call for the preacher to avoid context, the apostle Paul calls for the preacher to be expository. When the great preacher arrived at Thessalonica, he "as his custom was, went in to them, and for three Sabbaths reasoned with them from the Scriptures" (Acts 17:2). As

Luke penned these words to describe Paul's approach to preaching, he chose the word *dielexato*, which in our English Bibles is translated "reasoned." It is a compound word in Greek, the language of the New Testament. It is made up of the preposition *dia*, which means "through," and the verb *lego*, meaning "to speak." Paul's approach to the preaching event was to "speak through" the Scripture. He was an expository preacher! It is alarming how few in the pulpit today are reasoning ("speaking through") the Scriptures. Many reason with their hearers through current events, popular psychology, and through such things as certain habits of highly successful people. Yet too few of these Baptist preachers "reason through the Scriptures" in the Biblical pattern of exposition.

It is the Word of God that brings conviction. Simon Peter stood at Pentecost, took his text from Joel 2:28–32, illustrated it with Psalms 16:8-11; 68:18; and 110:1 (Acts 2:25–28, 34–35) and preached a Bible message. He established a scriptural, biblical basis for what was happening in the manifestations of the Spirit at Pentecost and for what he desired his hearers to do in response to what they had seen and heard. Like his, our preaching should be biblical and expository. It is alarming that the Bible is so little used in the worship experience of the modern church in the Western world. A preacher who does not use the Bible in his proclamation of the gospel is akin to a surgeon going into the operating room to perform surgery on his patient without a scalpel. The preacher attempting to speak without his Bible is like a carpenter attempting to build a house without his hammer. God still speaks to us today through the prophet Jeremiah: "Is not My Word like a fire? . . . and like a hammer that breaks the rock in pieces?" (Jeremiah 23:29). It is little wonder that so many churches are empty and powerless today. Relevancy has replaced the revelation of the Word in many modern pulpits.

The result of Simon Peter's Bible-based exposition at Pentecost was that his hearers "were cut to the heart" (Acts 2:37). Our English word, *cut*, in verse 37 translates a compound Greek word made up of the preposition *kata*, which means "through," and the verb *nusso*, which means "to pierce." Thus, their hearts were "pierced through." We have a word for this: we call it *conviction*, and it has become one of the lost words in our Christian vocabulary. When the men and women at Pentecost heard Peter's gospel message and realized they were personally responsible for the crucifixion of the Lord Jesus, their hearts were broken and they began to ask, "What shall we do?" (Acts 2:37). Why aren't more people "cut to the heart" in our churches today? It is because they do not realize they must take personal responsibility for their sin. Why are they ignorant of this fact? Many of them have never heard a preacher "speak through" the Scriptures and allow the Word of God to bring conviction. By not being expository in their approach these preachers are no longer personal in their application. Biblical, expository preaching is what the Holy Spirit uses to bring about conviction of sin. God said that His Word "will not return to me empty, but will accomplish what I desire and achieve the purpose for which I sent it" (Isa. 55:11, NIV).

Too many sermons today are preached only in first person plural (*we*) or in third person plural *(they)*. This has been the emphasis of much of the teaching related to preaching in the last generation. There has been a definite move away from second person singular (*you*) in the preaching event. A careful observation of the apostolic preaching model in Acts reveals that these early and anointed preachers preached often in second person so as to call upon their hearers to take personal responsibility for their own sin in order to find the freedom that issues from genuine repentance and forgiveness of sins. Listen to Simon Peter as he preached at Pentecost: "Jesus of Nazareth was a man accredited by God to *you* by miracles, wonders and signs, which God did among *you* through him, as *you* yourselves know. This man was handed over to *you* by God's set purpose and foreknowledge; and you, with the help of wicked men, put him to death" (Acts 2:22–23, NIV emphasis added).

Many preachers today are afraid of offending baby boomer mind-sets, deacons, elders, large givers, civic leaders, politicians, and various others. Their preaching avoids confrontation with others and personal responsibility for personal sin. Thus, their proclamation is impersonal. It is indirect and nonconfrontational. It does not bring about true conviction of sin, nor does it point men and women to their need of a personal Savior. Charles Finney said, "Preaching should be direct. The gospel should be preached to men, and not about men. The minister must address his hearers. He must preach to them about themselves, and not leave the impression that he is preaching to them about others."[2] Simon Peter preached, "You, you, you!" He was confrontational and challenged his hearers. And the result? "When the people heard this, they were cut to the heart" (Acts 2:37, NIV). God used Peter's expository proclamation to prick the hearts of the hearers with conviction of sin.

Conviction always precedes conversion. My first pastorate was in Hobart, Oklahoma. There, on the plains of Southwestern Oklahoma among those good and godly wheat farmers, I began to beat out on the anvil of personal experience the preaching event. I learned much from those dear old men who had spent a lifetime in two places, their fields and their Bibles. They taught me that there were four things necessary in order to grow a good crop. First, the ground had to be broken. They would ride their tractors, plowing up and down the fields turning the sod over and over, breaking up the hardened earth. Second, the seed had to be planted. Third, the wheat had to be cultivated, watered, and nurtured. Fourth, around the first of June every year, the harvest was gathered.

Many churches today wonder why they never reap a harvest. Perhaps they have not broken the ground in a long time. It is the Word of God that cuts the human heart. Our preaching must so "reason through the Scriptures" that it becomes to our heart like the plow that breaks open the hardened earth. We will never see the harvest without the preaching of the Word of God.

The preacher's job description has not changed through the centuries. Our task is to "speak through the Scriptures" as Paul did in Thessalonica and as Peter did at Pentecost. In a day when many are encouraging young preachers to avoid context, Paul's words come echoing down through the corridors of the centuries: "Be expository! Reason with your hearers! Speak through the Scriptures!"

Be Explanatory

While some modern preaching techniques call upon the preacher in our contemporary culture to avoid confessions, the apostle Paul calls for the preacher to be explanatory. Luke, the writer of Acts, tells us that Paul was not only reasoning with his hearers from the Scriptures, but he was also "explaining" the Word to them (Acts 17:3). The word we translate "explaining" in our English Bibles is from the Greek word, *dianoigon*, which comes once again from the preposition meaning "through" and the verb *anoigo*, which means "to open." Thus, we see that for Paul gospel preaching was not simply "speaking through the Scriptures" in an expository fashion but also entailed the "opening through of the Scriptures" in an explanatory way. This same Greek word is used in other places in the New Testament to describe the opening of the womb or the opening of the door. It also appears in Luke 24:32 to describe how the Emmaus disciples' hearts began to burn within them as the risen Lord Jesus began to "open the Scriptures" to them. This is the preacher's task, to speak through and open through the Scriptures for the hearers.

There at Thessalonica, Paul was "explaining" the gospel, the death, burial, and resurrection of the Lord Jesus Christ. He "reasoned with them from the Scriptures, explaining and demonstrating that the Christ had to suffer and rise again from the dead, and saying, 'This Jesus whom I preach to you is the Christ'" (Acts 17:2–3). There is no true biblical preaching without the gospel, the good news of the death, burial and resurrection of our Lord. Paul "explained" this to his hearers. He had two themes in his preaching at Thessalonica, the cross and the resurrection. He was an astute theologian, but he never preached theology. He used theology to preach the Lord Jesus. At the heart of our message is that Christ "had to suffer" (*dei*, which indicates it was a necessity) and that, as the apostle states,

He is "the one and only Christ" (definite article in Greek). There is no other savior, no other way to the Father.

When Paul preached, he "opened through the Word" to his hearers. He was explanatory. This, too, is our job, whether it is in the pulpit, in the classroom, across the counseling table or wherever. And, parenthetically, it is very difficult to do so without a working knowledge of the language of the New Testament. Does it make sense that the preacher whose task it is to "speak through and open through the Scriptures" has at his disposal the language in which his Bible was written, yet he is not willing to pay the price of study in order to know it? In a day of superficiality when modern preaching techniques call upon the preacher to avoid context and confessions of doctrinal truth, Paul's words are poignant, pertinent, and practical. He still calls upon us to be expository and to be explanatory, to open up doctrinal truth to our hearers and to preach that Jesus is *the* Christ.

Be Explicit

While some modern preaching techniques call upon the preacher in our social society to avoid controversy, Paul calls upon the preacher of the gospel to be explicit. Luke continues his account of Paul's preaching style by saying he not only was "reasoning" and "explaining" but also "demonstrating" the Scriptures to his hearers (Acts 17:3). In the language of the New Testament, Paul chooses the Greek word *paratithemos*, which we translate "demonstrating" in our English Bibles. This word comes from the preposition *para*, which means "beside," and the verb *tithemi*, which means "to lay down" or to "lie down." Hence the word literally means "to lie down alongside." It is used in legal terms to describe one who gives evidence, who "lays alongside" the facts certain evidence to support his or her cause. Paul admonishes the preacher here to not be afraid of "laying it out," to speak the truth in love—even if it is offensive and controversial. In the context of Acts 17:1–4, Paul is "demonstrating," "laying out," the evidence that Jesus is, indeed, the Christ and that He did indeed rise from the dead. He presents evidence to back up the fulfilled prophecies of Isaiah 53 and Psalms 22 and 69 as well as the various Old Testament shadows and types of the coming Christ. He was explicit in his approach.

The preacher of the gospel message should "lay out alongside" the facts of the gospel his own life that "demonstrates" the validity of the message. Our lives should certainly be evidence of the validity of what we preach and proclaim. Paul "laid it out." He presented the evidence. That is the preacher's task. It entails a systematic theology and a knowledge of Bible doctrine as well as a life that matches our utterances.

In a day when many shy away from any and all types of controversial subjects from the pulpit, the apostle's words ring loud and clear. He is saying to every preacher of the new millennium: "Be explicit; tell it like it is; lay it out, and with holy boldness speak the truth to contemporary culture and speak it in love."

Be Expeditious

While some argue that the preacher should avoid context, avoid confessions, and avoid controversies, others warn to also avoid confrontation. To this Paul states flatly: be expeditious in your approach to preaching the gospel. The Bible records that he "went in to them. . . . and some of them were persuaded; and . . . joined Paul and Silas" (Acts 17:2, 4). The great apostle began with the end in mind. He was possessed with the gospel message and had a sense of urgency. He "went in to them" at Thessalonica, "persuaded" them, and they "joined" him in the faith.

The preacher's task is to "persuade" his hearers. This English word translates the Greek word *epeisthesan*, which means "to induce one by words to believe." It carries with it the connotation of yielding to or complying with a certain persuasion.

Paul did not shy away from bringing his hearers into a confrontation with the Lord Jesus Himself. Paul gave an appeal. He was winsome and persuasive in his preaching and the result was that many "joined" him (Acts 17:4). Our English word "joined" translates the Greek word *proseklerothesan*. It comes from the preposition, *pros*, meaning "with, unto, or among," and the verb *klero*, meaning "to obtain an inheritance." These Thessalonians heard the gospel preaching of Paul and made a conscious decision to take as their very own private possession the Lord Jesus Christ. Paul "persuaded" them, and they "joined" him in the faith. This is still happening today wherever the Bible is preached in a manner that is expository, explanatory, explicit and expeditious.

All through the New Testament we find this pattern for biblical proclamation. Recorded in Acts 11, in connection with the great missionary church in Antioch, is another poignant apostolic pattern of biblical preaching. In describing the Bible preaching ministry in Antioch by those of the diaspora following the stoning of Stephen as well as that of such well-known first-century preachers as Barnabas and Paul, three very important words are found. They "preached" (Acts 11:20) the Word at Antioch. The Greek word here is the familiar *euangelizomenoi*, which carries with it a note of pathos and passion as they preached and called for evangelistic decisions. Also, in the same context we read the word *parekalei* (v. 23), which describes the way they used the preaching of the Word to encourage and exhort the believers in Antioch. But this was not all. They also "taught" (*didaxai*, v. 26) a great number of people from the Word of God.

We continually see evidenced throughout the early church a balanced ministry of the Word of God. Many conservative churches have only evangelized. They seldom encourage or teach the Word but are tenacious in their attempts to use it to evangelize. To become out of balance in the preaching ministry on the side of evangelizing can mean that we may become overly confrontational in our approach to the preaching of the gospel. On the other hand, those who have only taught to the virtual exclusion of evangelism and encouragement may have a tendency to become overly confessional. Throughout the decades of the twentieth century, Baptists have enjoyed the supernatural blessing of God upon their congregations because, by and large, they have maintained a balanced and biblical approach to the task of preaching the gospel. They have been known for their evangelistic zeal and passion as well as their ministry of encouragement and their strong emphasis upon the teaching of Bible doctrine.

Preaching in Today's World

Engaging the culture into the new millennium is the church's greatest challenge. We are called upon to reach an entire generation, most of whom have never been inside a Bible preaching church nor have they sung a Christian hymn. They are searching for meaningful relationships. Many young adults in the Western world have never known a meaningful relationship in life. They are homesick for a home they have never had. They want immediate gratification and guilt-free living. The church must reach out to this lost generation, but the church must not sacrifice the Word on the altar of relevancy.

The apostles were called to reach a world more and more like our own, that is, a pagan, godless, humanistic, secular society. Recently, while visiting the reconstructed ruins of the ancient metropolis of Ephesus, I was struck by the fact that Paul entered this city with just a couple of friends and engaged its culture and transformed the entire city. How? He did not incorporate in his strategy even one of the superficial church growth principles prevalent in our day. He did not engage in marketing strategies to determine what the people of Ephesus "wanted" to hear and do. He did not tailor his ministry and programs to meet the "wants" of the people of Ephesus. He preached the Word of God to them, teaching them doctrine, reproving their sin, correcting their false paths, and instructing them in righteousness. Later, from a Roman incarceration, he wrote to Timothy, the young pastor at Ephesus, and instructed him to do likewise (2 Tim. 3:16–17). When the apostle Paul concluded his ministry in this great city, it is recorded by Luke as one of the most touching scenes in the Bible. The Ephesian church leaders followed Paul down to the seaside as he boarded his ship. "He knelt down and prayed with them all. Then they all wept freely, and fell on Paul's neck and kissed him, sorrowing most of all for the words which he spoke, that they would see his face no more. And they accompanied him to the ship" (Acts 20:36–38). Paul had spent his years in Ephesus building his people up in the Word of God, and his last words to them were, "So now, brethren, I commend you to God and to the word of His grace, which is able to build you up and give you an inheritance among all those who are sanctified" (Acts 20:32).

The apostolic preaching pattern that Paul demonstrated was one of explanation and application. When the modern-day preacher has finished preparing his sermon, he should ask himself three questions before the actual preaching event: What? So what? Now what?

- *What?* That is, what does the message say? Is it true to the text? What is the specific object? Is it clear to the hearer?
- *So What?* Is it relevant to the lives of men and women who are hearers? Does it meet and serve the contemporary needs of the congregation?
- *Now what?* Does the sermon move the hearer to do something? Is it applied to our daily lives? Does the hearer have a "handle" by which he or she can take the point of the sermon and put it into practice in the normal traffic patterns of his or her daily life?

It will do the preacher of the twenty-first century well to heed the words of Paul, who said, "Imitate me, just as I also imitate Christ" (1 Cor. 11:1). This is especially true of his model of biblical preaching. Instead of avoiding context, be expository. Instead of avoiding confessions, be explanatory. Instead of avoiding controversy, be explicit. Instead of avoiding confrontation, be expeditious. It still pleases God by "the foolishness of preaching to save them that believe" (1 Cor. 1:21, KJV).

Endnotes

1. Altar Calls: Appropriate for Appealing to the Lost? Baptist Press, 13 May, 1996.

2. Ibid.

3. Charles Grandison Finney, *Lectures on Revival of Religion* (1835; reprint, New York: Revell, 1968), 223.

CHAPTER TEN

The Necessity of Being Salt and Light

RICHARD D. LAND

When people come to a saving knowledge of Jesus Christ, the Holy Spirit begins to develop their Christian character and they begin to have new responsibilities as citizens of the Savior's kingdom. Jesus tells His disciples that they are to be "the salt of the earth" and "the light of the world" (Matt 5:13–14).*

The larger content of the passage tells that Jesus saw "the multitudes." Jesus truly saw the people. He saw them in their lostness, in their degeneration, in their darkness. He, and He alone, sees the complete havoc of sin, because He not only sees

* Unless otherwise noted, all Scripture quotations in this chapter are from the King James Version of the Bible.

what they are, but He sees what God intended for them to be, if not for sin. He beholds the world's individual and collective ruin, and He tells His disciples that they are to be salt and that they are to be light, stressing the fact that the believer *is* salt and light. The Christian's character described in Matthew 5:3–12 reveals the gospel internalized. Since the world is corrupt and degenerating, Christians are commanded to be salt, the agent that preserves from decay and putrefaction. Since the world is in darkness, Christians are to be light, to illuminate the pathway to life. Salt is essentially defensive. It stops the decay. "You do not salt a living thing. You salt a dead one that it may not be a rotting one."[1]

Christians who are fulfilling their role as salt retard evil by their presence. They are people in whose presence it is harder to say or do the wrong thing and it is easier to say or do the right thing. They act as "a moral disinfectant" in a deteriorating world.[2]

To be salt, Christians must remain pure. If the salt loses its savor, then it is good for nothing." Light, unlike salt, cannot cease to be light. However, it can be covered. It can be obscured. If these words of Jesus teach us anything, it is that "to be a true Christian in all secrecy, comfortably and enjoyably, is as impossible as firing a cannon in all secrecy."[3]

These words of Jesus, spoken in a type of "installation sermon" for citizens of His kingdom, "are a perpetual rebuke to all Christians who suppose either that they can, like hermits, withdraw from the world, or that, entering it, they can conceal their true allegiance."[4] Jesus leaves no room here either for monastic withdrawal or syncretistic cultural accommodation. As Martyn Lloyd-Jones so aptly put it: "The true Christian cannot be hid, he cannot escape notice. A man truly living and functioning as a Christian will stand out. He will be like salt; he will be like a city set upon a hill, a candle set upon a candlestick."[5]

The Christian must be in the world. (Remember salt must touch and make contact with what it preserves or purifies, and light that is to "shine before men" must be seen by men.) The Christian must be *in* the world but not *of* the world (James 1:27).

The Christian who fulfills his or her commission to be salt and light will provoke two responses from the world.[6] Many in the unregenerate world will find the salt irritating and the light disconcerting. That is why this particular passage (Matt. 5:13–16) is preceded by a passage that warns of rejection and persecution. The Beatitudes not only portray a differing value system from the value system of the world, but a totally opposite one. As John tells us, when the light came "into the world . . . men loved darkness rather than light, because their deeds were evil" (John 3:19). Paul warned Timothy that "all who desire to live godly in Christ Jesus will suffer" (2 Tim. 3:12, NKJV). Suffer from whom? From the world that is irritated and disconcerted.

However, Jesus predicts yet another wholly different response by some. As we let His light shine through us, some will see our "good works" and will "glorify" God.[7] The word for "good" in Matthew 5:16 is a Greek word for goodness that is winsome and attractive, a stronger, better word than merely "good." As we fulfill our divine purpose as light, Paul tells us we "adorn the doctrine of God our Savior in all things" (Titus 2:10).[8]

As we face our neopagan cultural milieu under the command to be salt and to be light, we must realize that an ability to do so successfully will be governed not only by His presence in our lives, but also by the extent we surrender on a daily basis to His lordship. As Paul challenged the Romans, when we unreservedly "present" ourselves for service, we discover "that good, and acceptable, and perfect, will of God" for our lives which, as we have seen, includes being salt and light as a priority of the highest order (Rom. 12:1–2).

Never before has our nation more needed for Christians to shoulder their kingdom responsibilities to be salt and light. As individuals, as Christians, as Americans, as human beings, we face an appalling crisis—a crisis of the mind, of the heart, and of the spirit. Our homes, our communities, and our nation are buffeted by centrifugal forces and wracked by life—diminishing philosophies. Evidence of decay and collapse inundate us on every side.

People from all shades of the political spectrum, from many divergent disciplines, and from myriad walks of life have sounded the alarm with increasing urgency. Something is terribly, tragically, perhaps terminally wrong. George Gallup Jr., surveying the vast amounts of information at his disposal about America gleaned from exhaustive polling data, concludes, "I would venture to say that the great problems of our time are not economic and political, but they are religious and moral. . . . We are in a moral crisis of the first dimension."[9]

America confronts crippling epidemics of alcohol and drug abuse, mindless violence, and a rampant materialism that often becomes nothing less than idolatrous worship of the "good life" of material affluence. The nation is beset with virtually ubiquitous sexual immorality and a pornography-fed vortex of violent sexual crimes against women and children both inside and outside the home.

The family in America is increasingly dysfunctional as it reels under the impact of societal blows and pagan parental behavior. The nuclear family as it has been experienced in the Judeo-Christian West is so shattered that concerted efforts are now being made to redefine it to fit the new, fractured and broken reality.

All the while, the dominant idea in the most powerful public-opinion making sectors of American society was to isolate religion to the realm of personal piety and the "religious" area of life. Stephen Carter's recent *The Culture of Disbelief* summarizes and explains some of the many ways in which our culture has come to belittle religious devotion, to humiliate believers, and discourage religion as a serious activity!

Christians are commanded by Jesus to be the "salt" of the earth and the "light" of precisely this kind of world—a society teeming with immorality and seething with secularist hostility. Christians are called to active engagement with society, preserving as "salt" and illuminating as "light."

The *Baptist Faith and Message* confession of faith affirms this call to involvement with the world when it states that "every Christian is under obligation to seek to make the will of Christ supreme in his own life and in human society." The confession also says Christians not only "should oppose, in the spirit of Christ, every form of greed, selfishness and vice," but "should seek to bring industry, government, and society as a whole under the sway of the principles of righteousness, truth and brotherly love."

This statement clarifies our *responsibilities* as Christians and our *rights* as citizens. When we bring our religious and moral convictions into the public marketplace of ideas and involve ourselves in the political arena, we are standing solidly within the best of our traditions as Americans and as Baptists. Far too often in recent decades we have allowed ourselves to be driven from the arena of debate by false understandings and misleading applications of church—state separation and religious liberty.

President Kennedy once said, "The great enemy of truth is very often not the lie, deliberate, contrived and dishonest, but the myth, persistent, persuasive and unrealistic." One such "persistent" myth that has afflicted us as a nation is the belief that you cannot, or at least should not, legislate morality.

Nothing could be more false. As a practical matter, all governments legislate immorality. Government must legislate morality in order to fulfill its God—ordained purpose of punishing evildoers and rewarding those who do right (Rom. 13:1–7). God requires that Christians hold government responsible to its purpose of punishing evil and protecting its citizens. Laws against murder, theft, rape, and racism *are* the legislation of morality. And when Christians seek to make murder, theft, rape and racism illegal, they are not so much trying to impose their morality on murderers, thieves, rapists, and racists as they are trying to keep murderers, thieves, rapists, and racists from imposing their immorality on their victims. And that is not only the Christian's right, but his responsibility.

A total separation of morality and politics is as debilitating of moral values and public virtue as a complete dominance of a church by the state or the state by the church is of personal and religious freedom. Our forbearers intended—and the Constitution of the United States provided for—a balance between morality and public virtue and a separation of the institution of the church and the institution of the state. This delicate constitutional balance, solidified and anchored by the First Amendment, is endangered at present, and it will not be put right unless people of faith insist upon it. The First Amendment is in the Constitution in large measure because our Baptist forbearers insisted upon it as a prerequisite for their support of the Constitution's ratification. The First Amendment says, "Congress shall make no law respecting an establishment of religion, or prohibiting the free exercise thereof." All the restrictions are on the *government*, not individual Baptists or other Americans of religious faith. The government must not establish a religion and must not interfere with its free exercise.

To say the First Amendment's guarantees of religious freedom and separation of church and state were intended to restrict the political participation of people of faith or to disqualify their religious convictions and beliefs from consideration in the public arena of ideas is to twist and distort the First Amendment's intent and meaning beyond all recognition.

This is amply demonstrated both by the words and deeds of our political and spiritual ancestors. When our forbears declared their independence from Great Britain, they asserted their firm belief in such moral/political convictions as all human beings being "endowed by their Creator with certain unalienable rights" such as "life, liberty and the pursuit of happiness." They declared their appeal "to the Supreme Judge of the World for the rectitude of our intentions" with "a firm reliance on the protection of divine providence." One Declaration signatory, Samuel Adams, said "We have this day restored the Sovereign to Whom all men ought to be obedient, and from the rising to the setting of the sun, let His Kingdom come." When they issued the Declaration of Independence, they never intended to declare their independence from God, only from Great Britain.

In his "Farewell Address" George Washington declared, "Of all the dispositions and habits which lead to political prosperity, religion and morality are indispensable supports. In vain would that man claim the tribute of patriotism who should labour to subvert these great pillars of human happiness." Washington's successor, John Adams, reiterated the role of religion and morality in our nation's life. In 1798 President Adams said, "We have no government armed in power capable of contending in human passions unbridled by morality and religion. Our Constitution was made for a moral and a religious people. It is wholly inadequate for the government of any other."

Religious conviction has profoundly influenced our nation throughout its history. There would have been no abolitionist and antislavery movement without the leadership and support of people of faith. There would have been no child labor reform movement without the impetus of religious conviction. There would have been no civil rights movement without the moral imperative provided by people of religious conviction. Our Baptist ancestors were active in all of these movements. They believed their moral convictions left them no choice but to be involved. They found no contradiction between such action and their commitment to church/state separation.

Clearly, as American citizens, Christians have the *right* to be involved in the legislative arena. As obedient Christians, they have the *responsibility* to be involved.

Christians are called upon not just to enjoy, but to exercise; not just to preach, but to practice their liberties. Surely, there could be no better thing for Americans and for America than for Citizen Christians to awaken to the *exercise* of their *rights* and to the *fulfillment* of their *responsibilities.*

In 1947 C. S. Lewis, in *The Abolition of Man*, wrote that in the properly ordered composition of human beings the head ruled the belly (which represented the sensual appetites) through the chest. Lewis defined the chest as consisting of "emotions organized by trained habit into stable sentiments."[10] The chest, in Lewis's view, was the "indispensable liaison between cerebral man and visceral man."[11] Lewis noted that moral relativism removes man's moral character, producing moral eunuchs.[12] "In a sort of ghastly simplicity we remove the organ and demand the function. We make men without chests and expect of them virtue and enterprise. We laugh at honor and are shocked to find traitors in our midst. We castrate and then bid the geldings to be fruitful."[13]

We must offer hope to men who have been raised without chests and give them an answer for the emptiness of their lives. We must be ready to tell of a God who loves them, and of an "abundant" life in which "We are not the sum of our possessions. They are not the measure of our lives."[14]

Rather, salvation, meaning, and purpose is found in the One who said, "he that loseth his life for my sake shall find it" (Matt. 10:39b).

Having realized how far the family has fallen from God's divinely ordained institution composed of a husband (father) and wife (mother) and children, we must reawaken among believers a clear understanding of God's design. Husbands are to love their wives, Paul told the Ephesians (Eph. 5:25) with the revolutionary, self-sacrificing, other-directed *agape* love with which God first loved us (John 3:16; 1 John 4:10) and which is produced by the Holy Spirit in the hearts of yielded believers (Gal. 5:22). Leadership, in the gospel of Jesus Christ, is servant leadership. It is sacrificial leadership. It is foot-washing leadership that spends itself in service to others.

This *agape* love was "a concept baptized and consecrated within the church."[15] The *agape* love of Christianity "is shed abroad in our hearts" (Rom. 5:5) and thus should be "the decisive reality in our existence" if we are followers of Jesus of Nazareth.[16]

Those characterized by *agape* love "should show love without expecting it to be returned, lend where there is little hope of repayment, give without reserve or limit" and "accept the enmity of the world willingly, unresistingly and sacrificially"[17] (See Luke 6:28).

Such love will revolutionize relationships inside and outside the family and will enable parents to obey the command not to "provoke" their children "to wrath," but instead to "bring them up in the nurture and admonition of the Lord" (Eph. 6:4).

We must not only reawaken, we must reconstruct within our churches and communities of believers a truly biblical understanding of the family as God meant for it to function. That understanding must lead to a greater reinstitution of its practice. Individuals need, families need, America needs much greater application of "family practice," not just family theory. We need to practice being family. As Christians we must recognize the family's absolute indispensability. Nothing can replace the family as the nurturing environment for healthy human growth and emotional and spiritual development.

Consequently, we must reassert the Christian family's unique value and place in society. Suffused in the self-sacrificing, spirit-produced *agape*, the Christian family is essential. Thus having reconstructed, reinstituted, and reasserted the Christian family, we must reach out and replace the family for those who either do not have one, or who belong to one that is dysfunctional.

Through the power that is available in Jesus, we must allow Christ to use us as instruments of healing in families and as instruments of healing in persons. As individuals, as couples, as families, as churches, we must allow our Heavenly Father to use us as the fathers, mothers, sons, daughters, husbands, wives, brothers, and sisters that bruised spirits and wounded souls need and miss so desperately.

It will not be, it never has been, sufficient merely to say these things. We must live them. We must live our *agape* love of self-sacrifice to which we are called. As Francis of Assisi put it, "Preach the Gospel all the time. If necessary use words." How is that to be done? Perhaps one of his prayers provides an answer.

Lord, make me an instrument of thy peace,
Where there is hatred, let me sow love,
Where there is injury, pardon,
Where there is doubt, faith,
Where there is darkness, light,
And where there is sadness, joy.

Divine Master,
Grant that I may not seek to be consoled,
as to console.

To be understood, as to understand;
To be loved as to love;
For it is in giving that we receive;
It is in pardoning that we are pardoned;
It is in dying that we gain eternal life.18

To those enslaved by besetting addictions we must witness to, and live before them, the veracity of "And ye shall know the truth, and the truth shall make you free" (John 8:32) as proclaimed by the One who said, "I am the way, the truth, and the life; no man cometh unto the Father, but by me" (John 14:6).

We must confront them with truth, and we must comfort them with the fact that we have a Savior who is a "merciful and faithful high priest" (Heb. 2:17) [the Book of Hebrews goes out of its way by mentioning this twice—in Heb. 2 and in Heb. 4] and who is "touched with the feeling of our infirmities" and "was in all points tempted like as we are, yet without sin" (Heb. 4:15). In responding, in reacting to the relentless twentieth-century assault on the deity of Jesus Christ, we within the orthodox faith have too often allowed those attacks to rob us of a full understanding and comprehension of the true and complete humanity of Jesus Christ. He who "thought it not robbery to be equal with God" humbled Himself and was made of "no reputation" and was "found in fashion as a man" and was obedient even to a cross kind of death so that God has "given him a name which is above every name"—not Immanuel, not King of Kings, not Lord of Lords, but Jesus, His human name.[19] We have not a high priest who is cold and distant, a high priest from Olympian heights who doesn't understand, who hasn't been touched by our humanity. Rather, our high priest is human as well as God. We need that comforting hand. We need that certain antidote to the solitary existence of the twentieth century. "No, never alone?" Amen! No, we are never alone because He is with us and He understands, and He has life and power and a new beginning in His touch.

Consequently, we are all encouraged to "come boldly unto the throne of grace, that we may obtain mercy, and find grace to help in time of need" (Heb. 4:16).

It will not be sufficient merely to believe the right thing. It will not be sufficient merely to say the right thing. It will not be sufficient merely to do the right thing. In order to comply with our Lord's command to be the light of the world, we must do the right thing and do it for the right reason with the right motive. As Jesus reminded the church at Ephesus, we must do what we do because we love Jesus, and we want to please Him.[20] How can we hate the sin and what it does to the sinner, yet love the sinner? Those we are seeking to love know if we're just trying or if we really love them, if we accept them but not their behavior. We do this because we do what we do because we love Jesus Christ and we want to please Him. We love them because He loves them. We serve them because He serves them. We do what we do because it pleases Him. And if we don't, we "grieve" the Holy Spirit.[21]

As John Stott has concluded,

> The church has no light without love. Only when its love burns can its light shine. Many churches . . . today have ceased truly to exist. Their buildings remain intact, their ministers minister and their congregations congregate, but their lampstand has been removed. The church is plunged in darkness. No glimmer of light radiates from it. It has no light, because it has no love. . . .
>
> So the church today, like the church of Ephesus, has a work to be done, a fight to be fought and a creed to be championed. But above all, it has a Person to be loved, with the love we had for Him at first, a "love undying."[22]

May that love savor the salt and energize the light that our Savior has called us to be.

Endnotes

1. Alexander Maclaren, *Expositions of Holy Scripture* (Grand Rapids: Baker, 1982), 2:179.
2. R. V. G. Tasker, *The Gospel According to St. Matthew* (London: Tyndale Press, 1961), 63.
3. Soren Kierkegaard, quoted in *Daily Devotional Bible Commentary* (Nashville: Holman, 1974), 3:24.

4. A. M. Hunter, *A Pattern for Life*, rev. ed. (Philadelphia: The Westminster Press, 1965.), 46.

5. D. Martyn Lloyd-Jones, *Studies in the Sermon on the Mount* (Grand Rapids: Wm. B. Eerdmans, 1971), 1:174.

6. Robert A. Guelich, *The Sermon on the Mount* (Waco: Word Books, 1982), 132-133.

7. Cf. John 8:12, "I am the light of the world; he that followeth me shall not walk in darkness, but shall have the light of life."

8. Cf. also Peter 4:11b.

9. *Choices*, documentary produced for the National Broadcasting Company by the Radio and Television Commission of the Southern Baptist Convention, 1990.

10. C.S. Lewis, *The Abolition of Man* (New York: The Macmillan Co., 1965), 34. Originally published in 1947.

11. *Ibid.*

12. *Ibid.*, 35.

13. *Ibid.*

14. Ronald K. L. Collins, "Ad bucks hook the kids—on fads, fashions, spending," *The Atlanta Journal and Constitution*, 4 March, 1990, G-3, quoting President Bush.

15. Negel Turner, *Christian Words* (Nashville: Thomas Nelson, 1981), 265.

16. *Theological Dictionary of the New Testament.* Ed. Gerhard Kittel. Translated Geoffrey W. Bromiley. (Grand Rapids: Wm. B. Eerdmans, 1964), 1:49.

17. *Ibid.*, 46.

18. Quoted in R. L. Middleton, *The Gift of Love* (Nashville: Broadman Press, 1976), 21.

19. Phil. 2:5-11.

20. Rev. 2:1-6.

21. Eph. 4:30.

22. John R. W. Stott, *What Christ Thinks of the Church* (Grand Rapids: Wm. B. Eerdmans, 1958), 33-34.

CHAPTER ELEVEN

Family Values in Baptist Life

DOROTHY PATTERSON

From the beginning, God has used the home as the primary classroom and object lesson for teaching His people about Himself and the holy lifestyle He demands of His followers. Without a spiritually healthy family, the work of producing Spirit–filled, mature believers is greatly handicapped. Samuel Davies described the home as "the nursery of the church and state."[1]

God sets the solitary in families;
He brings out those who are bound into prosperity;
But the rebellious dwell in a dry land. (Ps. 68:6)[*]

* Unless otherwise noted, all Scripture quotations in this chapter are from the New King James Version of the Bible.

God has chosen to make His presence available in unique ways within the family circle. He established the home when He created the man and woman and brought them together in the Garden of Eden (see Gen. 2:18–24) before there were civil governments or assemblies of worship. The Lord designed the family unit as a close–knit group made up of parents, children, grandparents, uncles, aunts, and cousins.

The family has also been the natural setting for molding and nurturing a child in the ways of the Lord (Prov. 22:6). The fertilizing and pruning experienced by the child in the "greenhouse" of his parents prepared that child for his direct accountability to God (see Deut. 6:4–9). Such commitment to scriptural nurture in the home in no way diminishes the importance of the family's involvement in the local church as an arena in which there is collective edification and encouragement, as well as equipping for the development and use of spiritual gifts (1 Tim. 3:4, 5).

Venerable pastors have warned fathers against secular pursuits—wealth or fame or pleasure—at the expense of spiritual leadership in the family. Parents have been admonished to get control of their children; they are instructed to direct their children to God early; they are warned to move their children from parent–control through self–control to God–control (Prov. 23:15, 16).

The boundaries of a young child are established by his parents (Prov. 3:12; 13:24; 22:6, 15; 23:13, 14; 29:15, 17; Eph. 6:4). During the maturing process, the child assumes responsibility for making decisions based upon the godly principles he has been taught by his parents. However, the ultimate goal is to move the child to an accountability to God (Ps. 119:9–11).

The eighteenth–century preacher Jonathan Edwards was a dedicated pastor, gifted theologian, and prolific writer. His most important accomplishment in the kingdom was the leadership he assumed in the Great Awakening Revival. Yet he and his wife Sarah reared eleven children, and the generations that have come from this union even overshadow Edwards's worthy contributions to the kingdom. By 1990, an overview of the descendants of Sarah and Jonathan Edwards included sixty-five professors and thirteen college presidents; one hundred attorneys; sixty-six physicians; eighty government leaders, including thirty judges, three senators, and one vice president of the United States; in addition to a host of pastors and missionaries.[2] By taking time for their family, Jonathan and Sarah Edwards left a godly heritage that has extended over the generations just as surely as did the patriarch Abraham (Gen. 18:17–19).

The Primacy of the Home in Scripture

Genesis records God's plan for Christian marriage (Gen. 2:24) and the account of His establishment of the home as His first institution. In Exodus, the commandments of the Decalogue each touch upon some aspect of life within the family circle (Exod. 20:3–17). In Leviticus, the penalty for betraying the home is clear (Lev. 19:20). In Numbers, the numbering of the people is done by families (Num. 1:17–19). Deuteronomy has much on family worship and contains the second giving of the Law, with special emphasis upon the responsibility of parents to instruct their children (Deut. 6:4–12).

The Book of Joshua presents a patriarch who leads his family to commit themselves to God (Josh. 24:15). In Judges, Samson's unbridled lust brings tragic consequences to him, his family, and the entire nation (Judg. 16:1, 18–20); whereas in Ruth, romantic love and family devotion are clearly presented (Ruth 1:16, 17).

In the history of Israel recorded in the books of Samuel, Kings, and Chronicles, the impact of the home is seen in the lives of the kings. The wickedness of Ahab was increased under the influence of his wife Jezebel (1 Kings 21:5–16); while the godliness of Samuel was certainly encouraged by the influence of his devout mother, Hannah (1 Sam. 1:27, 28).

In Ezra, Nehemiah, and Esther, the family unit preserved godly seed even in the midst of the dark days of captivity (Esther 2:20; 4:14). Satan's attack on the home is nowhere more apparent than in the Book of Job (Job 1:13–21; 2:7–10). Promises for the home abound in the Book of Psalms (Ps. 127), and both Proverbs and Ecclesiastes are saturated with godly wisdom about the home and family (Prov. 14:1; 22:6; Eccl. 4:9–12). The Song of Solomon is devoted to an intimate account of that most exclusive love between a husband and wife (Song 4:1–7). The home is also present throughout the Prophets as God warns His people about the open violation of His principles (Isa. 3:12; Jer. 31:29, 30; Lam. 4:10; Ezek. 16:44, 45; Hos. 4:1–5; Joel 2:28, 29; Mic. 7:5, 6; Mal. 2:14–16).

The Gospels present many families of the New Testament. Questions concerning divorce are answered by Jesus Himself (Matt. 19:3–9). In John's Gospel, Jesus performed His first miracle at a wedding in Cana (John 2:1–11). The Book of Acts introduces contrasting couples: Ananias and Sapphira, who agree to withhold from God that which they had promised to Him (Acts 5:1–11) and Aquila and Priscilla, who offered themselves and what they had to the Lord and His work (Acts 18:2, 3, 18, 26). Family relationships are often addressed throughout the Epistles (1 Cor. 11:1–16; Eph. 5:21–6:4; Col. 3:18–21; 1 Thess. 4:1–7; 1 Tim. 3:1–12; Titus 2:1–5; Heb. 12:5–11; 1 Pet. 3:1–7). The Book of Revelation (Rev. 3:20) also has a word for the home.[3]

The value of family–centeredness and the tragedy of a lack thereof is readily apparent in Scripture. The encouragement to exclusiveness within the family (Exod. 10:2–8; 20:2–6; Deut. 5:16–21; 7:1–6), the expectation of obedience to authorities within the family (Josh. 24:14–18), and the respect for time-tested wisdom within the generations were all part of the family tradition described in Scripture (Prov. 1:8).

God gave the Ten Commandments (Exod. 20:3–17) as a concise summary of supreme virtues and ultimate moral duties. The first four of these Commandments concern the individual's relationship to God, and the remaining six address relationships within the human family. Within the latter category, three are directed to the family circle: children are to honor their parents (Exod. 20:12); husband and wife are to honor their commitments to one another (Exod. 20:14); all are to honor God not only in their overt actions but also in the thoughts and intents of their own hearts (Exod. 20:17).

The Bible has many examples of worship within the family. For whatever reason, it pleased God to transmit the faith through domestic means. From the beginning, His covenant was from father to son, and every covenant has included succeeding generations. In the Old Testament, Job made family religion a priority (Job 1:5). Noah built an altar to the Lord, and his family responded to his preaching by joining him in commitment to and worship of the Lord (Gen. 7:1; 8:20). Abraham and Sarah not only received God's promise together but must have linked hand and heart in prayer and praise as Abraham raised altars and made sacrifices (Gen. 18:9–15). Isaac continued in the tradition of his father and built an altar at Beersheba (Gen. 26:25). Jacob also worshiped with his family, and he assumed responsibility for cleansing his household of idols (Gen. 35:1–3).

The Passover was an observance for the family (Exod. 12:24–27). Joshua must have brought his family together in worship in order to inspire them to follow his example of public commitment to the Lord (Josh. 24:15). David was aware of the importance of including his home in his worship of the Lord (2 Sam. 6:20; Ps. 101:2). Daniel's commitment to private devotion to the Lord had its moorings in the family religion that had been a part of his own childhood home (Dan. 6:10).

The church has often been described as a family, but in actuality, the church is made up of the individual family units to which it offers ministries. Therefore, family ministries are absolutely imperative. These should not be limited to seasonal programs but must be extended to ongoing nurturing activities that encourage parents in their responsibilities within the family circle.

The home environment has long been recognized as one of the most powerful factors in determining even the academic learning of children. Scientists have long since determined that differences in learning abilities are not solely based upon the genetic code or the location of the community in which the child lives. Rather, the values, habits, and dynamics of relationships within the household are more significant influences.[4]

A View of Family Worship in History

As early as 1557 Menno Simons wrote a brief tract. Its title was translated from the Dutch as "A Sound Instruction and

Doctrine As to How All Pious Parents are, According to the Scriptures, Required to Govern, Chastise and Educate Their Children, and to Nurture Them in a Pious, Virtuous, and Godly Life." The title page also notes these passages of Scripture—Proverbs 23:13, 14; 29:15, 17; 1 Corinthians 3:11. Simons argued fervently and effectively for acquainting "all the brethren" with the importance of the "education of children, in order that every one may comply and in the nurture and instruction of his children observe and obey the same"[5]

Simons used the impetus of the native disposition toward sinfulness, which can only be addressed with the fear of the Lord as the beginning of wisdom. He contrasted the world's desires for children as "earthly and perishable, money, honor, fame, and wealth" with those born of God who would desire "that which is heavenly and eternal . . . the nurture and admonition of the Lord." Not only did he use the admonition of Moses that parents teach their children the law and commandments of the Lord as they "sat down in their house and when they walked by the way, when they lay down and when they rose up," but he reminded parents that to allow their children to follow their evil and corrupt natures without correction would be in a real sense to silence their own testimonies, calling forth the testimony of Eli, who was punished by the Lord on account of the disobedience of his sons.[6]

In 1557, Simons published another brief treatise, "Table Prayers for Mealtime," including meditations and prayers saturated with Scripture for both before and after a meal.

The early Reformers left testimony of their commitment to family devotion. Martin Luther considered the family a model for the church and society—a workshop in which Christian nurture was to develop. The prayers he uttered in his house are widely recorded by his biographers. Though the family was the first institution in creation, preceding centers for worship and government, Luther ranked it as the most indispensable social unit following the church and state. For Luther seemingly to place the church and state before the family in importance has been considered by many to be a weakness in his theology of the family.[7]

Parents have been commanded to incorporate spiritual training in the warp and woof of homelife through prayers and Bible reading or what has been called "family worship" (see Deut. 6:4–9). In fact, the goal of Christian parents should be to nurture their children spiritually in such a way as to lead their children to be more committed and more spiritually prepared than they were themselves (1 Kings 1:37; Ps. 78:4, 6). Baptists, together with other evangelicals, have contributed to this effort by producing many materials to encourage family worship.[8]

Isolated families in frontier America faced numerous challenges as they tried to provide religious training. If they had neighbors at all, they were frequently rough and worldly. Frontier towns were noted for drinking, dancing, gambling, and fighting. Within the Christian households, families had to develop spiritual nurture, binding themselves together through prayer and Bible study. Usually even times of relaxation centered in thought-provoking pursuits, and the family look pleasure in adding to their biblical knowledge and praising the Lord with inspirational singing, filling their minds with inspiring influences. Leadership during these times of family worship was the duty of the head of the family—the husband and father.

These families were often dependent on circuit riders for religious support. The ministry of an early Methodist circuit rider was described in this way: "The whole family where he visited would often be bathed in tears. He appeared to understand the character and the peculiarities of every child. He prayed for all, and we thought he prayed for everything."[9] It was common to witness conversions during family prayers as the gospel was proclaimed in the most plain and simple manner and its appeal bathed in prayer.

Southern Baptists have always considered ministries to families a priority. The "Home Daily Bible Readings" that accompanied the International Sunday School Lessons in the Uniform Series were adapted for use in family worship and published in the Convention's *Home Life* Magazine. The magazine itself was compiled and published by the denomination "to interpret the values of Christian family life and give motivation and help to parents for Christian home building." Its distribution goal was to reach all Southern Baptist families, and this was pursued diligently throughout the Sunday school program in the local church.[10]

In addition, the Wednesday night gathering of the church involved a common meal and other activities geared to the participation of the entire family, such as graded choirs, missionary educational organizations, prayer meeting, etc. The midweek activities were often called "Family Night."[11]

Beginning in 1959, family ministry was assigned to the Sunday School Board: "The objective of the Program of Family Ministry is to interpret and promote the standards and values of Christian family life and to provide assistance to churches in their ministry to families."[12]

The local Baptist church's emphasis on ministries to the family was organized around three major areas: (1) preparation for marriage and family life, (2) specific ministries to families in need, and (3) motivation for family members to participate in worship, witness, spiritual instruction, kingdom ministries, and a Christlike lifestyle.[13]

In 1975, messengers to the Southern Baptist Convention meeting in Miami Beach, Florida, expressed concern that "the restoration of happy and biblical family relationships is one of the most critical moral imperatives of our time." Convention action urged appropriate agencies "to give top priority to providing resources for Christian family living." The restoration of family relationships was identified as "one of the most critical moral imperatives" facing Southern Baptists.

Added to the Sunday School Board's assignment was a directive to the Christian Life Commission to produce materials for distribution, to organize workshops and conferences, to offer consultation to churches and agencies concerning family values and relationships within the home, and to seek to shape in a positive way public policy for the family.[14]

Characteristics of Family Worship

Sincerity is one of the most important characteristics of worship within the family circle. People who know each other best participate in the daily routines of life under the constant scrutiny of one another. For genuine Christianity, this demands accountability (Gen. 35:2, 3; 1 Sam. 2:30).

Someone once wisely said: "To give children good instruction and a bad example is but beckoning to them with the head to show them the way to heaven, while we take them by the hand and lead them in the way to hell."[15] Considering God's overwhelming graciousness to us in pouring out His blessings above measure, how can parents do less than express their gratitude and lead their children in declaring thanks to Him (1 Sam. 12:24).

Unity calls for all members of the family to come together in worship. By definition and as the name suggests, family religion is joint worship rendered by all the members of the family.

Such worship should be participatory. The husband/father is to lead the time of worship, but the mother should take some part, as should each child who is old enough to recite a memorized verse or read a verse of Scripture. Listening in reverence is an early lesson to be learned. Yet the time should elicit deep and delightful interest on the part of all. Its content should extend to everything that might help in the formation of character.

Gigi Graham Tchividjian testifies that the love, fear, and reverence she and her siblings developed for the Lord Jesus was the fruit of seeing the examples of her parents, Billy and Ruth Graham, as happy, fun–loving, and spirit–filled Christians. Daily family devotions were not lengthy and boring but varied and adjusted to the attention span of children—a meaningful time of spiritual sharing.[16] Spiritual life cannot be separated from daily routines nor relegated to church activities. Rather it must be woven throughout every day's activities.

The reading of Scripture is the most important part of the family devotional period. Baptists through the centuries have prided themselves on being people of the Book. They have rightly refused to withhold the Word of God from the laity. The constant sharing of God's Word cannot help but make its mark in even the hardest heart, just as the continual flow of water wears down a rock. Whether chapter by chapter consecutively or carefully selected passages or the reading of a devotional book page by page, the biblical text should be central. Perhaps this is the time for each family member to bring a Bible to the family circle, whether one reads and the others follow or the passage is read around the circle.

Prayer, too, is essential. In the circle of family, little children are taught to pray, asking God for their needs and the desires of their hearts. Prayer requests and intercession are precious indeed in this most intimate setting. Every routine of ordinary life is enhanced by preparation in prayer. J. W. Alexander describes prayer as "an intellectual discipline" because one cannot pray without gaining "control over his thoughts."[17]

Instruction in the things of the Lord is not ultimately the responsibility of the church but finds its most fertile ground within the family circle (Ps. 78:1–4; 2 Tim. 3:15). There is no better training ground and channel for transmitting God's truth from generation to generation than family religion. This instruction must include teaching them to know God in a personal way and to understand His principles in order to discern between good and evil. Children must also be taught to worship the Lord through reading the Word, praying, and expressing thanksgiving (Exod. 10:9; Matt. 21:15, 16). Children must be led to honor the Lord's Day.

Daily, regular consistency underscores the importance of the family's gathering around the altar of prayer and Bible reading. Each day calls for renewal of commitment and seeking again God's direction and blessing. To put aside the time of family worship for whatever reason—to attend an activity, to prepare for the school classroom, etc.—is to suggest that other things are more important than the time of worship within the family. Such neglect is to place yourself under the judgment of God (Jer. 10:25). To put God first takes planning and commitment (Ps.

92:1, 2). What better way to assign this priority to Him than to begin and conclude the day with God.

Timing is important—whether early in the morning before the day's activities begin or at mealtime when all gather naturally and regularly, or in the evening as the day draws to a close (Ps. 55:17; Prov. 8:17).

Family mealtimes offer parents a regular ritual as one possible setting for all learning experiences. Emotional ties between parent and child are strengthened through the parent's involvement in the child's life at every level. Parents must be good stewards of their influence over their child's learning, and accordingly they must assume their primary role as their child's first and most important teachers.

Detriments to Family Worship

Long gone are the generations who lived in communities of the extended family protecting traditions and heritage. The interruption of a family's continuous life together is sometimes due to protecting livelihood—moving in order to fulfill responsibilities of employment. The mobility of this era permits a family member to be long absent and far removed from the family circle merely in the course of events. Children, too, are often removed from their homes at the most impressionable age to pursue "higher" education. Often they are pulled away from the values and virtues taught in their childhood homes, never to return to the home or the values it spawned. The dissolution of family ties through divorce precipitates the most tragic exodus from the family circle (see Mal. 2:14–16). The pattern and demands of society have too often superseded the formation and needs of the family.

Most Christian homes are in the lukewarm category when it comes to family worship—neither hot nor cold. Often such homes appear to be the picture of spiritual devotion because of their involvement in church activities, but the desire for God's presence is not found at the core of their existence.

Perhaps the neglect of this vital ministry throughout the formative years would cause one to hesitate to enter such a commitment in later years. Tragically, even some pastors and deacons have no family worship in their homes and thus no deliberate instruction of their children in spiritual matters.

To use the neglect of former years as an excuse for continuing neglect would seem to be even more reprehensible. The only caution is that once introduced, the discipline of meeting together around God's Word should be carried forward with resolution and consistency. When the sentence of condemnation has not been sealed for a wayward member of your family, you cannot be certain it has been executed. As long as there is life and breath, there is hope, and you are to be even more zealous and faithful in prayers and deeds to draw your children to faithful service to the Lord.[18]

Parents are to sow in hope, knowing that sometimes they must wait through years of disappointment and despair to experience the longed-for harvest. God is ever faithful to remember "your work and labor of love," however feeble and ineffective may be the one performing that work (Heb. 6:10, NKJV).

Every family has those who have no willingness to read God's Word, yet they will daily hear the Word under the most favorable conditions when there is regular family religion in the home.[19]

Augustine, the bishop of Hippo in North Africa and the most prominent theologian of the early centuries, testified of the anxious and faithful concern of his own dedicated and pious mother who received these words from a comforting minister, "Woman, it is impossible that a child of so many prayers and tears should be lost."[20]

The Need for Family Religion

Family religion is the stuff of which strong, God-fearing families are made. Parents cannot expect their children to take seriously that which is meaningless and unimportant to them.The Christian home should be the best and most readily available theological textbook, presenting a "word about God" (Gk. *theos*, "God"; Gk. *logos*, "word") to all who enter its portals or look in upon its daily routine.

Baptists in this generation may ask: Why is a theology of the family so important? One answer is that the family, by way of divine fiat, is designed to be a mouthpiece for the Lord in revealing Himself and His purposes to all.

The Lord demands separation from the world. Certainly this depends largely upon the education of children—not merely in the teen years but from earliest childhood. Parents should be motivated to this responsibility just for the spiritual nurture of their own children. However beyond that, parents should have a concern for their own spiritual accountability for the evil ways of their children. The example of Eli is clear (1 Sam. 2:22–24; 3:12, 13). Though blameless himself, he neglected to discipline his own sons, and God held him responsible.

King David, too, fell prey to the consequences of neglecting to restrain his sons (1 Kings 1:6). Many parents are quick to demand obedience as long as it is convenient, but they cannot be bothered by continual watchfulness and tedious training. They encourage Bible study and the memorization of Scripture once the child is old enough to do it himself, but they do not take time to teach and nurture the child in God's Word from infancy. Ultimately, parents can expect their children to take seriously only what they themselves take seriously.

For whatever reasons, God chose to reveal Himself to His people through family language: He used the metaphor of the home to describe His heavenly dwelling, where believers shall join Him for all eternity. He selected the analogy of family relationships (husband/wife and parent/child) to illustrate how believers are to relate to Him: God is the Father; Jesus is the Son; the church is the bride of Christ; believers are His children. He clearly taught that the most basic and consistent spiritual teaching, character development, and discipleship training should be within the family circle (Deut. 6:4–9).

In a real sense the home is the seminary of God's church (Ps. 22:29, 30). A faithful missionary to China on the last day of his life whispered a poignant prayer, "Lord, grant that my children may arise and fill their father's place."[21]

Family religion is often the last bastion for influence upon a wayward family member. A single spark or simmering coal may die out; however, when the coals unite, a blazing fire can ensue. When the family is called together with consistent regularity, the one who neglects private devotional time is drawn into the family setting to hear Scripture and prayers in the circle of love.[22]

Family religion makes spiritual matters a focus of daily interest and importance. It is as if God's name is imbedded on the household door and His altar established within the walls of the home. The enjoyment of the comforts of home must be coupled with the duty of spiritual growth. Someone once wisely said that the "parade of delights" within the haven of home should be also the "school of virtue."[23]

Can anyone question the impact of family religion throughout Christian history? The churches of the New Testament apparently met first in homes, which would suggest that family members were the first congregations (Acts 18:7; 1 Cor. 16:19; Col. 4:15; Philem. 2). Even until the present, the family ought to be a domestic congregation or the "church in the house."[24] Cornelius did not neglect to involve his family as he sought the Lord (Acts 10:2, 30).

Family religion is a service due the Lord for His gracious providence to families; it is essential for the protection of the family from temptations and dangers; it is a source of strength and comfort for the difficulties and tragedies of life in a sinful world. If the family fails in this awesome responsibility, subsequent generations will move further and further away from the Creator/Redeemer.

Endnotes

1. *The Godly Family: A Series of Essays on the Duties of Parents and Children* (Pittsburgh: Soli Deo Gloria Publications, 1993), 1.

2. Elisabeth Dodds, *Marriage to a Difficult Man* (Philadelphia: Westminster Press, 1971), 38.

3. *Believer's Study Bible* (Nashville: Thomas Nelson, 1991), 1850–51.

4. *Family Policy* (Washington: Family Research Council) 8, no. 4:2.

5. Menno Simons, *The Complete Writings of Mennos Simons* (Scottsdale, Penn.: Herald Press, 1956), 948.

6. *Ibid.*, 949–50.

7. See Gerald Strauss, *Luther's House of Learning: Indoctrination of the Young in the German Reformation* (Baltimore: Johns Hopkins University Press, 1978).

8. Everett C. Goodwin, *The New Hiscox Guide for Baptist Churches* (Valley Forge: Judson Press, 1995), 172.

9. A. Gregory Schneider, "Focus on the Frontier Family, *Christian History* 45:38.

10. *Encyclopedia of Southern Baptists*, vol. 1, 634–35.

11. *Ibid.*, 436.

12. *Ibid.*, vol. 3, 1,696.

13. *Ibid.*

14. *Ibid.*, 4:2, 199-2,220.

15. *The Godly Family*, 220.

16. Gigi Tchividjian, *Thank You, Lord, for My Home* (Minneapolis: World Wide Publications, 1979), 46.

17. J. W. Alexander *Thoughts on Family Worship* (Ligonier, Pennsylvania: Soli Deo Gloria Publications, 1990), 88.

18. *The Godly Family*, 74, 237.

19. Alexander, *Thoughts on Family Worship*, 203.

20. *The Godly Family*, 265–66.

21. *Ibid.*, 259.

22. Alexander, *Thoughts on Family Worship*, 32–33.

23. James, 168.

24. Alexander, *Thoughts on Family Worship*, 219.

CHAPTER TWELVE

Holding the Ropes: A Strategy for Christian Stewardship

MORRIS H. CHAPMAN

The principle of cooperation is a stroke of genius: both the strength of the rope and the beauty of harmony came from the mind of God. Southern Baptists discovered this principle by studying God's Word and being led by God's Spirit. The strength and beauty of our togetherness, to whatever degree it is reality, is a gift from God to Southern Baptists and through Southern Baptists to the world.

Throughout history, many religious organizations have resulted from combining strengths for the sake of achieving desired goals, relinquishing the autonomy of the smaller to the authority of the larger. Southern Baptists chose a different, more fragile, organizational style. Since 1845, a worldwide evangelistic witness and nurturing ministry has resulted from the choice of many individuals and churches to weave the strands of their strength together without forfeiting the priesthood of each believer or the right of self-determination of each church or fellowship of churches under the lordship of Jesus Christ. By cooperating, Southern Baptists have helped to fulfill the desire in the heart of Jesus that the will of His Father be done and His kingdom "come on earth as it is in heaven."

The title of this chapter uses the rope analogy in the manner of William Carey, the English cobbler whose compassion for the lost people of India directed his life toward going to them personally. In a passionate appeal to his Baptist friends, he asked that they hold the rope while he ventured into the darkness of a land whose people did not know the Lord of the universe and the Savior of life. To hold the rope, according to missionary Carey, was to be bound together in continual prayer support and to share the costs in financial support.

The rope analogy was also used by James L. Sullivan to describe how Southern Baptists came to be able to support annually thousands of missionaries throughout America and the world, provide education for thousands of pastors and other ministers to churches, start more and more churches reaching growing numbers of persons, and offer ministry to millions of persons in many circumstances of distress. He called it a "rope of sand with strength of steel." With the rope of sand idea, Sullivan affirmed the voluntary, cooperative, autonomous nature of Southern Baptist life, and with the strength of steel he celebrated the capacity for accomplishment that it produces. He knew that in order for there to be a rope to hold, people must be willing to come together in cooperation with a common sense of mission and vision. Southern Baptists did that in 1845 when they adopted a constitution that set forth the plan of the Southern Baptist Convention for "eliciting, combining, and directing the energies of the whole denomination in one sacred effort to the propagation of the gospel." Sullivan knew that Southern Baptists must regularly renew commitment to that plan and the principle of cooperation it requires.

Since 1845, Southern Baptists have continued to weave the strands of cooperation into ropes of missions and ministry. We have continued to hold the ropes while others go to the distant and difficult places to make Jesus known, by words and deeds, to everyone everywhere. This chapter focuses on how Southern Baptist individuals, churches, associations of churches, state conventions, and the national convention are doing that today and how we can and must do it more effectively until our Lord comes again in glory. The biblical basis and the biblical mandate provide a strategy and an urgency for such whole-life stewardship.

The Believer's Stewardship

Then God said, "Let us make man in our image, in our likeness, and let them rule over the fish of the sea and the birds of the air, over the livestock, over all the earth, and over all the creatures that move along the ground." So God created man in His own image, in the image of God he created him; male and female he created them. God blessed them and said to them, "Be fruitful and increase in number; fill the earth and subdue it. Rule over the fish of the sea and the birds of the air and over every living creature that moves on the ground."

*(Genesis 1:26–28)**

Partnership and cooperation were in the mind of God from the beginning of creation. Man was created a steward of God's creation, free to relish the joy of using all God made according to the directions of the Creator. To invest the energy of every day in managing oneself and all the resources God has made available, while meeting the basic needs for fellowship, creativity, and security, that is the essence of stewardship. That is cooperation with God. That is the good life.

While everything that God made was integrated in purpose and relationship (even the worms do their part in aerating and maintaining productive soil), only man was charged with consciously, intentionally nurturing creation. Stewardship began in

* Unless otherwise noted, all Scripture quotations are from the New International Version of the Bible.

God's gracious choice of man to be His partner in maintaining the glory of creation. Stewardship continues in man's deliberate, positive, active response to this privilege of partnership.

But the good life of stewardship was lost when Adam and Eve chose not to relate to that which God had created according to His (the Creator's) directions. They chose another director and lost their joy of stewardship, the joy of being partners with God. Life outside Eden was harsh. Almost every page of the Old Testament chronicles the price that is paid for choosing to be directed by the tempter in the Garden instead of the Creator of the Garden.

"I no longer call you servants, because a servant does not know his master's business. Instead, I have called you friends, for everything that I learned from my Father I have made known to you. You did not choose me, but I chose you to go and bear fruit—fruit that will last. Then the Father will give you whatever you ask in My name" (John 15:15–16.)

That which was lost by disobedience in the Garden was regained, and much more, by faith in Jesus Christ. Disciples of Jesus know the joy of restoration in addition to fellowship with God, partnership in the mission of God, and stewardship of the resources of God. What blessing! What privilege! Servants of God again and more—co-laborers!

Personal stewardship involves all of life: time, mind, body, abilities, property—all of life any way you describe it. Regarding time, all of the ticks of the clock belong to God. He alone knows how many each child of His will have to use. Using all of them, not just Sunday hours, in ways that honor Him is a mark of maturity in Christian stewards.

Minding the mind was a stewardship issue with Paul. Aware that Jesus had said that the greatest commandment included loving God with all your mind, he challenged the Philippians to apply their minds in thinking about "whatever is true, whatever is noble, whatever is right, whatever is pure, whatever is lovely, whatever is admirable . . . excellent . . . praiseworthy" (Phil. 4:8). A contemporary national fund-raising appeal uses the slogan "A Mind Is a Terrible Thing to Waste." How true that is for the

Christian steward who is challenged to guard the mind, quicken the mind, invest the mind creatively in praise to God and in service to others.

Paul appealed to the Romans to be good stewards of their bodies, to keep them holy, as belonging to the Lord, and to consciously offer them to God each day (see Rom. 12:1–2). That rules out all forms of abuse of our bodies—what we put into them, personal neglect, carelessly endangering them, or immoral behavior. It also rules out worshiping them. The constructive challenge is for daily investment of our ears, eyes, mouth, hands, and feet in God's service. God knows our bodies, how strong or weak we are, and offers to work with those who will work with Him in getting the very best use of them. That is a stewardship challenge.

Each Christian is a steward of talents and abilities. Like minds and bodies, they are gifts from God. Some have talents and abilities that are used publicly and earn recognition and applause. Most do their creative things that bless people and make life better in more private ways. Sometimes the steward of the ministry is not even known by those who have been served by the steward. The model is Jesus, about whom it is said, "He went around doing good" (Acts 10:38).

More is said in the Bible about cooperating with God in the use of personal property, particularly money, than any other expression of stewardship. Jesus actually talked more about how people use their possessions than about heaven or hell. He got to the subject early in His public ministry, soon after His baptism, while teaching His disciples on the mountainside. "Do not store up for yourselves treasures on earth," He said. "Store up for yourselves treasures in heaven. . . . For where your treasure is, there your heart will be also. . . . No one can serve two masters. . . . You cannot serve God and money" (Matt. 6:19–24).

Southern Baptists are instructed by the Scriptures in matters of faith and practice, and the Scriptures speak clearly regarding the responsibility for tithing personal income. As in every directive God gave about personal behavior, tithing is instructed because of what it does for the steward as well as what it does for the kingdom of God. In Old Testament days, days of law before many people knew the grace of God, the primary law of the tithe required giving one-tenth of the firstfruits of one's labor into the storehouse to be used in caring for the temple, those who served in the temple, and people with special needs (see Mal. 3:8–12). Failing to give the tithe regularly demonstrated disregard for the law of the Lord and prevented God from protecting and blessing the people as He desired.Faithfulness in giving the tithe meant respect and faithfulness to God, a relationship that allowed God to pour out His blessings on the steward. Jesus pronounced woe on the Pharisees in regard to tithing (see Matt. 23:23). While affirming the partnership principle of tithing as a practice they should continue faithfully, He declared that tithing did not free them from the call to live graciously with all people.

Most surveys indicate that Southern Baptists contribute approximately 2.5 percent of their income to their churches. This level of giving prevents God from showering blessings on His people called Southern Baptists. It means that many needs of people (churches exist to minister to people by lifting up Jesus in their midst) go unmet. In the absence of tithing, churches resort to fund-raising appeals in order to meet the needs God challenges them to meet. The God who owns the cattle on a thousand hills, and every one of the thousand hills, is able to provide the resources needed in the ministry of every church, but He has chosen to give the resources through His children so we can be active partners with Him.

If a tithe of the income of Southern Baptists were received by the churches, there would be no limit to our ability to share the gospel in every place and in every effective way to assure that every person in the world has the opportunity to know and respond to Jesus Christ as Lord. In 1992–93, Southern Baptists gave $5,054,436,650 in gifts through their churches. If that amount were increased four times to the level of the tithe, the churches would have $20,217,746,600 for sharing the gospel throughout the world and ministering to the needs of all the people in Jesus' name. Such is the potential in the principle of cooperation in financial stewardship.

Southern Baptist church members are sometimes heard to reject the principle of the tithe by insisting that it is an Old Testament law that has been superseded by grace principles of the New Testament. However, I have never heard that from a person who was giving to the Lord as much as a tithe. In fact, tithers who know the grace of our Lord Jesus give in celebration and rarely limit their giving to the tithe. They enjoy hilarious giving that Paul encouraged and respond to needs and opportunities to give offerings in addition to tithes.

Southern Baptists are hindered from giving tithes and offerings, not so much by inadequate income as by poor personal money management. Christians are not immune to the consequences of unwise financial decisions. Even though they know God, who according to Haggai 2:8 owns all the silver and all the gold, and even though they have access to the Bible, the greatest financial guide ever written, Christians still make unwise decisions that lead to financial captivity. Consequently, many are unable to tithe or give to God because their money is controlled by others.

In order to make it possible for Christians to give obediently to God, they must be set free financially. The Bible provides guidance concerning earning money, consumer debt, spending choices, lifestyle standards, saving, investing, and other financial considerations. When Christians commit themselves to live according to God's standards, they can anticipate divine assistance in resolving financial problems. This is not just a temporary escape from crushing debt, but a pathway to financial freedom. This will not only produce a less stressful lifestyle, but it will make it possible to be obedient to the Lord with tithes and offerings. And that makes the faithful believer a full cooperating partner in carrying out the Great Commission to go into all the world with the gospel and with the healing that Jesus brings.

When Churches Hold the Ropes

The Holy Spirit did not breathe the New Testament churches into existence to be a burden to Christ's disciples, but to be a blessing. As Jesus declared that His mission was to serve and not to be served (see Matt. 20:28), so churches come to serve the people rather than to be served by the people. What a good thing God did when He designed New Testament churches! What blessings He bestowed on believers by bonding them together for mutual support as they worshiped together, testified to the teachings of Jesus and God's grace, prayed for one another, encouraged each other in witnessing, and broke bread together in fellowship. They needed churches then, and we need churches now.

Sermons about church loyalty and personal stewardship sometimes present the church as an institutional burden to be borne by persons who must give money to pay the church bills and take the jobs in the organization in order to keep the church going. The old "give to pay the preacher" concept of stewardship rears its ugly head all too often. It is no wonder that godly joy and hilarious giving are lacking in churches nurtured with that concept of churchmanship.

Southern Baptist churches find their vision and their mission in the Great Commission that Jesus gave on at least four occasions. Matthew recorded His commission as "go and make disciples of all nations, baptizing them in the name of the Father and of the Son and of the Holy Spirit, and teaching them to obey everything I have commanded you" (Matt. 28:19–20a). Mark reported that He instructed His disciples to "Go into all the world and preach the good news to all creation" (Mark 16:15). In Luke 24:47, Jesus reported the prophecy that "repentance and forgiveness of sins will be preached in his name to all nations, beginning at Jerusalem," and identified His disciples as the witnesses. And Luke, recording the acts of the apostles, revealed the mission in the teachings of Jesus just before He ascended to the Father: "But you will receive power when the Holy Spirit comes on you; and you will be my witnesses in Jerusalem, and in all Judea and Samaria, and to the ends of the earth" (Acts 1:8).

What privilege! What opportunity! To be called to join hearts with other believers in regularly taking the salvation message to neighbors and on out to the "ends of the earth." Southern Baptists have embraced both the mission assignment of the New Testament and the means demonstrated in the New Testament through which each church member can participate in that mission. By being a good steward of all that God has entrusted, and using the New Testament church model of linked lives, each person can be an active participant in inviting all persons everywhere to personal faith in Jesus Christ and eternal salvation.

The newly born church in Jerusalem was a rope of lives bound together and extended in care to all those who had needs. "All the believers were one in heart and mind. No one claimed that any of his possessions was his own, but they shared everything they had" (Acts 4:32). With that same compassion, the young church in Antioch responded to instructions to set Paul and Barnabas apart "for the work to which I have called them" (Acts 13:2). While the Antioch church held the rope of blessings and support, Paul and his colleagues traveled throughout Asia Minor, Macedonia, and Greece telling people about Jesus and gathering believers into churches. With that same compassion, the young churches of Asia Minor responded to the needs of believers in Jerusalem by sacrificially supporting them in their needs with love offerings, which messengers delivered on their behalf. They held the rope of generosity and spread abroad the grace of God.

The New Testament model is the stewardship model for Southern Baptists today. Christians have the privilege to partner with God in declaring and demonstrating God's love to the ends of the earth. Individuals can do that more effectively with the strength created by cooperation with others in churches. In churches, individual needs are met, and individual resources are combined and extended to reach out to the world.

There are more than forty thousand Southern Baptist churches today with more than 15.5 million members. What potential for missions and ministry throughout the world exists with so many who name the name of Jesus and have committed themselves to His commission!

Earlier in this chapter, the focus was on the potential income Southern Baptist churches could anticipate if members gave a tithe of their income through the churches. That scenario can also be applied to churches and the impact they have as they share their financial resources with local associations of Southern Baptist churches, state conventions of churches, and the Southern Baptist Convention for use in ministry to the world beyond the church community. Most Southern Baptist churches support the ministry of a local association of churches with monthly association missions gifts, usually based on a percentage of the church's undesignated receipts. They also contribute to the statewide ministry of their state convention and the worldwide ministry of the Southern Baptist Convention. That is in keeping with the language of Acts 1:8—"both in Jerusalem, and in all Judaea, and in Samaria, and unto the uttermost part of the earth" (KJV). The work of state conventions is supported through monthly Cooperative Program gifts, annual state missions offerings, and annual offerings for special ministries such as children's homes (Mother's Day). State conventions determine a percentage of their Cooperative Program receipts to be used to fund their work and a percentage to be forwarded to the Southern Baptist Convention to support ministry in America and the rest of the world. Churches also receive from members annually a special offering for home missions (Annie Armstrong Offering) and a special offering for foreign missions (Lottie Moon Offering) which they send through state convention offices to the Southern Baptist Convention.

The scenario introduced earlier in this chapter involves church support of state, national, and international ministries through the Cooperative Program. In 1995–96 (October 1–September 30) Southern Baptist churches gave $411,926,628 in support of missions through the Cooperative Program. That represented 8.14 percent of undesignated receipts of all the churches. If church giving had been 10 percent of undesignated receipts, the Cooperative Program would have channeled $453,889,860 to state, national, and international ministries. However, if church members were tithers through their churches as instructed in the Bible (they could support special causes with grace giving above the tithe), and the churches shared 10 percent of those undesignated receipts through the Cooperative Program, the state conventions and Southern Baptist Convention would have had more than $2 billion to support the Great Commission mandate Jesus gave His followers. It is clear. The problem is not with God's resources, but with decisions about the use of God's resources made by church members and churches that are not consistent with God's intention and instructions.

Why do churches use so much of their resources on themselves and invest so little in reaching the lost world beyond their communities? To some extent it reflects the "me first" attitude that permeates our society. Many church members bring to church budget discussions a disproportionate interest in local comforts and conveniences for those who worship, study, and fellowship in their gathering places. While hundreds of millions have not heard that Jesus is the Savior, and while thousands of communities have not one evangelical church, and while thousands of churches throughout the world have not a gathering place away from the heat and wind and rain, it is not right for those who have a choice of accessible churches with comforts and conveniences to spend almost all of their resources on themselves.

Churches, like individuals, have an obligation to practice good money management principles. They must be characterized by integrity in all financial matters. Just as debt is one of the most serious problems in family finances, it is also an immense handicap to faithful church stewardship. Many churches are able to do little more than pay the mortgage and the staff. They have obligated themselves to 30 years of financial servitude.

There are many creative alternatives to financing building projects that have enormous advantage over long-term debt. Fund-raising programs like "Together We Build," serviced by the Sunday School Board of the Southern Baptist Convention, enable churches to meet building needs without such long-term servitude to indebtedness. When challenged, under divine leadership, God's people have proven the ability to give very sacrificially. The blessings of this approach are marvelous. It saves money by eliminating long-term interest payments. The church budget is not overextended by a large monthly mortgage payment. Perhaps the greatest blessing is the spiritual growth experienced by people who see and experience the miraculous power and provisions of God.

A phenomenon of the last half of the twentieth century is the dependence of churches on employed persons for every service, from the maintenance of property to worship leadership. In times past, volunteers were enlisted and trained for property maintenance as well as teaching, ministering to persons with special needs, leading music, working with youth, and other tasks common to churches. The emergence of two-salary households makes fewer volunteers available, and those who are available have fewer discretionary hours for volunteer service. However, records of contemporary volunteerism, particularly on the part of senior adults, shows a willingness of persons to give generously of their time to those ministries that appeal to their minds and match their skills. The more use churches can make of volunteers, the less obligated they are as a personnel-intensive organization on ever-increasing salaries and benefits. That, too, is good stewardship that may free a church to play a larger partner role in reaching beyond itself and hold the rope for witness in Christ's name to more of the world.

Churches Together in Associations

Southern Baptist is the name given to a denomination of churches carrying out the Great Commission. Southern Baptist churches are supported by three denominational entities.

The Associational Base Design, 1988 update, addresses the unique nature of each of these four denominational units, as follows:

> The whole Southern Baptist denomination is strengthened by each entity—churches, associations, state conventions, Southern Baptist Convention agencies—fulfilling its own unique role. Apparent strength ultimately reveals itself as a weakness when any Baptist body attempts to strengthen itself at the expense of another Baptist body. That means each body must not only give

attention to fulfilling its own purpose, but also to the strengthening of every other Baptist body.[1]

A Baptist association is "a fellowship of churches with a common faith and active on mission in its setting, and is governed by messengers from those churches."[2] Baptist associations have been in place in America since the Philadelphia (Regular) Baptist Association was organized in 1707. The concept of associations took root in Baptist life in America with a primary focus on fellowship among churches, uniformity in faith and practice, and the cooperation of churches in their broader ministries. In recent years, associations have also served as interpreters of denominational services to the churches and centers of training for church leadership.

Whatever the shape of Baptist associations is and whatever it is to become should be determined by four underlying principles:

1. Associations are doctrinally-based fellowships of churches that are on mission—both individually and together—in their unique setting.
2. Associations, as self-governing Baptist bodies created by the churches, have an inherent responsibility for developing a comprehensive strategy for mission to their own particular areas.
3. The denomination cannot hope to involve all the churches in anything without the active participation of associations.
4. While self-governing is an indisputable right of every Baptist body, it is tempered by the necessity for, the spirit of, and the duty to practice interdependence and cooperation.[3]

Associational ministry to churches is made possible as members of churches provide leadership for associational programs; churches contribute financially to the costs of maintaining associations; and state conventions and the Southern Baptist Convention, particularly the North American Mission Board, contribute funds toward the cost of both personnel and projects. As principle 4 above states, the association plays a strategic role in holding the denominational rope as Southern Baptists reach a lost and hurting world because of the dynamic tension between self-governing and interdependent.

The State Convention Connection

At no point has the rope of sand been more tenuous than in the relationship between the Southern Baptist Convention and state conventions. Autonomous churches, sending messengers to annual meetings of autonomous state conventions and to annual meetings of the autonomous national convention, forged the steel that gave it strength. It has been known as the Southern Baptist way to organize for communicating the love of Christ to a world still reeling from the moral disaster in Eden. If it is a stroke of genius, the genius is God's.

Baptist state conventions predate the Southern Baptist Convention. According to the 1993 *Southern Baptist Handbook*, published by the Baptist Sunday School Board, nine state conventions that came to cooperate with the Southern Baptist Convention were formed prior to the 1845 organization of the Southern Baptist Convention: South Carolina (1821), Georgia (1822), Alabama (1823), Virginia (1823), North Carolina (1830), Missouri (1834), Maryland-Delaware (1836), Mississippi (1836), and Kentucky (1837).

Between 1845 and 1900, conventions of Southern Baptist churches were organized in six states: Arkansas (1848), Louisiana (1848), Texas (1848), Florida (1854), Tennessee (1874), and the District of Columbia (1877).

Only three state conventions were organized between 1900 and 1925: Oklahoma (1906), Illinois (1907), and New Mexico (1912). Illinois was the first midwestern state in the Southern Baptist family, reaching to the Great Lakes; but Southern Baptist work was limited to the southern part of the state due to an informal comity agreement with the Northern Baptist Convention.

In the 1925–50 period, Southern Baptists organized conventions as far reaching as Hawaii (1943) and Alaska (1946). Other additions to the list of conventions in this period were Arizona

(1928), California (1940), Kansas-Nebraska (1946), and the Northwest, including Oregon and Washington (1948).

Four conventions were organized in the 1950s: Colorado, Indiana, Michigan, and Ohio. New York and Utah-Idaho were organized in the next decade. The 1970s added Nevada, Pennsylvania-South Jersey, and West Virginia. Three other conventions, Minnesota-Wisconsin, New England (six states), and Wyoming, were added in the 1980s. Southern Baptists in Iowa organized as a state convention in 1994.

Fellowships of Southern Baptists are organized in areas where church membership and financial strength is not sufficient for a convention. Fellowships presently assist the churches in the Dakotas, Montana, and the Caribbean Islands.

Before 1925, state conventions with their academies, colleges, universities, children's homes, and a variety of other agencies of ministry and outreach, as well as the growing number of agencies of the Southern Baptist Convention, turned to church leaders for opportunities to make fund-raising appeals to the churches. Churches were torn between their desire to be cooperative and their need to be free from incessant interruptions in the conduct of their worship and study.

Agencies of both state conventions and the national convention, knowing the importance of their ministry assignment, often overextended themselves in debt and burdened the churches with guilt regarding the unmet needs. This ever-present pressure caused national leaders to respond to the appeals of the churches for relief in the form of the Seventy-Five Million Campaign, "a five-year program, 1919–24, which provided greatly increased support for missionary, educational, and benevolent work in the states and Southern Baptist Convention and set a new pattern for Baptist cooperation."[4]

The financial statement on the Seventy-Five Million Campaign, reported in the proceedings of the 1925 Southern Baptist Convention begins, as follows:

> Final returns upon the 75 Million Campaign as reported to the general headquarters office shows total cash collections in the sum of $58,591,713.69. While the Campaign did not attain its

> total financial goal, it came more nearly doing so than almost any other forward movement conducted by any of the large denominations during the period immediately following the war. Of special interest to our constituency will be the fact that an exceptionally low expense account was maintained throughout the inauguration and conduct of this forward movement.[5]

Although not reaching its financial goal, the campaign made giant strides toward resolving the crisis and opened the eyes of Southern Baptists to the wisdom of cooperation in pursuing far-reaching missions and ministry goals. The time was ripe for a truly cooperative effort involving churches, state conventions, and the Southern Baptist Convention. So, in the 1925 annual meeting of the Southern Baptist Convention, messengers endorsed the report of the Future Program Commission which included the recommendation "that from the adoption of this report by the Convention our co-operative work be known as 'The Co-operative Program of Southern Baptists.'"[6]

The Cooperative Program has linked churches, state conventions, and the Southern Baptist Convention in a partnership of world missions since 1925. Churches decide the amount of their undesignated receipts (usually a percentage) they will send to their state convention for both state convention and Southern Baptist Convention work. State conventions decide in annual business sessions the percentage of Cooperative Program receipts they will use in their programs and the percentage they will send to the Southern Baptist Convention Executive Committee for distribution among the national agencies.

Both the cooperative program of work and the Cooperative Program of funding the work require continuous planning and evaluation. Cooperative efforts in planning denominational support to churches is as important as cooperative efforts in funding the work of state conventions and the Southern Baptist Convention.

Bold Mission Thrust, launched in 1976 with state conventions and the Southern Baptist Convention in full partnership, is the best developed and most comprehensive church support plan in our denomination's history.

The cooperative funding plan has had different forms since 1925. At times, all that churches gave in support of state and national causes—Lottie Moon Offering for Foreign Missions, Annie Armstrong Offering for Home Missions, state missions offerings—were included in the Cooperative Program. At times, state conventions considered some operations or projects as preferred items and subtracted their costs from monies received from the churches before applying the principle of percentage distribution with the Southern Baptist Convention. At times, state conventions worked diligently to get their distribution percentage to a 50/50 level. A few states reached that level for brief periods of time.

The variations and the changes all testify to the reality that churches, state conventions, and the Southern Baptist Convention relate as autonomous participants in a mission support plan God placed on the hearts of Southern Baptists in 1925. As James L. Sullivan said, that approach to denominational life is as fragile as a rope of sand and as strong as steel. Thirty-seven state conventions, two fellowships, and a national convention bound together in a common Great Commission task.

National Convention—Worldwide Mission

Messengers from Southern Baptist churches gathered in Augusta, Georgia, May 8–10, 1845, and constituted the Southern Baptist Convention for the purpose of "carrying into effect the benevolent intentions of our constituents by organizing a plan for eliciting, combining, and directing the energies of the whole denomination in one sacred effort, for the propagation of the gospel."[7]

That vision, even with later editorial changes, has remained with Southern Baptists for 150 years. The words speak of putting our benevolent intentions into reality, organizing and channeling ("eliciting, combining, and directing") our energies for maximum effectiveness, and the sacred effort that moves beyond mere human organization to the touch of God and to the significance of eternity. That remains the challenge of the Southern Baptist Convention.

In order to accomplish this enormous task, faithful stewardship with limited resources was and is a necessity. "The question facing these founding Southern Baptists was not why but how—how to organize a convention that could effectively carry on a broad program of work and not infringe on the authority of the churches."[8]

Starting with the Home Mission Board and Foreign Mission Board in 1845, Convention organization grew to four boards, seven institutions, seven commissions, one missions auxiliary, and the Executive Committee. In 1997 the Southern Baptist Convention restructured into four boards, six institutions, one commission, one mission auxiliary, and the Executive Committee. (See the organizational chart.)

All of the entities of the Southern Baptist Convention focus on assisting churches in carrying out the Great Commission. That means providing helpful information and tools that inspire and enable churches to do well that which they are to do with their own resources. It also means representing churches collectively to reach people in places beyond their reach and to provide services they cannot provide alone: equipping and sending missionaries; providing seminaries for training persons God has called to start churches around the world and serve them; providing literature, Bibles, and books; managing wills, trusts and endowments; administering retirement funds; televising and broadcasting the gospel message to the world; collecting the records of our history and preserving them; and many other services.

This strategy for Christian stewardship could not have lasted more than 150 denominational years or more than 70 Cooperative Program years had not the breath of God inspired the designers, the developers, and the preservers. Today the impact of Southern Baptists on the world is great, not to any person's credit, but to the glory of God. The combined energies of Southern Baptists has turned millions toward Christ and eased the pain of millions more. But we have not pushed back the gates of hell as we should or as God has made us able. When Southern Baptists become stewards of our possessions as the Bible

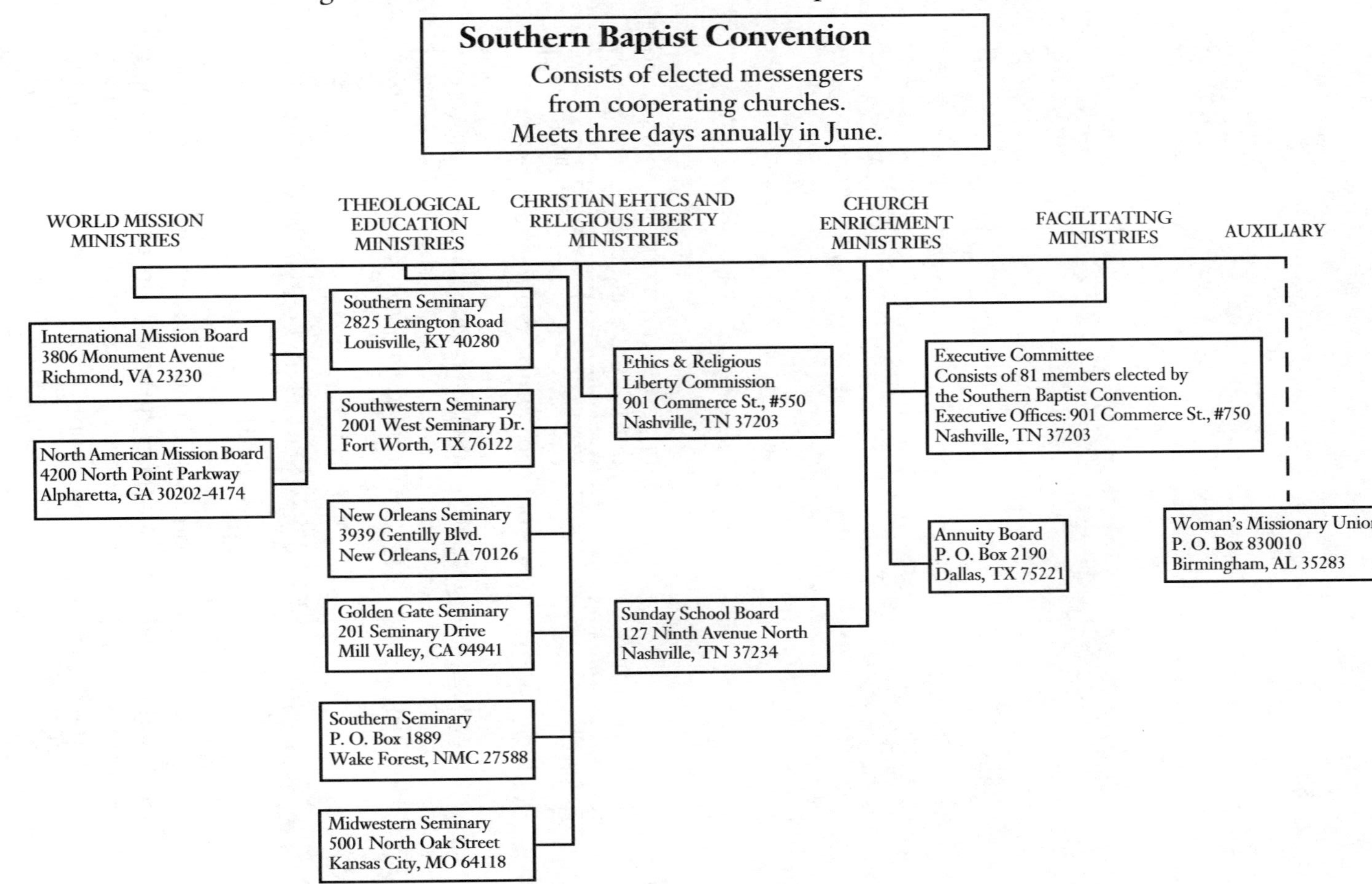
Organizational Chart of the Southern Baptist Convention
Southern Baptist Convention
Consists of elected messengers
from cooperating churches.
Meets three days annually in June.
WORLD MISSION MINISTRIES
THEOLOGICAL EDUCATION MINISTRIES
CHRISTIAN EHTICS AND RELIGIOUS LIBERTY MINISTRIES
CHURCH ENRICHMENT MINISTRIES
FACILITATING MINISTRIES
AUXILIARY
International Mission Board
3806 Monument Avenue
Richmond, VA 23230
North American Mission Board
4200 North Point Parkway
Alpharetta, GA 30202-4174
Southern Seminary
2825 Lexington Road
Louisville, KY 40280
Southwestern Seminary
2001 West Seminary Dr.
Fort Worth, TX 76122
New Orleans Seminary
3939 Gentilly Blvd.
New Orleans, LA 70126
Golden Gate Seminary
201 Seminary Drive
Mill Valley, CA 94941
Southern Seminary
P. O. Box 1889
Wake Forest, NMC 27588
Midwestern Seminary
5001 North Oak Street
Kansas City, MO 64118
Ethics & Religious
Liberty Commission
901 Commerce St., #550
Nashville, TN 37203
Sunday School Board
127 Ninth Avenue North
Nashville, TN 37234
Executive Committee
Consists of 81 members elected by
the Southern Baptist Convention.
Executive Offices: 901 Commerce St., #750
Nashville, TN 37203
Annuity Board
P. O. Box 2190
Dallas, TX 75221
Woman's Missionary Union
P. O. Box 830010
Birmingham, AL 35283

describes stewardship, we will look on all that we have done in the past as a flickering candle, a feeble thing. Then the ropes we hold will reach to all the world. Then we will celebrate the Great Commission with joy enriched by sacrifice.

Endnotes

1. Association Base Design, 1988 update, 1:27.
2. *Ibid.*, 11:3.
3. *Ibid.*, 1:27.
4. *Encyclopedia of Southern Baptists*, vol. 2 (Nashville: Broadman Press, 1958), 1196.
5. Annual of the Southern Baptist Convention, 1925, 23.
6. *Ibid.*, 31.
7. Proceedings of the Southern Baptist Convention, May 11–15, 1988, 3.
8. Cecil Ray and Susan Ray, *Cooperation: The Baptist Way to a Lost World*, (Nashville: Stewardship Commission of the Southern Baptist Convention, 1985), 19–20.

CHAPTER THIRTEEN

Implementation of the Covenant for a New Century

(MESSAGE TO SOUTHERN BAPTIST CONVENTION, JUNE, 1996)

ROBERT RECCORD

At this defining moment in our 151 years of history, I know we stand together with open minds, receptive hearts, a prayerful attitude, and a like-minded commitment to living the Great Commandment and fulfilling the Great Commission.

Machiavelli said, "There is nothing more difficult to take in hand, more perilous to conduct, or more uncertain in its success, than to take the lead in the introduction of a new order of things." With the rapid change in our world and our own personal lives, it is sometimes a challenge to keep up. Experts tell us the decisions made today must happen twice as fast as in 1990. The race of life and ministry seems to be fast, difficult, and demanding. But *how* we run it makes all the difference. In the

Academy Award winning film *Chariots of Fire*, Eric Liddle and his sister, Jenny, were talking. She was desperate for him to return to the mission field in China where his parents faithfully served. Finally, taking her on a walk in the Scottish highlands and sitting her overlooking a beautiful valley, he said, "Jenny, I'm going to China." Almost bursting with joy, he interrupted her ecstasy by continuing to say, "But first, I'm going to run. The same God who made me for a purpose also made me fast. And, Jenny, when I run I feel His pleasure."

The writer of Hebrews tells us that we are indeed in a race to feel God's pleasure. He says it this way: "Therefore, since we are surrounded by such a great cloud of witnesses, let us throw off everything that hinders and the sin that so easily entangles, and let us run with perseverance the race marked out for us. Let us fix our eyes on Jesus, the author and perfecter of our faith, who for the joy set before him, endured the cross" (12:1-3).*

For 151 years Southern Baptists have been running the race and desiring to feel God's pleasure. It has been a relay race with multiple legs. In a relay race the first runner hands the baton over to the second runner, the second to the third, and so forth, in order for the team to have the best chance of winning. The participant not only runs his lap to the best of his ability, but also helps his teammates get the very best start possible by skillfully passing the baton. As the baton is passed, the runners are in motion, with each runner loosening his grip while the new runner accelerates, reaches back, and grabs the baton while bursting forward with speed. *Today we come to you with the baton in hand.*

Participation

As you hear the writer of Hebrews, we too are surrounded by a great *cloud* of witnesses. The word *cloud* here is used only once in the New Testament and it means a rolling bank of clouds that goes as far as the eye can see. It is speaking of a stadium filled with spiritual Olympians who have run the race before us. As we

* Unless otherwise noted, all Scripture quotations are from the New International Version of the Bible.

look back at our cloud of witnesses, we must immediately return to 193 messengers who gathered in the late spring of 1845 to start the first leg of our race. Since then gifted runners have kept us at a strong pace, sensing the pleasure of God as they ran their respective legs. Runners such as James Boyce, J. M. Frost, B. H. Carroll, and Basil Manly ran untiringly. Taking the baton and pressing forward were runners such as E. Y. Mullins, W. T. Conner, Lottie Moon, and Annie Armstrong. And to this day, hundreds still persevere and run a race marked out for us. Among these are those who serve faithfully on boards, educational institutions, commissions, and multiple Southern Baptist entities. We appreciate and applaud you running your race well in the midst of change.

In the 1995 Convention in passing the Covenant, you instructed the Executive Committee (who then instructed us) to implement the necessary changes, including all legal and organizational revisions, and to oversee such changes. We thank you for that opportunity. It is not our primary task as we come to you today simply to reflect on the past but, more importantly, to chart the course for the future. The temptation for our Task Force would have easily been to kick off our leg of the race as the baton was handed to us from you through the Program and Structure Study Committee and the Executive Committee by merely moving to planning and strategizing and changing.

Instead, we began by fasting, praying, and seeking God's presence. First Corinthians 9:25 says, "Everyone who competes in the games goes into strict training." The writer of Hebrews says in order to run your race well, you must first "throw off everything that hinders and the sin that so easily entangles." As a result, two of our Task Force, unknown to each other, began forty days of prayer and fasting before we ever met for the first time. Another has recently done so. Together we studied from the Word of God and books that dealt with our own holiness and walk before Jesus Christ. As an athlete trains to run his best, so we understood that change is not an event but a journey, not a sprint but a relay. Believing also that the Lord's work must be done with excellence, we began with our own personal lives before we moved to Convention business.

We are now closing in on approximately four thousand man hours that have been spent by your Task Force in carrying out the Convention's mandate. These are hours in addition to responsibilities back home in ministry. Knowing also that we could not be presumptuous of the Southern Baptist Convention's vote today on Bylaw 15, we did our preparation through three major aspects: gathering information, understanding information, and communicating information.

Gathering Information

- We communicated with all affected agencies face to face, by phone, letters, and fax.
- We sought legal counsel concerning the thousands of issues involved.
- We developed personnel questionnaires that were completed by the agencies and forwarded to us.
- With your help we brought aboard consulting facilitators, experienced and ultimately qualified in the area of change management, media technology, and cost/benefit analysis.

Understanding Information

As we sought to understand information, we spent our time listening, researching, evaluating, and interpreting. This was done so that we could make good and informed decisions. As an example, it aided us in realizing the North American Mission Board is indeed to be a new entity, combining the best of all present entities into a fresh, innovative unit, rather than reshuffling the present organizations with one being a stack-pole and the others simply attached.

Communicating Information

In trying to keep you informed we used, on a regular basis, our Convention's Baptist Press.

Cooperation

As we have run our leg in the race, we determined early on that the spirit in which the leg of implementation is done is critical. Although at times there have been points of disagreement, we have resolved that at no time would things become disagreeable. Victor Frankl reminds us, "The last of human freedoms is to choose one's attitude in any given set of circumstances."

Baptists do best what they do together. In 1925, we established a Cooperative Program. Again in 1959, we established the state Cooperative Agreements. Even the Covenant for a New Century says such cooperation should be maintained and enhanced. We have worked hard to minimize competition and to maximize cooperation.

We must be reminded that we are not running against each other. One of my favorite stories is of two young men who were hiking on the Appalachian Trail. They had been hiking for several days and were weary when they came to a beautiful mountain stream. It was there they sat down, took off their shoes, and dangled their feet in the cool water. They reached into their knapsacks and began to pull out food and eat it. Just as they were relaxing, they heard the biggest rumble and roar behind them they had ever heard. As they turned, they were stunned to see the largest bear imaginable rising out of the bushes. It had caught wind of the hikers and their food and was preparing to enjoy a snack—them.

Immediately, one of the hikers reached over into his knapsack. Instead of getting his hiking boots, he put on his running shoes. The other hiker looked at him and said, "What are you doing? Are you nuts? You can't outrun the bear." The friend hurriedly tied his shoes and quickly said, "I don't have to outrun the bear, I just have to outrun you!"

That is not the way Southern Baptists must run the race. Instead, we must be like the Special Olympics hundred-yard dash of Down Syndrome kids a few years ago. As the starter's gun fired and each participant began pounding down the track toward the goal, it was amazing to watch their concentration and joy. Everything went fine until they reached the three-quarter mark when, suddenly, one of the children fell and sprawled in the clinders of the track. Rather than continuing the race, every participant stopped, went back, and picked up their fallen friend and walked across the goal line together. That's what Southern Baptists are all about!

Track coaches say a good runner in a relay has to learn to "feel" the other runner. Since everyone runs at different speeds and hands off in different ways, it is critical that the "feel" of a good exchange of the baton be built on trust, dependency, and confidence. Across our nation we have heard Baptists express their trust, their dependency, and their confidence in the spirit of the Covenant. I will guarantee you today there has been no sitting in smoke-filled rooms, summarily deciding the fates of people or entities. Instead, the Task Force has been working hard to involve people in the directions and to arrive at win-win solutions.

- Early on, I divided the Implementation Task Force into multiple teams, each team assigned a person to communicate and stay in touch with at the entities.
- People like Hollis Johnson at the Foundation, Bill Summers at the Library and Historical Archives are being kept in key roles, though the structure is changing.
- A joint strategy, using Incorporators to give the North American Mission Board a solid start, was forged by not just the Implementation Task Force, but with the presidents, trustees, and chairman of transition committees for the Brotherhood Commission, Radio and Television Commission, and Home Mission Board.
- Concerning men's ministry, the Brotherhood Commission and the Southern Baptist Convention are helping form a strategy for the Sunday School Board to minister to men in the areas of discipleship, growth, and ministry—while the North American Mission Board will minister with men through mission, disaster relief, mission education, and will work jointly to discover points of joint cooperation.

- The Home Mission Board, the Foreign Mission Board, and the Canadian Convention of Southern Baptists have joined us in hammering out a transition strategy for Canada.

The plan you hold strives to assure wise and prudent stewardship in Convention assets, attempts to respond practically to personnel needs and issues, and moves toward the efficient transfer of work of affected agencies in an orderly and fiscally responsible way. Speaking to the essential of teamwork, Carl Lewis said, "I love relays—I love depending on other people and being depended upon. Victory flows from the desire to be part of a larger work and do your part in making a great team." That's what Southern Baptists have been doing in seeing the big picture of the Covenant and not nit-picking.

Concentration

In any good relay every team member knows concentration is required. The defining moment in a relay is the exchange. It is the moment of risk. The exchange zone is only twenty meters long, and one runner at full speed must pass the baton to the other runner at full speed within the twenty meters or be disqualified. It is like two cars traveling at twenty-five miles an hour trying to pass a small stick from one window to another without dropping it, all in only twenty meters of running space.

It is the risk that often paralyzes action. We must remember that in every opportunity there is difficulty and in every difficulty, there is opportunity. The exchange zone of the Covenant of the New Century is between now and 1997. The future Southern Baptist Convention is like a runner poised and beginning to move to receive the baton from the present Southern Baptist Convention. Both are in motion and moving forward, ready for the hand-off. Is there risk? Yes! We must be reminded, though, as Henry Blackaby says, "You cannot follow God and stay where you are at the same time."

For 151 years Southern Baptists have run to feel God's pleasure, but we must not be overly confident with God's pleasure of the past. Success in the past does not guarantee success in the future. The 1988 Olympic four-hundred-meter relay team would clearly warn us of that. As they entered the Seoul games, they looked back at a history in which the U.S. had won 13 of 16 Olympic four-hundred-meter relays. But in Seoul, in spite of the successes of the past, they did not properly pass the baton within the exchange zone and were disqualified. Let's not miss the effective and successful passing of the baton.

Celebration

Again, the writer of Hebrews reminds us that, in a well-run race, there is always celebration that comes on the other side of sacrifice. It was "for the joy set before him" that Christ "endured the cross." The tougher the challenge the greater the triumph. What we gain too easily we esteem too lightly.

We come to you today with baton in hand and with God's mission for Southern Baptists in our heart. Today, as we pass the baton to you, it is not an easy pass, for we stand today with:

- 70 percent of our Southern Baptist churches plateaued or declining according to the April issue of *Fact and Trends;*
- Since 1985, one in every six Southern Baptist churches did not report one baptism;
- We have moved from it requiring 20.3 members to produce one baptism in 1955 to today it requiring 41.3 members to produce one baptism.

Yet today we have many points to celebrate, including these:

- As a Convention we have a mission statement that moves us toward being purpose-driven rather than just program-managed.
- We move to streamline our entities from nineteen to twelve.
- We pick up pace toward enhanced effectiveness by combining the key elements of ministry, mission, technology, and evangelism needed in North America and Canada under one roof called the North American Mission Board.

- We take a giant step toward strengthening the effectiveness of our agencies and institutions, better serving our churches, simplifying our processes, and stretching our dollars.
- And as a result, we project an estimated savings in the first five years of the new Covenant of between 34 to 41 million dollars to be reallocated toward the front lines of evangelism, missions, and church planting as determined by Southern Baptist budgeting process.

We cannot become what we need to be by remaining what we already are. I ask you today:

1. Pray for the renewal of a passionate thirst for God in your own life and in your own church.
2. Remain faithful to the Cooperative Program and cooperative mission emphasis—we can still do more cooperatively than individually.
3. Prayerfully and positively support the Covenant for a New Century and its implementation—a team divided against itself will never finish strong.

Edwin Moses, a two-time Olympic medalist, summed up the whole challenge before us when he said, "It all comes down to having one shot . . . one shot to do it right! There is only one perfect time to pass the baton. . . . you can run a great race, but if you mess up on the hand-off, you lose the whole thing."

Today, as we hand you the baton and as the great cloud of witnesses urge us on, this is our one shot—one shot to do it right for the future. Grab it and sprint into the twenty-first century!

Questions for Group Discussion and Personal Reflection

Chapter One

1. What does the 1963 *Baptist Faith and Message* state about the Bible?
2. Discuss the comments about the Bible made by James P. Boyce, John Dagg, J. M. Frost, J. B. Tidwell, Basil Manly, John A. Broadus, John R. Sampey, A. T. Robertson, E. Y. Mullins, and John Locke.
3. What is the meaning of the word *inerrant*?
4. What is the meaning of *Biblia*?
5. Explain the "Plenary Theory" and the "Dynamic Theory."
6. What does Dr. Hobbs write about the historical accuracy of the Bible?

7. Ponder the work of Sir William Ramsey. Who was he? What did he discover? Why is this important?
8. What does the author mean by this statement: "The Bible is not a textbook in science"?

Chapter Two

1. What is meant by "generic religion" and "dog-tag Christianity"?
2. What are the "two major diseases of the contemporary church"?
3. Describe the SBC as far as "diversity" and "adversity."
4. Why do so many "Baptist" groups exist? Discuss some of these.
5. Who was David Benedict and what did he do?
6. Describe the "erosion of theological consensus." What does this mean?
7. Ponder each of the following "identity markers":
   - Orthodox convictions
   - Evangelical heritage
   - Reformed perspective
   - Baptist distinctives
   - Confessional context

Chapter Three

1. What was one of the first resolutions passed at the founding of the SBC in 1845?
2. What is "the task of evangelism"?
3. At first, what was the primary evangelistic strategy of Southern Baptists?
4. What is "church planting"?
5. What happened when, at the 1904 convention, Len Broughton, a Georgia pastor, made a motion that Southern Baptists form a department of evangelism? Why was the idea controversial?
6. What is Landmarkism?
7. How was the Department of Evangelism started?
8. What are the four Southern Baptist methods of evangelism? Describe each one.
9. What is the history of Sunday school? Why was the program developed, where, and by whom? When did Southern Baptists start

to embrace the Sunday school idea? Why did it take so long to "catch on"?

10. What does Dr. Kelley mean by "Old McBaptist Had a Farm"?
11. According to this chapter, what is the future of evangelism in the SBC? What do we need to do to reach people in the future for Jesus Christ?

Chapter Four

1. What exactly is "the Great Commission"? Why is it called the "Master's mandate"?
2. What is the difference between "commission" and "mission"? Describe the difference between "apostello" and "pempo."
3. What are the nine "distinctive Baptists beliefs" as identified by Dr. May? Discuss each.
4. When were the "seeds of Southern Baptist missions sown"? Who were some of the key leaders and organizers?
5. What brought about the Southern Baptist Convention in 1845.
6. What is the intended work of the Foreign and Home Mission Boards?
7. Describe some of the milestones that Dr. Naylor mentions. List the importance and significance of each one as it concerns the work of Southern Baptists.
8. What is the purpose of Bold Mission Thrust?
9. Tell how Dr. Rebekah Naylor came to be a missionary.
10. What does she mean by "profession" and "witness," and why does she consider them "inseparable"?
11. What is meant by "World A," "World B," and "World C"?

Chapter Five

1. Ponder the following statement: "Theology is not an ivory-tower exercise for sturdy academics; it is the serious responsibility of every Christian and every church that seeks to be faithful to its Lord."
2. What does Dr. Dockery mean by "the multi-faceted nature of Baptist theology"?
3. What is the purpose of the Constitution of the Southern Association of Baptist Colleges and Schools?

4. How many schools did Southern Baptists own, control or have a substantial governing interest in 1977? How many students have been graduated from these schools since their founding? What was the property value at that time?
5. How many "varieties" of Southern Baptists existed on the 1990 census? What does the Baptist heritage stress?
6. Describe the "hyper-Calvinistic Primitive or Old-School Baptists."
7. What were American Baptists "among the first to realize"? Why?
8. What is the most notable change in Baptist higher education? Why?
9. Why did Jerry Falwell, in 1971, found Liberty Baptist College? What did he envision for the school?
10. What happened among religious colleges upon "the Great Awakening"? Describe.
11. Why did Roman Catholics develop schools?
12. Discuss this comment: At midcentury, "it would have been taken for granted that the Bible should occupy a central place in Religious Education."
13. Discuss the modern "controversy over education."
14. What were the results of the publication of Alan Bloom's book, *The Closing of the American Mind?*
15. What did Soren Kierkegaard warn about the "professors of theology"?
16. Dr. Henry writes: "In evangelical Protestant circles the sermon has probably least of all attained its immense educational possibilities." What does he mean by this statement? Do you agree and why?
17. What are some of the many facets of religious education?
18. What has happened to the "parental instruction of children" in modern times? How does this differ from the past?
19. What did Robert Ulich of Harvard mean by his statement: "Millions of Christians profess what they no longer believe"?
20. What are some of the great theological themes that "press for clarification" as Baptists approach the twenty-first century?
21. Consider the education developed by ancient Hebrews in Palestine. What was the purpose of the synagogue?

22. Discuss the issue of infant baptism as presented by Dr. Henry.
23. Why would "the recent loss of the Bible by Western academic institutions of higher learning" have astounded the Reformers?
24. What "golden opportunity" did Chicago-area Baptists lose, according to Dr. Henry?

Chapter Six

1. "Baptists are not a creedal people." What does Dr. Patterson mean by this statement?
2. What things do Baptists hold in general agreement with many of the churches of other denominations?
3. What is meant by *sola gratia* and *sola fide* and *sola scriptura?*
4. What is *Volkskirche*?
5. What is a church?
6. Describe the practices of "restricted communion," "immersion", and "infant baptism."
7. What is the concept of church in the New Testament?
8. What is the meaning of "ekklesia"?
9. What does Dr. Patterson write about: The People of God; The Body of Christ; The Fellowship of the Spirit; and The Temple of God?
10. What is the "function of the church" according to the author?
11. What is the recent controversy over "Lordship Salvation"?
12. Describe the "public witnesses of the church."
13. What is the Anabaptist idea of the ordinances as "zeugnis"?
14. Describe the organized life of the church.
15. What is meant by "the priesthood of believers"? What is it and what is it not?
16. What is the meaning of "deacon"?
17. The author makes strong statements about the place of women in the church. Discuss. Do you agree? Why or why not?
18. What are some special issues for the church?
19. What is meant by "the New Testament Church"?

Chapter Seven

1. What is usually meant by the phrase "worship service"? What does it mean to you?

2. Do you agree that "worship is the foundational activity of the Christian church"? Why or why not?
3. Read Acts 1:14; 2:42-47; 4:31; 5:12, 42; 20:7-12; and 1 Cor. 10-14. If time allows, discuss each.
4. Answer the following: "Standing high in the list of features that marked out Christian worship from its antecedents in the Old Testament and Rabbinic Judaism and from the contemporary world of Greco-Roman religion is the _____ _____ of the _____ _____ whose promise to be with His people who assembled in His name was claimed and known. (Read Matt. 18:20; 28:20).
5. What is the vertical and horizontal movement of worship? Why is worship "a community act"?
6. What were the three groups the early church developed out of, and discuss each.
7. According to the author, what is meant by "worship"?
8. According to the author, what is meant by "the essence of worship"?
9. How and why have worship patterns developed and changed within Baptist worship over the years?
10. Describe each of the following:
    - The traditional "Charleston" worship
    - The revivalistic "Sandy Creek" worship
    - "Contemporary" worship
11. What is "worship renewal" and why is it needed?
12. In your opinion, how can worship be improved?
13. According to Dr. Dockery, what are the effects of renewal in our worship?
14. Discuss what encountered in Isaiah 6:1-8 after the prophet had "authentically encountered God."

Chapter Eight

1. What is the purpose of intercessory prayer in the local church. Why is it important? Why should it be church-centered? How will the entire church be blessed because of this prayer program?
2. How should we, as a church, prepare to pray? How are the attributes of God understood in prayer?

3. What two ways does God want us to identify with Him in prayer? Discuss each.
4. Describe God's holiness.
5. What is the difference between "worship" and "praise"?
6. Why is thanksgiving important to prayer?
7. What does Dr. Hunt write about "asking" in prayer? What are the two kinds of asking the Bible teaches? What is the difference between petition and intercession?
8. What did Jesus call the temple? Why?
9. What are some ways to establish and maintain the prayer ministry?
10. What is different about a prayer ministry in a small church versus a medium-sized or large church? Why is prayer essential in all churches?
11. What is a total prayer ministry and of what does it consist? Describe each type of prayer meeting and discuss the advantages of each.

Chapter Nine

1. Why is "the preaching event" a "true Baptist distinctive"?
2. Discuss this statement made by Dr. Hawkins: "The pulpit in a Baptist church is most always on center stage." Why is this true?
3. What is the "prefix generation"?
4. Why is there a "blatant emphasis today to avoid context," "to avoid confessions," "to avoid controversy," and "to avoid confrontation"? What does the author mean by these terms?
5. What is the difference between what people "need" and what people "want"?
6. Why do some "pulpit ministries go to seed on doctrine"?
7. Take a moment to examine the "Pentecostal proclamation."
8. What is the "apostolic preaching model"?
9. How does the author compare the preaching of the apostle Paul with modern day preaching and preachers?
10. What does it mean for the preacher to be "expository"?
11. Why are today's preachers "afraid of offending baby boomer mind-sets"?
12. What did Charles Finney say about preaching?

13. Fill in the blanks: "While some modern preaching techniques call upon the preacher in our contemporary culture to ______ __________, the apostle Paul calls for the preacher to __ _______."
14. Why is "engaging the culture into the new millennium" the "church's greatest challenge"?
15. Describe the "apostolic preaching pattern" as one of "explanation" and "application." What does this mean?
16. Ponder the meaning of 1 Corinthians 1:21.

Chapter Ten

1. Read Matt. 5:13-14 and discuss its meaning.
2. Read Matt. 5:3-12, and describe "the Christian character."
3. What is meant by "being salt"? What must the Christian do to be "salt"?
4. What is meant by "being light"?
5. "The Christian who fulfills his or her commission to be salt and light will provoke two responses from the world." What are they and why?
6. What did the apostle Paul mean in Titus 2:10?
7. What statement does Dr. Land make about "the family in America"? Do you agree, and why or why not?
8. What are "our responsibilities" as Christians and "our rights" as citizens?
9. Ponder and explain the meaning of the First Amendment: "Congress shall make no law respecting an establishment of religion, or prohibiting the free exercise thereof."
10. What is meant by "agape love"?

Chapter Eleven

1. What did God use as the primary classroom and object lesson for teaching His people about Himself?
2. Why is the home described as "the nursery of the church and state"?
3. Why is the family "the natural setting for molding and nurturing a child in the ways of the Lord"? What did it accomplish?
4. Ponder the contribution of Jonathan Edwards's family. What, in your opinion, made this all possible?

5. Why should Scripture be taught in the home? Discuss.
6. Describe some examples of worship within the family as described in the Bible.
7. What was the meaning of Passover in a Jewish family?
8. Ponder: "The home environment has long been recognized as one of the most powerful factors in determining even the academic learning of children."
9. How did the early Reformers leave "testimony of their commitment to family devotion"?
10. What three main areas do Baptist churches emphasize on ministries to the family? Discuss the importance of each.
11. What was the concern expressed in 1975 by messengers to the Southern Baptist Convention?
12. What are the characteristics of family worship?
13. Why does J. W. Alexander describe prayer as "an intellectual discipline"?
14. What are some of the detriments to family worship as stated by Dr. Dorothy Patterson? Do you agree or disagree? Can you think of others?

Chapter Twelve

1. What is meant by "a rope of sand with the strength of steel"?
2. What is the "believer's stewardship," and how does Dr. Chapman address it?
3. Why were "partnership and cooperation" "in the mind of God from the beginning of creation"?
4. What is meant by "personal stewardship"?
5. Describe personal tithing and what Dr. Chapman writes about it.
6. Fill in the blank: "Most surveys indicate that Southern Baptists contribute approximately _____ of their income to their churches." Does this figure surprise you?
7. How many Southern Baptist churches are now existing and operating? How many members do Southern Baptists claim?
8. Explain the two special offerings in Southern Baptist churches: Annie Armstrong and Lottie Moon. How did each come about?
9. What is meant by "Together We Build"? How does this program work?

10. What is the "phenomenon of the last half of the twentieth century"?
11. Explain how Southern Baptist churches come together in associations.
12. What are the four underlying principles that shape Baptist associations?
13. What is the "state convention connection"?

Chapter Thirteen

1. Read Hebrews 12:1–3. What does this passage say to you?
2. What is meant by the "great cloud of witnesses"?
3. According to the author, what is needed as Southern Baptists strive to implement a covenant for a new century?
4. Discuss the following issues:
   - Cooperation
   - Concentration
   - Celebration

APPENDIX

Covenant for a New Century

The Spirit and Structure of the Southern Baptist Convention

The Report of the Program and Structure Study Committee, February 1995

The Mission of the Southern Baptist Convention

"Go Ye." The Southern Baptist Convention was established in 1845 by missionary Baptist churches who were committed to cooperation in the propagation of the gospel of Jesus Christ. In the spirit and substance of its founding, the new convention of Baptist churches made clear its missionary commitment, evangelistic vision, and its Baptist convictions.

Thus, the Convention stated clearly and forcefully its purpose as "eliciting, combining, and directing the energies of the Baptist denomination of Christians, for the propagation of the gospel."[1]

That sacred purpose has stood unaltered for 150 years—a century and a half of faithful service and God-blessed cooperation.

We are convinced that this founding vision remains the passion and purpose of the Southern Baptist Convention and its churches. The vision has remained vivid and clear through times of trial, testing, and triumph. It has stood unchanged through 150 years of remarkable change and social transformation. That commitment has been maintained though the world itself has changed.

Even in this age of transformation, the mission of our Convention remains the same—to cooperate in mission and ministry so that the gospel of Jesus Christ may be preached throughout the world. Before turning to issues of structure, we must focus upon the spirit of the Convention—its essential mission.

The Convention is most fundamentally a fellowship of churches—not a bureaucratic organization. The Lord Jesus Christ commanded His church to go and make disciples. That commission, "Go Ye," is the Lord's instruction to the church for which He died. In obedience to that commission, and in keeping with Baptist polity, we believe that the mission of the Southern Baptist Convention is as expressed in this statement:

> **The Southern Baptist Convention exists to facilitate, extend, and enlarge the Great Commission ministries of Southern Baptist churches, under the Lordship of Jesus Christ, upon the authority of Holy Scripture, and by the empowerment of the Holy Spirit.**

This mission statement is consistent with the founding vision of the denomination. It is faithful to the congregational polity of our churches, and it expresses the evangelical faith of our fundamental theological affirmations. This mission statement is worthy of a covenant, a solemn agreement among Southern Baptists that resources of the Southern Baptist Convention will be invested effectively to assist churches in carrying out the Great Commission with unwavering submission to the Lordship of Jesus Christ, the authority of Holy Scripture, and the empowerment of the Holy Spirit. By this standard, we must measure our denominational structures, institutions, and programs. In the spirit of this covenant, we must create and maintain structure that serves the accomplishment of our shared mission to the greatest standard of faithfulness and our most careful stewardship.

Over the past one and one-half years, this committee has reviewed our programs and structures in light of this central mission. We have considered these issues in light of both the historical context and contemporary challenges. Our commitment has been to keep this sacred mission as our constant focus and guide. The following is our report:

150 Years of Mission

When first organized, the Southern Baptist Convention had established only two mission boards: a Foreign Mission Board and a

Domestic Mission Board. Though many in the Convention were ambitious to see the young denomination establish work in publications and theological education, the Convention focused its energies and structures toward the task of home and foreign missions.

The world of 1845 is far distant from the world in 1995 as we now look into the twenty-first century. The nation was largely rural, and Southern Baptist churches were concentrated in just a few southern states. Not yet a century old, the young nation was divided by sectional strife. Travel was difficult, the economy was largely agricultural, and the population was dispersed in towns, villages, and farms.

The massive social transformations of the last 150 years can be seen in the changing work of the two mission boards. The domestic missions task of 1845 was focused upon the evangelization of Native Americans and spreading the gospel on the expanding frontier. The Foreign Mission Board sent mission-aries to distant lands, when travel was a dangerous journey by boat, and communication was rare and difficult.

Now, even as the nation has expanded, Southern Baptist churches are serving in all 50 states. The demographic shifts toward the West, into urban centers, and throughout the Sunbelt have been matched in impact by the racial, ethnic, and cultural diversity which now marks the American people. The gospel has not changed—but the mission field has changed radically.

The same is true for foreign missions. The technological revolutions of the modern age have opened avenues of mission advance and allowed both rapid deployment and immediate communication. We have shifted from a seafaring mission force located in a handful of nations to an airborne global mission force, with over 4,000 missionaries serving in more than 125 nations. Missiological technologies and strategies have been transformed, but the mission remains the same.

Our concern is that the Convention keep its primary focus on its founding vision—and on our shared mission. Every question, no matter how difficult; every issue, no matter how complex, must be measured by this standard: How can Southern Baptists accomplish our mission to the greatest level of faithfulness and the highest standard of stewardship?

The Mission Expands

Over 150 years, the Convention has expanded its work from the two mission boards to a system of specialized agencies. Theological education was an early concern, but it was not until 1859 that The Southern Baptist Theological Seminary was established. By the 1960s, Southern Baptists were served by six seminaries, located in Kentucky, Texas, Louisiana, North Carolina, California, and Missouri.

The Sunday School Board, founded in 1891, is now the world's largest religious publisher and church service organization. Its publications and programs are designed for the churches of this Convention and the strengthening of their ministries.

Other structures were added throughout the years as the Convention expanded its work and responded to the challenges of the day. These include the American Baptist Seminary Commission (1913), the Christian Life Commission (1913), the Education Commission (1915), the Executive Committee (1917), the Brotherhood Commission (1918), the Annuity Board (1918), the Radio and Television Commission (1946), the Southern Baptist Foundation (1947), the Historical Commission (1951), and the Stewardship Commission (1960).

Some structures, such as the Baptist Hospital Commission, served for a period but were later discontinued—not because Southern Baptists retreated from the challenge, but because the structure no longer served the Convention's central mission.

Constant Mission/Changing Times

We are no longer a small, rural, southern denomination of churches. The Southern Baptist Convention is now the nation's largest non-Roman Catholic denomination, with over 39,000 churches and over 15,000,000 members. Our challenge as a Convention is to review and measure our structures and programs by our first commitment—our constant mission.

Charged with this task, our committee has conducted a thorough process of study and review. We have interviewed the executives of our agencies and met with representatives of various constituencies and the executive directors of the state Baptist conventions. We have asked and received from our agencies their own reflections and projections concerning their work and mission.

We have asked hard questions and faced complex issues. At this historic juncture, we believe that Southern Baptists are ready to face the future by entering into this Covenant for a New Century with structures and programs that are forward-focused, mission-centered, and committed to excellence. As a people, we will maintain our covenant with each other to exercise the most careful stewardship of the resources Southern Baptist churches invest in mission through the Southern Baptist Convention, and we will seek in every way to be most faithful to the gospel and our missionary mandate.

This is the time for Southern Baptists to act—to address these issues with the confidence that Christ has called us to an ever expanding mission. In so doing we face one of the striking paradoxes of our age: In an era of expanding mission, we are convinced that we need a streamlined structure.

Ministry Assignments

We believe that our focus should no longer be on program assignments, but on ministry assignments. By such an assignment, the Convention directs its agencies to serve the mission of its churches through focused ministry responsibilities. The goal is the fulfillment of ministry—not the accomplishment of mere programs.

Thus, the structures of the Southern Baptist Convention should minister to the churches and facilitate the mission and ministries of those churches. The structures should emerge out of the mission—never should the mission be conformed to the structures.

The International Mission Board of the Southern Baptist Convention

In light of the contemporary mission challenge, we recommend that the two mission boards be redefined in strategic purpose and focus. We recommend that the Foreign Mission Board be renamed The International Mission Board of the Southern Baptist Convention and that it maintain its historic focus upon mission advance outside the United States and Canada. The shift in missiological context from national definitions to the identification of "people groups" recognizes changes which have already taken place on mission fields. Furthermore, the older dichotomy between "foreign" and "home" missions has been transcended by more contemporary designations.

The North American Mission Board of the Southern Baptist Convention

We recommend that the Home Mission Board, the Radio and Television Commission, and the Brotherhood Commission be consolidated into The North American Mission Board of the Southern Baptist Convention to be located in Atlanta, Georgia. This new agency would be assigned primary responsibility for evangelistic witness and mission advance in the United States and Canada.

The assignment of this new agency is reaching the United States and Canada for Christ, using every appropriate means of evangelization and church planting. By bringing the assignment and resources of the current Radio and Television Commission into this structure, the new board will include as a strategic focus the use of communication technologies in the evangelization of North America.

The current Brotherhood Commission will bring to this new board the focus upon the mobilization of volunteers for mission, disaster ministries, and missions education.

The North American Mission Board of the Southern Baptist Convention will consist of three major divisions:

A. North American Evangelization

B. Mission Technologies and Communications

C. Mission Volunteers and Education

The Board of Trustees of the North American Mission Board will elect a president who will serve as chief executive officer of the new board and will provide administrative leadership for the total board structure. Each of the three major divisions will be led by a vice president/chief operating officer.

The agency will be governed by a 75-member Board of Trustees composed of the president of the Southern Baptist Convention and 74 trustees elected by the Convention.[2] Beginning in June 1997, this board shall consist of the trustees of the current entities serving a second term.[3] Thereafter, the Board will assume a normal rotation pattern.

The Southern Baptist Convention should remain a national body with churches located in the United States of America. The Convention should continue to relate to the Canadian Convention of Southern Baptists as a separate and autonomous Baptist convention. We recommend that the North American Mission Board be assigned responsibility for representing the Southern Baptist Convention in its relations with the Canadian Convention of Southern Baptists in the development of a mission strategy. The focus on North American missions will maximize the cultural, language, and geographic relationships between the American and Canadian peoples.

Cooperation between the North American Mission Board, the Canadian Convention of Southern Baptists, and Baptist state conventions will be essential to the development of a North American missions strategy for the twenty-first century. Cooperative Agreements between these bodies will continue to frame the working relationships which will facilitate mission advance. Such agreements should be maintained and enhanced in terms of cooperation and stewardship.

In 1959, the Southern Baptist Convention adopted a denominational strategy which encouraged the state conventions to assume primary responsibility for developing and funding mission strategies within their state boundaries, thus avoiding duplication and confusion of strategy and resources. This principle, though never fully implemented, remains valid and should be reflected in the Cooperative Agreements adopted by the North American Mission Board and the state conventions.[4]

We recommend that the North American Mission Board be charged to focus upon direct and cooperative mission strategies with primary attention to evangelism and church planting. Thus, the four major gains accomplished by this new structure and focus are:

A. A clearer definition of the relationships between the state conventions and the North American Mission Board and an affirmation of the responsibility of established state conventions for work in their own areas.

B. A comprehensive front-line communications strategy for evangelism and missions, made possible by the consolidation of the Home Mission Board and the Radio and Television Commission.

C. The ministry responsibility for Church Growth in established churches is clearly assigned to the Sunday School Board—and the North American Mission Board is freed to focus on church planting and the growth of new congregations.

D. The total number of NAMB trustees is approximately one-half of the total serving the present agencies, thus saving expenses and streamlining governance.

Coordination

We are convinced that greater coordination and cooperation between the two mission boards will be necessary in our rapidly changing global environment. Tremendous shifts on the world stage and developing national and international patterns indicate that such cooperation will be required, even as the pace of change makes such cooperation more difficult. Though some have suggested the consolidation of the Foreign Mission Board and the Home Mission Board, we are convinced that such a union would compromise two different missiological strategies and confuse our missions vision.

Nevertheless, redefinition, refocus, and rethinking are in order as we approach the third millennium. The recommendation detailed above combines the strengths of our established pattern of two mission boards with the benefits of an updated and focused missions strategy.

We recommend the formation of a Great Commission Council which will serve the International Mission Board and the North American Mission Board by meeting regularly for consideration of mission strategies and the deployment of mission resources. The goal will be maximum faithfulness in our Great Commission task. This 14-member council will consist of the two board presidents, three vice presidents from each of the boards, the chairpersons of the two Boards of Trustees, and two other trustees chosen by the chairpersons of each board.

The Great Commission Council will advise the Convention and its Executive Committee concerning mission issues, needs, and advance.[5]

Church Enrichment Ministries: Strengthening Congregations in Ministry and Mission

The primary focus of the Sunday School Board should be on assisting and enriching Southern Baptist churches as they minister in the name of Jesus Christ. The Board's six present ministries of Bible Teaching/Reaching, Discipleship Training, Church Music, Church Administration, Church Media Library, and Church Recreation should be understood within one comprehensive ministry assignment. The goal should be to provide a complete and balanced program of assistance for local churches as those congregations develop their own ministries.

The Sunday School Board will continue in its established ministry assignments, but it is also charged with new assignments, including ministries to men and women, stewardship education, and capital fund raising.

We identify the need for a comprehensive strategy of ministry to men and women as one of the priority issues for the denomination's future. We recommend that the Sunday School Board be responsible for assisting churches in providing ministries that are specifically designed for contemporary men and women. The Sunday School Board is already charged with responsibility for family ministry, and this ministry for men and women will also relate well to the Board's work in discipleship development and publishing.

We also believe that Stewardship Education is best assigned to the Sunday School Board as part of its church services responsibility. Stewardship is a vital concern for the local church, and curricular materials should fit within the Board's charge to provide a comprehensive ministry to the local church. We recommend that this assignment, currently assigned to the Stewardship Commission, be a ministry assignment of the Sunday School Board.

Capital Fund Programs should complement the Church Architecture assignment of the Board and would be best promoted and coordinated through the established structures of the Sunday School Board.

The Sunday School Board will assist churches in understanding our Baptist history and heritage and in using that understanding in decision making and planning.

We also recommend that the Sunday School Board be assigned responsibility for Church Growth in keeping with the assignment to assist churches in the development of church ministries. Thus, Church Growth—focused on established congregations—is distinguished from Church Planting, which is assigned to the North American Mission Board.

Theological Education:
The Training of Ministers

We underscore that Southern Baptists are committed to quality theological education for the training and preparation of ministers for our churches. We affirm the essential role of the seminaries in ministerial education and preparation. Southern Baptists now conduct programs of theological education through six national seminaries, which are servants of our churches.

The Executive Committee will assist in the coordination of theological education in cooperation with the presidents of the seminaries. We recommend that the six seminary presidents comprise a Council of Seminary Presidents which will represent the cause of theological education and provide coordination of the total program of theological education.

The seminaries will continue to provide programs of theo-logical education by extension, with the Council of Seminary Presidents providing governance and direction. The proposed theological education ministry assignments are consistent with current program assignments.

The American Baptist Theological Seminary

Established in 1924, the American Baptist Theological Seminary is a Nashville institution supported by both Southern Baptists and the National Baptist Convention, Inc. The school, which offers baccalaureate and pre-baccalaureate studies, was founded "for the training of Negro ministers and religious workers."[6] The SBC is represented in this work by the 16-member Southern Baptist Commission on the American Baptist Theological Seminary, elected by the Convention. Currently, 175 students are enrolled in regular programs of study and 570 students study by extension.

The American Baptist Theological Seminary is a legacy of an age of racial discrimination, when African-American students were not allowed to enroll in the Convention-supported seminaries. At present, black students are enrolled in significant numbers in all six of our seminaries. We recommend that Southern Baptists move further toward racial inclusion by dissolving The Southern Baptist Commission on the American Baptist Theological Seminary and granting sole responsibility for the institution to the National Baptist Convention, Inc. We celebrate the contributions made by the American Baptist Theological Seminary over the past seven decades, but we are convinced that this is no longer the appropriate structure for Southern Baptist support of African-American Baptist leadership. Instead, the appropriate programs of such study and preparation are conducted by the six SBC seminaries and their program of Seminary Extension.

Preserving the Denominational Heritage

We affirm the importance of preserving our denominational history and heritage. We must protect the legacy which we have inherited from our Baptist forebears and trace the lineage of faithfulness which has marked the Baptist experience.

Since 1951, the Historical Commission of the Southern Baptist Convention has served the denomination by providing an historical emphasis. We are convinced that these important services can and should be provided by other Convention agencies.

The proliferation of separate commissions was characteristic of an era of organizational expansion, when separate entities were considered necessary for each distinctive purpose. We believe that this impulse should not frame our current denominational strategy or structure. The standard of stewardship demands that we reconsider these issues in terms of the total denominational mission and structure.

Thus, we recommend that the six seminaries of the Southern Baptist Convention, already charged with responsibility for teaching Baptist history, be assigned to preserve the history of our denomination; that the Council of Seminary Presidents provide oversight and administration for the operation of the Southern Baptist Historical Library and Archives to be located in the SBC Building in Nashville; and that the Sunday School Board be assigned responsibility for assisting churches in the study and promotion of Baptist history through its church curricula.

Baptist Higher Education

We believe that the criteria of mission fulfillment and maximum stewardship also require that Southern Baptists reconsider the work of the Education Commission. This commission, established in 1915, is responsible for five programs, including Christian education leadership and coordination, college studies and services, teacher-personnel placement, student recruitment, and convention relations. The Education Commission also serves in cooperation with the Association of Southern Baptist Colleges and Schools, an autonomous body sponsored by the cooperating institutions.

Southern Baptists are no longer a denomination of small and struggling educational institutions. The state conventions sponsor more than 50 colleges and universities, and the need for the Education Commission is no longer what was seen by those who established the commission in 1915. We recommend that the Education Commission be dissolved, and that its programs, except for the administration of funded scholarship programs, be discontinued or transferred to the Association of Southern Baptist Colleges and Schools, should that body determine to exercise such leadership and assume these programs. The administration of funded scholarship programs will be assigned to the Southern Baptist Foundation that presently manages the investment of the funds.

Specifically, the Association may maintain the teacher-personnel placement registry, assume responsibility for representing their own interests in legal and governmental settings, and sponsor whatever training and promotional events as the Association may choose.

We affirm and appreciate the good work of the Cooperative Services International Educational Consortium, which has extended the work of Southern Baptists into many foreign nations through teacher and student exchanges. Nevertheless, we believe that the important work of the

CSIEC is best conducted through the Association of Southern Baptist Colleges and Schools in coordination with The International Mission Board of the Southern Baptist Convention.

Christian Ethics and Religious Liberty

The central responsibility of The Christian Life Commission of the Southern Baptist Convention is to apply Christian truth to the moral issues of the day and to promote religious liberty as a cherished Baptist distinctive. The Southern Baptist Convention has expanded the important work of the Christian Life Commission in recent years, including the explicit assignment of religious liberty promotion.

We recommend that the name of The Christian Life Commission of the Southern Baptist Convention be changed to The Ethics and Religious Liberty Commission of the Southern Baptist Convention, thus reflecting its expanded assignment and clarifying its ministry to the Convention and on behalf of its churches. This name will more accurately and clearly identify the nature and purpose of the commission's assignment and will help the general public and government agencies to understand the commission's work.

Facilitating Ministries: Supporting the Convention and the Churches

In our consideration of the programs and structures of the Convention, it was clear that a fundamental distinction should be drawn between those entities which ministered directly to the churches or extended the missionary reach of those churches and the entities which served to facilitate the work of the churches and the Convention.

The Executive Committee of the Southern Baptist Convention

The Executive Committee of the Southern Baptist Convention serves as the Convention ad interim (between annual sessions) and manages the affairs of the Convention not otherwise assigned. It is also specifically charged to provide a denominational news service and to represent the Convention to the public.

We recommend that the Executive Committee be assigned the responsibilities previously assigned to the Southern Baptist Foundation. This recommendation is made in light of financial stewardship and increased effectiveness. The Executive Committee would thus be assigned responsibility for estate planning consultation and investment management.

This transfer of assignment and responsibility would produce significant savings by reducing personnel and the costs of maintaining a separate board structure. Provision will be made for coordination of related issues among the entities of the Southern Baptist Convention, especially as these relate to estate planning and institutional investments.

We also recommend that the Executive Committee be charged to fulfill the Cooperative Program Promotion assignment currently held by the Stewardship Commission. This facilitating ministry of cooperative giving advancement is consistent with the Executive Committee's responsibilities for interpreting the work of the SBC to Southern Baptists and for receiving and distributing Cooperative Program funds.

These actions will save thousands of dollars each year through decreased personnel and trustee costs, with no loss of service or effectiveness. The Executive Committee will consult with state convention leadership in developing strategies and programs for the promotion of the Cooperative Program.

Annuity Board of the Southern Baptist Convention

We recommend that the Annuity Board of the Southern Baptist Convention be assigned its current programs of retirement annuities for churches and other denominational entities, insurance services, and ministers relief. We also recommend that the Annuity Board's programs be limited to (1) church employees qualified by state conventions, (2) employees of qualified Baptist associations, (3) employees of state conventions and their sub-sidiaries, and (4) employees of the entities of the Southern Baptist Convention and their subsidiaries.

Summary of Ministry Assignments

International Mission Board

1. Assist churches by appointing and supporting international missions personnel.
2. Assist churches by evangelizing persons and planting churches in other nations, except Canada.
3. Assist churches by meeting human needs and establishing need-based ministries in other nations, except Canada.
4. Assist churches by enlisting mission volunteers and coordinating the work of mission volunteers in other nations, except Canada.

North American Mission Board

1. Assist churches by the appointment and support of missionaries in the United States and Canada.
2. Assist churches in the ministry of evangelism.
3. Assist churches in the establishment of new congregations.
4. Assist churches through Christian social ministries.
5. Assist churches through the involvement and coordination of their members in volunteer missions throughout the United States and Canada.
6. Assist churches by involving their members in missions and missions education.
7. Assist churches by communicating the gospel throughout the United States and Canada through communications technologies.
8. Assist churches by strengthening associations and providing services to associations.
9. Assist churches in relief ministries to victims of disaster.

Sunday School Board

1. Assist churches in the development of church ministries.
2. Assist churches in ministries to college and university students.
3. Assist churches with Christian schools and home school ministries.
4. Assist churches in ministries to men and women.
5. Assist churches through the operation of conference centers and camps.
6. Assist churches through the publication of books and Bibles.
7. Assist churches through the operation of Baptist Book Stores.
8. Assist churches in stewardship education.
9. Assist churches through church architecture consultation and services.
10. Assist churches in capital fund raising.

Theological Seminaries

1. Assist churches by programs of pre-baccalaureate and baccalaureate theological education for ministers.
2. Assist churches by programs of masters level theological education for ministers.

3. Assist churches by programs of professional doctoral education for ministers.
4. Assist churches by programs of research doctoral education for ministers and theological educators.
5. Assist churches through the administration of the Southern Baptist Historical Library and Archives.

Ethics and Religious Liberty Commission

1. Assist churches in applying the moral and ethical teachings of the Bible to the Christian life.
2. Assist churches through the communication and advocacy of moral and ethical concerns in the public arena.
3. Assist churches in their moral witness in local communities.
4. Assist churches and other Southern Baptist entities by promoting religious liberty.

Executive Committee

1. Assist churches through conducting and administering the work of the Convention not otherwise assigned.
2. Assist churches by providing a Convention news service.
3. Assist churches by providing a Convention public relations service.
4. Assist churches, denominational agencies, and state conventions through estate planning consultation and investment management for funds designated for support of Southern Baptist causes.
5. Assist churches through cooperative giving advancement.

Annuity Board

1. Assist churches and denominational entities by managing retirement annuities for Southern Baptist ministers and denominational employees.
2. Assist churches and denominational entities by managing insurance services.
3. Assist churches through relief to ministers.

THE SOUTHERN BAPTIST CONVENTION

Spirit and Structure for the Third Millennium

The Spirit:

The Southern Baptist Convention exists to facilitate, extend, and enlarge the Great Commission ministries of Southern Baptist churches, under the Lordship of Jesus Christ, upon the authority of Holy Scripture, and by the empowerment of the Holy Spirit

The Structure:

World Mission Ministries

International Mission Board
North American Mission Board
Great Commission Council

Church Enrichment Ministries

Sunday School Board

Theological Education Ministries

Golden Gate Baptist Theological Seminary
Midwestern Baptist Theological Seminary
New Orleans Baptist Theological Seminary
Southeastern Baptist Theological Seminary
Southern Baptist Theological Seminary
Southwestern Baptist Theological Seminary

Christian Ethics and Religious Liberty Ministries

Ethics and Religious Liberty Commission

Facilitating Ministries

Annuity Board
Executive Committee

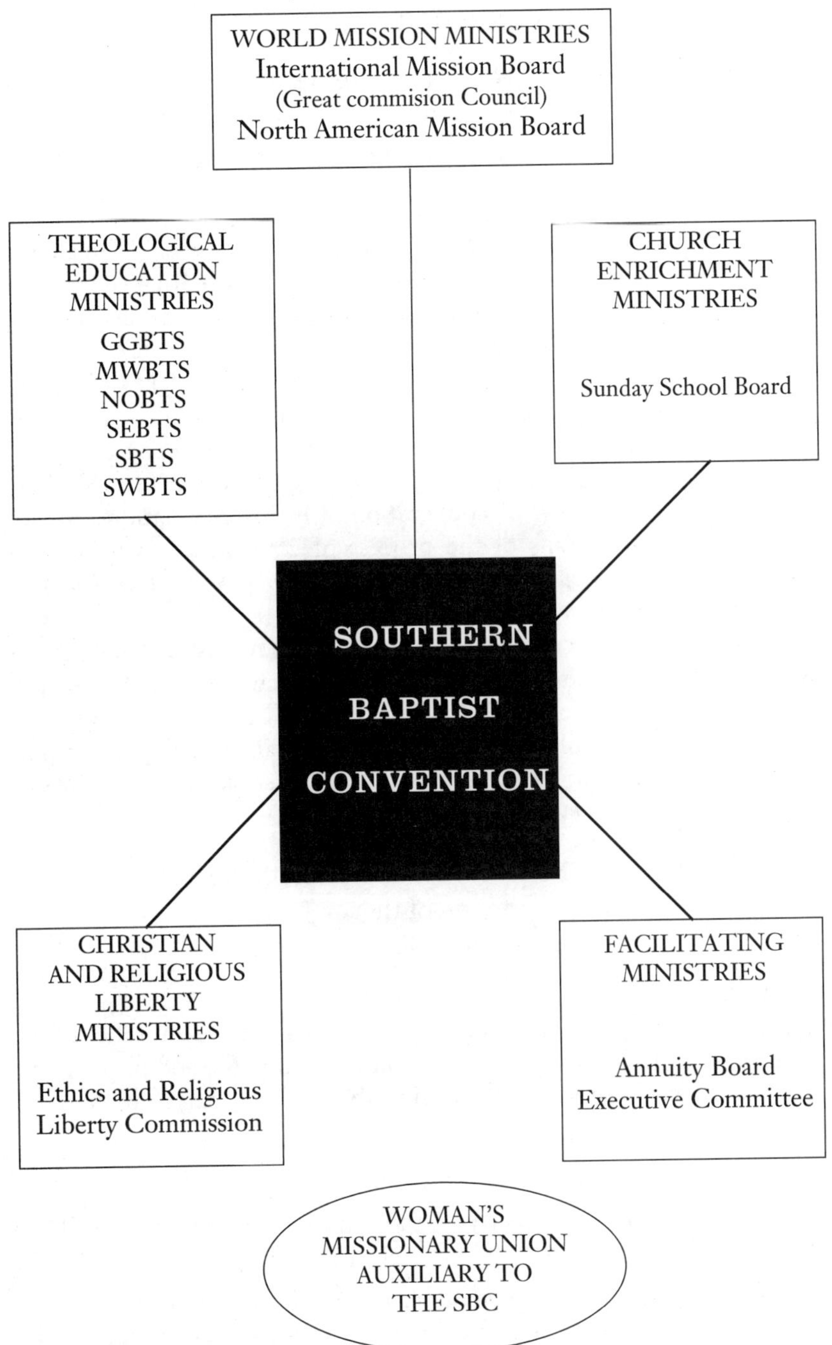
WORLD MISSION MINISTRIES
International Mission Board
(Great commision Council)
North American Mission Board
THEOLOGICAL
EDUCATION
MINISTRIES
GGBTS
MWBTS
NOBTS
SEBTS
SBTS
SWBTS
CHURCH
ENRICHMENT
MINISTRIES
Sunday School Board
SOUTHERN
BAPTIST
CONVENTION
CHRISTIAN
AND RELIGIOUS
LIBERTY
MINISTRIES
Ethics and Religious
Liberty Commission
FACILITATING
MINISTRIES
Annuity Board
Executive Committee
WOMAN'S
MISSIONARY UNION
AUXILIARY TO
THE SBC

SOUTHERN BAPTIST CONVENTION

Ministry Statements

to be included in the

Organization Manual of the Southern Baptist Convention

Ministry Statements assigned to each Southern Baptist Convention entity are rooted in and measured by our shared mission. The charge assigned to each entity is founded upon the conviction that the entities of the Convention exist to serve the churches, their ministries, and mission. The statements have been developed in order that each entity will serve the Convention's mission to the greatest standard of faithfulness and the maximum standard of stewardship.

These Ministry Statements will replace the present Program Statements as assigned to the entities of the Convention. The Ministry Statements, a statement of cooperation, a listing of relationships for cooperation, and details of the process of cooperation will be published in the *Organization Manual of the Southern Baptist Convention* as required by SBC Bylaw 20,(5),(m).[7]

Each entity will be required to file an Annual Ministry Plan with the Southern Baptist Convention through the Executive Committee in its budget planning process. The institutions will include a review and evaluation of the fulfillment of the Ministry Plan in each year's report to the Southern Baptist Convention, as published in the *Book of Reports* released at the Convention.[8]

THE INTERNATIONAL MISSION BOARD
of the
Southern Baptist Convention

Mission

The International Mission Board exists to assist the churches of the Southern Baptist Convention to be on mission with God in penetrating the unevangelized world outside the United States and Canada with the gospel and making Christ known among all people.

Ministries

1. ASSIST CHURCHES BY APPOINTING AND SUPPORTING INTERNATIONAL MISSIONS PERSONNEL.

   Find, appoint, arrange support for, equip, and send God-called Southern Baptist missionaries and other missions personnel who give evidence of piety, zeal for their Master's kingdom, conviction of truth as held by Baptists, and talents for missionary service.

2. ASSIST CHURCHES BY EVANGELIZING PERSONS AND PLANTING CHURCHES IN OTHER NATIONS, EXCEPT CANADA.

   Maintain a systematic and organized program for gospel proclamation and the winning of persons to Christ; give needed assistance to the organizing and strengthening of churches; develop or assist national Baptist unions in developing schools and other programs to prepare Christian leaders for churches; produce and distribute electronic and print media products that support evangelism and church development; facilitate translation and distribution of the Bible and Scripture portions in indigenous languages.

3. ASSIST CHURCHES BY MEETING HUMAN NEEDS AND ESTABLISHING NEED-BASED MINISTRIES IN OTHER NATIONS, EXCEPT CANADA.

   Provide, or support appropriate local entities in providing, health care and other human need ministries such as hospitals, clinics, community health programs, development programs, hunger relief, and other special projects.

4. ASSIST CHURCHES BY ENLISTING MISSION VOLUNTEERS AND COORDINATING THE WORK OF MISSION VOLUNTEERS IN OTHER NATIONS, EXCEPT CANADA.

   Inform Southern Baptists about the needs and opportunities for volunteers to assist in the ministries of the International Mission Board; provide a channel through which volunteers may become involved in projects of various durations; provide information and resources for volunteer training.

Relationships

The International Mission Board will work within the Southern Baptist Convention agency relationship guidelines approved by the Inter-Agency Council and the Executive Committee and printed in the Organization Manual of the Southern Baptist Convention.

THE NORTH AMERICAN MISSION BOARD
of the
Southern Baptist Convention

Mission

The North American Mission Board exists to proclaim the gospel of Jesus Christ, start New Testament congregations, and minister to persons in the name of Christ and to assist churches in the United States and Canada in effectively performing these functions.

Ministries

1. ASSIST CHURCHES BY THE APPOINTMENT AND SUPPORT OF MISSIONARIES IN THE UNITED STATES AND CANADA.

   Appoint, approve, support, and equip missions personnel; endorse chaplains; enlist and assist bivocational ministers in mission service.

2. ASSIST CHURCHES IN THE MINISTRY OF EVANGELISM.

   Serve as a channel in motivating and helping churches, associations, and state conventions to develop and implement effective strategies of evangelism; implement direct evangelism projects in strategic areas.

3. ASSIST CHURCHES IN THE ESTABLISHMENT OF NEW CONGREGATIONS.

   Work in partnership with churches, associations, and state conventions to start new congregations among all people groups; implement direct church starting projects in strategic areas.

4. ASSIST CHURCHES THROUGH CHRISTIAN SOCIAL MINISTRIES.

   Work with churches, associations, and state conventions in ministering to people with distinctive needs, seeking to bring them to wholeness in Jesus Christ; implement direct ministry projects in strategic areas.

5. ASSIST CHURCHES THROUGH THE INVOLVEMENT AND COORDINATION OF THEIR MEMBERS IN VOLUNTEER MISSIONS THROUGHOUT THE UNITED STATES AND CANADA.

Coordinate volunteer enlistment and training for volunteer mission and ministry projects in the United States and Canada; assist the International Mission Board in volunteer enlistment and training.

6. ASSIST CHURCHES BY INVOLVING THEIR MEMBERS IN MISSIONS AND MISSIONS EDUCATION.

   Develop organizations, services, and materials for establishing, enlarging, and improving missions and ministry learning and involvement experiences in churches, associations, state conventions, and Canada.

7. ASSIST CHURCHES BY COMMUNICATING THE GOSPEL THROUGHOUT THE UNITED STATES AND CANADA THROUGH COMMUNICATION TECHNOLOGIES.

   Produce and present radio and television programming that extends the message of Southern Baptist churches; provide counseling services to persons who respond to radio and television programs; assist churches, associations, state conventions, and Southern Baptist Convention entities to effectively use radio and television in accomplishing their tasks.

8. ASSIST CHURCHES BY STRENGTHENING ASSOCIATIONS AND PROVIDING SERVICES TO ASSOCIATIONS.

   Strengthen the work of associations by assisting them in developing, resourcing, and implementing effective strategies that undergird churches and their work.

9. ASSIST CHURCHES IN RELIF MINISTRIES TO VICTIMS OF DISASTER.

   Provide appropriate assistance to special disaster relief ministries such as the National Fellowship of Baptists in Missions and Disaster Relief.

Relationships

The North American Mission Board will work within the Southern Baptist Convention agency relationship guidelines approved by the Inter-Agency Council and the Executive Committee and printed in the Organization Manual of the Southern Baptist Convention.

THE SUNDAY SCHOOL BOARD
of the
Southern Baptist Convention

Mission

The Sunday School Board exists to assist churches and believers to evangelize the world to Christ, develop believers, and grow churches by being the best provider of relevant, high quality, high value Christian products and services.

Ministries

1. ASSIST CHURCHES IN THE DEVELOPMENT OF CHURCH MINISTRIES.

   Provide programs, products, and services that help churches grow in the areas of Bible study, discipleship, music, worship, administration, media/library, recreation, fellowship, and family ministry; consult with church leaders regarding total church growth concepts, strategies, and resources.

2. ASSIST CHURCHES IN MINISTRIES TO COLLEGE AND UNIVERSITY STUDENTS.

   Contribute to the effectiveness of churches and to individual spiritual growth by developing a program, products, and services that may be used in establishing, administering, enlarging, and improving ministry with college students, faculty, and administration.

3. ASSIST CHURCHES WITH CHRISTIAN SCHOOLS AND HOME SCHOOL MINISTRIES.

   Provide consultation, products, and services needed by churches with Christian schools and members educating through home schools.

4. ASSIST CHURCHES IN MINISTRIES TO MEN AND WOMEN.

   Contribute to the effectiveness of churches and to individual spiritual growth by developing a program, products, and services that may be used in establishing, administering, and improving ministries to men and women.

5. ASSIST CHURCHES THROUGH THE OPERATION OF CONFERENCE CENTERS AND CAMPS.

Develop, promote, and operate conference and resident camp facilities useful to Southern Baptist Convention entities, state conventions, associations, and churches in establishing, enlarging, and improving their ministries.

6. ASSIST CHURCHES THROUGH THE PUBLICATION OF BOOKS AND BIBLES.

   Produce, publish, and distribute products, including books, of Christian content and purpose and Bibles that contribute to the effectiveness of churches and individuals.

7. ASSIST CHURCHES THROUGH THE OPERATION OF BAPTIST BOOK STORES.

   Serve people and the churches, associations, state conventions, and agencies of the Southern Baptist Convention by distributing appropriate products through Baptist Book Stores.

8. ASSIST CHURCHES IN STEWARDSHIP EDUCATION.

   Produce, publish, and distribute products that help Southern Baptists to grow in commitment to Jesus Christ by applying biblical principles of stewardship.

9. ASSIST CHURCHES THROUGH CHURCH ARCHITECTURE CONSULTATION AND SERVICES.

   Develop products and services needed by Southern Baptist churches, associations, state conventions, and denomina-tional entities to assist them in planning, financing, furnishing, equipping, and utilizing property.

10. ASSIST CHURCHES IN CAPITAL FUND RAISING.

    Provide leadership to churches in securing funds for capital needs.

Relationships

The Sunday School Board will work within the Southern Baptist Convention agency relationship guidelines approved by the Inter-Agency Council and the Executive Committee and printed in the Organization Manual of the Southern Baptist Convention.

THEOLOGICAL SEMINARIES of the Southern Baptist Convention

Mission

Southern Baptist Theological Seminaries exist to prepare God-called men and women for vocational service in Baptist churches and in other Christian ministries throughout the world through programs of spiritual development, theological studies, and practical preparation in ministry.

Ministries

1. ASSIST CHURCHES BY PROGRAMS OF PRE-BACCALAUREATE AND BACCALAUREATE THEOLOGICAL EDUCATION FOR MINISTERS.

   Provide for students who have at least the equivalent of high school education biblical, theological, historical, and practical studies designed to develop ministerial competencies; provide extension study opportunities for persons in church vocations who have not completed college or seminary training, persons not in church vocations who desire theological training which is academically oriented, and seminary-trained persons desiring opportunities for continuing education.

2. ASSIST CHURCHES BY PROGRAMS OF MASTERS LEVEL THEOLOGICAL EDUCATION FOR MINISTERS.

   Provide theological education leading to a Masters Degree for those whom the churches recommend as called by God for a lifetime of leadership in the various ministries of the churches and other areas of Christian service.

3. ASSIST CHURCHES BY PROGRAMS OF PROFESSIONAL DOCTORAL EDUCATION FOR MINISTERS.

   Provide advanced theological education for persons who have earned a basic theological degree and have given evidence of capacity for effective performance in ministry to the churches.

4. ASSIST CHURCHES BY PROGRAMS OF RESEARCH DOCTORAL EDUCATION FOR MINISTERS AND THEOLOGICAL EDUCATORS.

Provide graduate theological education for persons who have completed their basic theological studies and have given evidence of academic ability and capacity for research, writing, and teaching.

5. ASSIST CHURCHES THROUGH THE ADMINISTRATION OF THE SOUTHERN BAPTIST HISTORICAL LIBRARY AND ARCHIVES.

   Operate the official Southern Baptist Convention library and archives as a national center for the study of Baptists.

Relationships

Southern Baptist seminaries will work within the Southern Baptist Convention agency relationship guidelines approved by the Inter-Agency Council and the Executive Committee and printed in the Organization Manual of the Southern Baptist Convention.

THE ETHICS AND RELIGIOUS LIBERTY COMMISSION of the Southern Baptist Convention

Mission

The Ethics and Religious Liberty Commission exists to assist the churches by helping them understand the moral demands of the gospel, apply Christian principles to moral and social problems and questions of public policy, and to promote religious liberty in cooperation with the churches and other Southern Baptist entities.

Ministries

1. ASSIST CHURCHES IN APPLYING THE MORAL AND ETHICAL TEACHINGS OF THE BIBLE TO THE CHRISTIAN LIFE.

   Provide research, information resources, consultation, and counsel to denominational entities, churches, and individuals with regard to the application of Christian principles in everyday living and in the nation's public life.

2. ASSIST CHURCHES THROUGH THE COMMUNICATION AND ADVOCACY OF MORAL AND ETHICAL CONCERNS IN THE PUBLIC ARENA.

   Represent Southern Baptists in communicating the moral and ethical positions of the Southern Baptist Convention to the public and to public officials.

3. ASSIST CHURCHES IN THEIR MORAL WITNESS IN LOCAL COMMUNITIES.

   Provide information resources that inform and equip churches for active moral witness in their communities.

4. ASSIST CHURCHES AND OTHER SOUTHERN BAPTIST ENTITIES BY PROMOTING RELIGIOUS LIBERTY.

   Provide information and counsel to denominational entities, churches, and individuals regarding appropriate responses to religious liberty concerns; represent Southern Baptists in communicating the positions of the Southern Baptist Convention on religious liberty issues to the public and to public officials.

Relationships

The Ethics and Religious Liberty Commission will work within the Southern Baptist Convention agency relationship guidelines approved by the Inter-Agency Council and the Executive Committee and printed in the Organization Manual of the Southern Baptist Convention.

The Executive Committee of the Southern Baptist Convention

Mission

The Executive Committee exists to minister to the churches of the Southern Baptist Convention by acting for the Convention ad interim in all matters not otherwise provided for in a manner that encourages the cooperation and confidence of the churches, associations, and state conventions and facilitates maximum support for world-wide missions and ministries.

Ministries

1. ASSIST CHURCHES THROUGH CONDUCTING AND ADMINISTERING THE WORK OF THE CONVENTION NOT OTHERWISE ASSIGNED.

   Manage according to the Southern Baptist Convention Bylaws, Bylaw 20, The Executive Committee; manage the operation of the Southern Baptist Convention Building according to guidelines adopted by Building occupants.

2. ASSIST CHURCHES BY PROVIDING A CONVENTION NEWS SERVICE.

   Provide regular news releases about Southern Baptists; serve as the Convention's press representative; coordinate news operations for annual meetings of the Southern Baptist Convention.

3. ASSIST CHURCHES BY PROVIDING A CONVENTION PUBLIC RELATIONS SERVICE.

   Interpret the Southern Baptist Convention to internal and external publics.

4. ASSIST CHURCHES, DENOMINATIONAL AGENCIES, AND STATE CONVENTIONS THROUGH ESTATE PLANNING CONSULTATION AND INVESTMENT MANAGEMENT FOR FUNDS DESIGNATED FOR SUPPORT OF SOUTHERN BAPTIST CAUSES.

   Consult with individuals, denominational agencies, and state conventions regarding wills, gifts, trusts, or deeds which benefit Baptist causes; provide investment management for a balanced portfolio of securities.

5. ASSIST CHURCHES THROUGH COOPERATIVE GIVING ADVANCEMENT.

   Consult with state conventions and Southern Baptist Convention entities regarding cooperative giving advancement; interpret the Cooperative Program as the basic channel of support for the ministries of the state conventions and the Southern Baptist Convention.

Relationships

The Executive Committee will work within the Southern Baptist Convention entity relationship guidelines approved by the Inter-Agency Council and the Executive Committee and printed in the Organization Manual of the Southern Baptist Convention.

ANNUITY BOARD of the Southern Baptist Convention

Mission

The Annuity Board exists to assist the churches and other denominational entities by managing retirement annuity services and providing programs of insurance for ministers and other full-time employees.

Ministries

1. ASSIST CHURCHES AND DENOMINATIONAL ENTITIES BY MANAGING RETIREMENT ANNUITIES FOR SOUTHERN BAPTIST MINISTERS AND DENOMINATIONAL EMPLOYEES.

   Make available and manage age-retirement annuity plans for all Southern Baptist ministers and other full-time denominational employees, supplementary widows annuity plans for all members of any retirement annuity plan, supplementary disability plans for all members of any retirement annuity plan, supplementary retirement plans, and added family protection.

2. ASSIST CHURCHES AND DENOMINATIONAL ENTITIES BY MANAGING INSURANCE SERVICES.

   Design, develop, and provide medical, hospital, life, and risk management insurance programs to respond to the needs of churches and denominational entities.

3. ASSIST CHURCHES THROUGH RELIEF TO MINISTERS.

   Provide a channel through which Southern Baptists can extend systematic financial help to Southern Baptist ministers or widows of ministers who are in need; interpret the channel to Southern Baptists for the purpose of eliciting financial support.

Relationships

The Annuity Board will work within the Southern Baptist Convention agency relationship guidelines approved by the Inter-Agency Council and the Executive Committee and printed in the Organization Manual of the Southern Baptist Convention.

Implementation

Full implementation of the "Covenant for a New Century" report will require revisions of the governing documents of the Southern Baptist Convention and time adequate to accomplish the transition.

Upon final approval of the Report by the Southern Baptist Convention (June 1996), the Executive Committee will implement the changes required by the Report on behalf of the Convention. The Executive Committee will implement the necessary changes, including all legal and organizational revisions, according to a Transition Plan it will report to the Convention in 1996. Barring legal complications, the new structure will be in place and functioning by the close of the Southern Baptist Convention annual meeting in June 1997. Further implementing in 1997-2000 will include the development of ministries.

Trustees of entities to be dissolved will continue in office until the dissolution or reorganization of the entity is completed.

We recommend that the Southern Baptist Convention authorize its Executive Committee, with the assistance of the Program and Structure Study Committee, to oversee and implement these recommendations—including all necessary legal action—in coordination with the entities of the Convention and report annually to the Southern Baptist Convention for five years, according to the following schedule:

Legal Process—Report to the SBC June 17-19, 1997

(1) September 1996—Executive Committee adopts implementation plans for revising legal processes.

(2) February 1997—Executive Committee reviews progress in legal processes necessary for full implementation of approved organizational structure.

(3) June 17, 1997—Executive Committee reports to SBC on legal process development and recommends approval of required legal documents.

New Organizational Structure—Report to the SBC June 9-11, 1998

(1) September 1997—Executive Committee reviews plans for completion of new organizational structure.

(2) February 1998—Executive Committee reviews progress in development of new organizational structure.

(3) June 8, 1998—Executive Committee reviews status of implementation of new organizational structure for presentation to SBC.

(4) June 9, 1998—Executive Committee reports to SBC implementation of new organizational structure.

New Ministries in Place—Report to the SBC June 15-17, 1999

(1) September 1998—Executive Committee reviews progress and plans for having new ministries in place by June 14, 1999.

(2) February 1999—Executive Committee reviews progress in implementing new ministries as assigned.

(3) June 14, 1999—Executive Committee reviews status of implementation of new ministries for presentation to SBC.

(4) June 15, 1999—Executive Committee reports implementation of new ministries to SBC.

Final Implementation—Report to the SBC June 13-15, 2000

(1) September 1999—Executive Committee reviews plans for final implementation of approved program and structure by June 2000.

(2) February 2000—Executive Committee reviews progress in final implementation of approved program and structure.

(3) June 13, 2000—Executive Committee reports to the SBC final implementation of approved program and structure for major advance in ministry in the third millennium.

This schedule provides that all processes will be completed and the Southern Baptist Convention will be fully prepared to fulfill this Covenant for a New Century with spirit and structure to match the needs of a rapidly changing world with the unchanging gospel of our Lord Jesus Christ.

Respectfully submitted,

Program and Structure Study Committee
Mark A. Brister, Chairman

Ronnie W. Floyd
William K. Hall
Greg Horton
R. Albert Mohler, Jr.
Robert L. Sorrell
Rex M. Terry

---

[1]Charter of the Southern Baptist Convention, 1845.

[2]The three current agencies are served by a total of 148 trustees. The 75 members of the Board of Trustees for the new North American Mission Board will include 44 members of the Home Mission Board, 15 commissioners of the Brotherhood Commission, and 15 commissioners of the Radio and Television Commission, plus the president of the Southern Baptist Convention.

[3]In adopting this report the Convention is interpreting Bylaw 16(9) to mean that a term on the North American Mission Board will be considered "an authorized subsequent term of service" on the Home Mission Board, the Radio and Television Commission, or the Brotherhood Commission. Thus, such persons will serve the remainder of their respective terms of service as previously elected by the Convention.

[4]An analysis of mission funding patterns among state conventions indicates that those conventions with total church membership which includes ten percent or more of their resident state populations have resources adequate to fund a greater portion of their evangelism and mission staff and programs. The North American Mission Board will, through the Cooperative Agreements, encourage these state conventions to fund a greater portion of their internal mission strategies while continuing to support the national and international ministries of the Southern Baptist Convention through the Cooperative Program and the recognized mission offerings. We are convinced that a greater percentage of total North American mission funds must be directed to pioneer mission areas and the major metropolitan areas of the United States and Canada.

[5]We recommend that the two mission boards assume primary responsibility for promoting their own mission offerings; the Lottie Moon Christmas Offering for Foreign Missions and the Annie Armstrong Easter Offering for Home Missions. We recognize and affirm the valued historic relationship with Woman's Missionary Union as an

auxiliary to the Convention, and welcome the continued voluntary contribution of Woman's Missionary Union in mobilizing mission prayer support, promoting missions offerings, and stimulating the missionary spirit within the Southern Baptist Convention.

[6]*Encyclopedia of Southern Baptists*, Volume 1 (Nashville: Broadman Press), p. 42.

[7]Ministry Statements are assigned only to Southern Baptist Convention entities governed by trustees elected by the Convention. Thus, the Womans Missionary Union, governed by directors elected by state WMU organizations, is not assigned a Ministry Statement.

[8]The reports will cover a three-year cycle. In a current year, the entity will report to the Convention concerning its evaluation and review of the fulfillment of the Ministry Plan for the previously completed year, and it will file with the Executive Committee a Ministry Plan for the next institutional year. The Executive Committee will receive the reports as information but will not approve, reject, or amend the reports.

Index